Curriculum
and Instruction
for All Learners

Curriculum and Instruction for All Learners

Blending Systematic and Constructivist Approaches in Inclusive Elementary Schools

Edited by

Beverly Rainforth, Ph.D.
&
Judy W. Kugelmass, Ph.D.

*Binghamton University,
State University of New York*

·P·A·U·L·H·
BROOKES
PUBLISHING CO.®

Baltimore • London • Sydney

Paul H. Brookes Publishing Co.
Post Office Box 10624
Baltimore, Maryland 21285-0624

www.brookespublishing.com

Typeset by Auburn Associates, Inc., Baltimore, Maryland.
Manufactured in the United States of America by
Versa Press, East Peoria, Illinois.

Most of the case studies that appear in this book are based on synthesized composites of the authors' experiences in inclusive elementary schools. However, a few of the case studies are based on actual cases; fictitious names have been used in most of these instances, and permission has been granted for the instances in which real names are used.

Figures 4.4, 4.5, and 4.6 are from *Stretching Student's Vocabulary* by Karen Bromley. Published by Scholastic Inc. Copyright © 2002 by Karen Bromley. Reprinted by permission.

Library of Congress Cataloging-in-Publication Data

Curriculum and instruction for all learners : blending systematic and
  constructivist approaches in inclusive elementary schools / edited by
  Beverly Rainforth & Judy W. Kugelmass.
    p.   cm.
  Includes bibliographical references and index.
  ISBN 1-55766-610-5
    1. Education, Elementary—United States—Curricula.   2. Curriculum
planning—United States.   3. Inclusive education—United States.
4. Multicultural education—United States.   I. Rainforth, Beverly, 1949–
II. Kugelmass, Judy W.
LB1570.C883845 2003
372.19—dc21

                   2003051981

British Library Cataloguing in Publication data are available from the British
Library.

CONTENTS

SECTION ONE

CHAPTER ONE

CHAPTER TWO

CHAPTER THREE

SECTION TWO

CHAPTER FOUR

ABOUT THE EDITORS

Beverly Rainforth, Ph.D.
Professor
School of Education and Human Development
Post Office Box 6000
Binghamton University (SUNY)
Binghamton, NY 13902

Dr. Rainforth is Professor of Special Education in the School of Education and Human Development at Binghamton University, State University of New York (SUNY). She has a bachelor of science degree in physical therapy from the University of Connecticut, a master of arts degree in special education from the University of Connecticut, and a doctorate in special education from the University of Illinois at Urbana-Champaign. She has worked as a physical therapist for children and adults with developmental disabilities and as a special education teacher for infants, preschoolers, and elementary-age children. She has presented at numerous conferences on inclusive education and educational teamwork and is co-author with Jennifer York-Barr of *Collaborative Teams for Students with Severe Disabilities: Integrating Therapy and Educational Services, Second Edition,* also published by Paul H. Brookes Publishing Co. (1997). She is a long-time member of TASH (formerly The Association for Persons with Severe Handicaps).

Judy W. Kugelmass, Ph.D.
Associate Professor
School of Education and Human Development
Post Office Box 6000
Binghamton University (SUNY)
Binghamton, NY 13902

Dr. Kugelmass is Associate Professor of Elementary and Special Education in the Division of Education, School of Education and Human Development, at Binghamton University, State University of New York (SUNY). She has been a teacher of young children, a school psychologist, and a program director of an early intervention agency. She has held academic appointments at Cornell University, Hobart and William Smith Colleges, and Goddard College.

Her teaching and research focuses on the development of educational approaches that respond to children's strengths and connect to their lives. Her interest in learner-centered, experiential education grew out of experiences as coordinator of the New York State Foxfire Teacher Outreach Network (1989–1994). Dr. Kugelmass's most recent publications include co-editorship of *Advocating for Children and Families in an Emerging Democracy*, exploring her work with teachers in developing inclusive schools in Eastern Europe. *I Couldn't Teach Anywhere Else*, investigates teacher empowerment and the development of inclusive schools (Teachers College Press, 2003). Dr. Kugelmass has had extensive international experiences, including being a Fulbright Scholar in Portugal, Indonesia, and Singapore and an International Research Associate for the National College for School Leadership in the United Kingdom. Her proudest achievement is, however, being a mother and grandmother of two wonderful children and two grandchildren.

CONTRIBUTORS

Karen Bromley, Ph.D.
Professor
School of Education and
  Human Development
Binghamton University (SUNY)
Post Office Box 6000
Binghamton, NY 13902

Robert L. Carpenter, Ph.D.
Associate Professor
School of Education and
  Human Development
Binghamton University (SUNY)
Post Office Box 6000
Binghamton, NY 13902

Laura Lamash, M.A.
Teacher
Binghamton City School
  District
287 Prospect Street
Binghamton, NY 13905

Monica Miller Marsh, Ph.D.
Assistant Professor
School of Education and
  Human Development
Binghamton University (SUNY)
Post Office Box 6000
Binghamton, NY 13902

Melissa A. Price, M.S.Ed.
Project Coordinator
New York Higher Education
Support Center for Systems
  Change
Syracuse University
150 Huntington Hall
Syracuse, NY 13244

Barbara L. Regenspan, Ed.D.
Associate Professor
School of Education and
  Human Development
Binghamton University (SUNY)
Post Office Box 6000
Binghamton, NY 13902

Jean Schmittau, Ph.D.
Associate Professor
School of Education and
  Human Development
Binghamton University (SUNY)
Post Office Box 6000
Binghamton, NY 13902

The principal walks me around his school. He stops in front of a classroom and gestures inside. "This," he says, "is our inclusive fourth grade. We have three inclusion children in this class."

I am, frankly, puzzled. If that's the "inclusion class" with three "inclusion children," I wonder what the other classrooms are. Are they the "exclusion classrooms," systematically excluding children who perform at different academic levels, speak a language other than English, or who have behavioral or emotional challenges? I wonder how we have reached a point in which the principal's statement makes sense to many teachers, administrators, and school boards.

What if we stopped talking about inclusion altogether? What if we talked, instead, about good teaching, about a rich and varied curriculum that engages students at multiple points of entry, about classroom communities that are supportive, kind, and respectful of all students? What if good teaching really is good inclusive practice? What if good inclusive practices are not separate and different from good teaching?

This book provides a hopeful vision of what schools and classrooms can be. Through rich and detailed classroom scenarios, the reader is invited to peek into classrooms that truly do meet the needs of all students, not by lowering expectations for all, but by setting high standards within a context of diversity. We meet teachers who draw on students' backgrounds and knowledge to develop curriculum that is relevant, culturally responsive, and inviting.

When I read, for example, Monica Miller Marsh's (Chapter 2) description of a teacher responding and teaching to the language diversity in her classroom, I am struck by the richness and depth of the curriculum. It is hard to imagine any parent who would not want his or her child included in such a classroom, not because it is an "inclusion class" but because the teacher is pedagogically skilled and the opportunities for learning are extensive. The classroom Miller Marsh describes truly epitomizes the T-shirt I bought that says, "I don't speak English only."

The Time Travel unit experienced by the fourth graders in Laura Lamash's class (Chapter 6) is exciting and captivating. The opportunities for learning and skill development are elaborately described. Again, the project is not an example of what can happen in an "inclusive classroom" but what can happen with 9-year-olds who learn in different ways when they are lead by a creative and flexible teacher. These are just two of the classrooms that this book visits. Although some of these classrooms might be labeled "progressive" and others more "traditional," they all share a commitment to viewing all children as learners, offering rich and inviting curricula, and providing instruction that meets a range of learning styles and strengths.

We have entered a period of great peril in education. The new focus on high-stakes testing enlarges and deepens the educational abandonment of a wide range of students. Teachers are reluctant to take students who will not test well because each teacher's evaluation hinges on students' performance on tests that often are irrelevant to children's lives and experiences. The tests are also often totally disconnected from their own learning and the teaching provided by teachers who know their students well. Perhaps even worse, many teachers are leaving the profession because the kind and quality of teaching they have come to value for their students is now considered unacceptable because it does not link directly to standardized tests. In Massachusetts, parents and teachers staged a protest of the standardized testing movement by erecting a graveyard of "lost educational opportunities." The teacher who used to hold the Shakespeare Festival, engaging all students in a variety of writing, acting, painting, mathematical and social activities, must now abandon that project in order to do test preparation. The biology teacher who used to do water sampling with students to investigate pollution and environmental conditions is told she can no longer take field trips. Unless the curricular and pedagogical changes described in this book are accompanied by political activism, the "standardization" of school may obliterate even the best designed and executed curricular projects.

The high-stakes testing movement erodes the relationship between teachers and students as well. A teacher told me, in tears, that she was forced to make her Russian-language immigrant student, in the United States for only 2 months, sit in front of a standardized test in English for 6 hours. The student looked at her with confusion and pain, understanding neither the task in front of him nor why the teacher who had been his ally was now his tormentor. We run the real risk that the "No child left behind" movement really will become the "No child left untested" initiative. Tested and then rejected. Tested and then abandoned.

We must create schools that are caring and responsive to all students and that provide a quality education within the context of a shared community. The alternatives, tracking and a return to ability grouping, will deepen the linguistic and racial divide in our country and impoverish us all. This book provides a clear vision of how schools and classrooms should be. Even more important, however, it provides us with examples of how this is already happening and can happen again and again. We are not left with vague promises or wishful thinking about how education can be, but with concrete examples that show grounded practice and compassionate teaching—therein lie the hopefulness and the urgency. We cannot afford, educationally or morally, to sacrifice any children, and there is no time to waste in making the world right for all.

Mara Sapon-Shevin, Ed.D.
Syracuse University

ACKNOWLEDGMENTS

The editors would like to thank the scores of teachers whose work is represented in this book. Their caring, creativity, and concern for children are reflected in the classrooms they have created. These commitments endure in spite of shifting instructional trends and ideological conflicts. Children remain the center of their instructional practice.

We also thank our graduate assistants, Svetlana Kononenko and Roberta Rosenberger, for hours of proofreading, re-reading, and bibliographic searching. Their assistance made our work possible.

Finally, we wish to acknowledge the support and good humor provided by our colleagues in the School of Education and Human Development at Binghamton University (SUNY). We appreciate their practices and ideals, their hard questions and encouragement, and their willingness to work with our deadlines and feedback. They are why we enjoy our work here.

To all children whose gifts go unrecognized

Designing Elementary Education for All Children

Once there were two teacher educators, Bev and Judy. They had different cultural backgrounds and grew up in different kinds of communities; they pursued higher education with different goals and enjoyed different learning paradigms; they had different kinds of professional and life experiences. They had different personalities. When they met in 1994, all of these differences might have caused them to reject one another, but they shared one important belief: All children are entitled to education that is meaningful, effective, and inclusive. Agreements about exactly what that meant and how to make such an education a reality in a conservative community were details to be discussed and negotiated.

Judy was, by nature, engaged in a more progressive paradigm. As an early childhood special educator and school psychologist, she had embraced child-centered and family-centered approaches and experiential learning. She had sought international experiences and multicultural understandings.

Bev was, by nature, engaged in a more behavioral paradigm. As a physical therapist and special educator, she had worked with students with significant cognitive disabilities for whom systematic and data-based instruction had become liberatory. Through her work, children once thought incapable of learning did learn, and the quantitative evidence of their learning helped secure greater resources for special education.

An integral part of Judy's and Bev's experiences was what Judy called "reflection" and what Bev called "analysis." These processes

1

provided insights and evidence that supported the women's respective paradigms but also led to growing recognition that each paradigm had limitations. Each seemed to lack what the other offered.

By the time Bev and Judy met, both had become aware that rigid adherence to and conflicts between paradigms were interfering with achieving their mutual goal of meaningful, effective, and inclusive education for all children. Therefore, rather than reject one another's paradigms, they recognized that both viewpoints could contribute to a more complete understanding of what works in today's schools with today's students. Thus began a partnership and exploration of what it would mean to blend "constructivist" and "systematic" approaches.

This book is a product of that partnership and exploration. At the same time, writing and editing this book has become part of the process of building the partnership and of exploring and deepening their understandings. Just as Judy and Bev have built this and other partnerships at their university, elementary school teachers are building similar partnerships while educating children with diverse learning abilities and needs. This book is intended to support teachers as they negotiate their partnerships and work to provide meaningful, effective, and inclusive education for all children.

The first section of this book explores the concepts of constructivism, systematic instruction, inclusive education, and cultural and linguistic diversity. Historical perspectives, theoretical underpinnings, and research related to these concepts provide the foundation for discussion of current practice and blending of practices and establish principles for designing educational programs that meet the concerns of all children.

CHAPTER ONE

Searching for a Pedagogy of Success

JUDY W. KUGELMASS & BEVERLY RAINFORTH

I n the current climate of school reform, policy makers are defining *success* as students' attainment of predetermined academic standards, which typically are measured by high-stakes testing programs. In spite of the political rhetoric surrounding such a definition, most educators, parents, and students understand that being successful requires much more than learning facts and developing skills. A successful student also knows how to get along with others, solve problems, think critically, and contribute to the school community. The ultimate assessment of this kind of success is determined by the ways students integrate their school experiences into life in the larger community, which includes family, neighborhood, city or town, state, nation, and the world. This book is designed to explore how classroom teachers can help students achieve both academic and social success. Rather than seeing these as incompatible, we believe neither can exist without the other.

The approaches presented in the following chapters represent rigorous instructional practices. The issue we hope to address is not whether rigorous instruction is necessary for both kinds of success but, rather, what constitutes rigorous instruction (a point on which few agree). Historically, educators have advocated for one of two approaches that have traditionally been perceived as incompatible. The first, the constructivist approach, has been identified as child centered, discovery oriented, and progressive. In this approach, content emerges from the child's interests and experiences. The second, the systematic

3

approach, has frequently been characterized as instrumental, behavioral, or teacher directed. In the systematic approach, the teacher or state predetermines curriculum content.

Our belief is that the endless debate between advocates of the systematic versus the constructive approaches has been counterproductive, depleting financial resources and energy from our schools. Instead, we see value in both when they are used purposefully to achieve a variety of outcomes, meet the concerns of different students, and offer all students diverse ways to learn.

We also believe that learning requires more than application of validated instructional strategies. Maslow (1987) asserted that children must have their survival needs (e.g., food, shelter, safety) met before they can achieve. Free and reduced-cost meals, school-based health services, and interagency social service supports have been designed to meet such basic needs. Maslow also asserted that meeting the need for a sense of belonging (i.e., to family, school, community) also precedes achievement. Throughout the 20th century, educators such as Dewey (1938; 1964/1902) and Kunc (2000) described the ways that schools routinely violate this tenet by insisting that children achieve academically in order to earn membership in their school community. Making academic achievement a prerequisite for social inclusion has had devastating outcomes that include

- Alienation
- Depression
- Suicide
- Gang or clique membership
- School drop out
- Segregation
- Social exclusion

The most insidious outcome may be the failure of large portions of individuals to achieve their potential. Paradoxically, the educational debates about the "correct" models of curriculum and instruction now dichotomize achievement and belonging. We agree with Maslow, Dewey, Kunc, and scores of researchers who advocate for "welcoming schools" that foster students' sense of belonging as the context for high achievement (UNESCO, 1997).

This book challenges the debates that have permeated education for decades, advocating instead for inclusive schools in which all children are welcomed. This unconditional acceptance of every child provides the foundation for success and for the application of curriculum and instruction that are both child centered and intensive, discovery oriented and systematic. We begin this discussion by presenting our definition of the term *inclusion*. Then, before turning to other foundational concepts, the historical debate that has created the need for this discussion is examined. That is followed by an exploration of the two conceptual themes of this book: constructivism and systematic instruction.

WHAT IS AN INCLUSIVE CLASSROOM?

In the United States, inclusion is generally used to describe the full and complete integration of children with disabilities in public schools and communities. Internationally, however, in both developing nations and those with well-established educational infrastructures and traditions, inclusion is being defined more broadly. Rather than reflecting an educational movement for children with disabilities, inclusive education is understood as an approach that supports and celebrates the diversity found among all learners. Globalization, increased immigration, and technological advances throughout the world are raising awareness of the implications of diversity in countries that once believed themselves to be homogeneous societies. Diversity in race, social class, ethnicity, religion, and gender have always existed everywhere, although to a lesser degree than in the United States. To a large extent, public education systems have ignored the significance of these differences on the success of diverse learners.

The knowledge gained during the 20th century regarding children's learning and development has combined with a growing understanding of the links among democracy, human rights, and publicly supported schools that serve all children. These insights are leading to recognition of the need for significant educational reforms that go beyond meeting academic standards. These kinds of systemic reforms must consider the diverse resources and concerns of every child and support a vision of inclusive education. Our definition of inclusive education is summarized in Table 1.1. The term *inclusion* will be used throughout this book to represent this broadened prospective.

Inclusive education ensures children's basic human right to an individually, culturally, and developmentally appropriate education and eliminates social exclusion. Inclusive schools do more than provide educational experiences for students whose cultures, social classes, learning styles, languages, intelligences, and physical and sensory capacities are different from one another. These kinds of schools also offer possibilities for enriching the experiences of every child while preparing them to live in an inclusive society. The practices

Table 1.1.   A broadened definition of inclusive education

All children attend the same schools and receive instruction in the same classrooms.

Remedial, special education, and related services are provided within general education settings. Specialists collaborate with classroom teachers to support all students and to provide adaptations and specialized interventions.

Accommodations are made in the general education curriculum that enable all students to learn skills appropriate to their chronological age and developmental needs.

The curriculum is conceived as promoting social-emotional and developmental growth in addition to helping every student meet age-appropriate and grade-level learning standards.

Technology is used to support all students' growth and development, academic learning, creativity, and social interactions.

All students are held to high expectations, while, at the same time, the need for individualization is acknowledged and accommodated.

Classrooms are learning communities in which all students are valued members who support one another.

Families are active and integral members of the school community.

Diversity in culture, language, ability, and student interest is celebrated and seen as enriching the educational experiences of all children.

described in this book offer examples of approaches that have been used by elementary school teachers in the development of classrooms that reflect this definition of inclusion. Their practices are built on the best of what is known about teaching and learning. These practices provide equal opportunities for excellence and support the participation of all children in their respective classrooms, schools, and communities. The purposes of this kind of inclusive education are summarized in Table 1.2. Features of curriculum and instruction designed to ensure a pedagogy of success for all children are described in Table 1.3. Although the specific examples presented in this book reflect the elements described in Tables 1.2 and 1.3 and support the unique development of every child, it is important to understand that our intention is not to offer "techniques" that can be duplicated by any teacher in any context. Rather, they are provided as examples of practices that represent visible and technical manifestations of inclusive school and classroom cultures in specific contexts. To be authentically inclusive in any setting, these approaches must also be built on an understanding and deep appreciation for diversity in all aspects of life. Inclusion means no child is excluded physically, psychologically, intellectually, academically, culturally, or socially. In an inclusive environment, the unique resources and concerns of every child in a classroom and a teacher's unconditional love of children are what guide instructional practice, rather than strict adherence to any one curricular model, specific theory, or ideology.

Table 1.2.   Purposes of inclusive education

Promote human rights and social justice through education

Provide all children their human right to education on a free and compulsory basis

Promote quality in teaching and learning

Promote quality of life

Provide equal opportunities to education

Acknowledge diversity of culture and social organization as a touchstone to human progress, tolerance, and change

Create positive values and attitudes that facilitate creative and satisfying social interactions with a wide range of individuals and groups

Develop the potential of community members so that they will be active participants in their families, communities, economies, and societies

From UNESCO. (2000). *Inclusive education and education for all: A challenge and a vision.* Paris: Author, Section for special needs education; adapted by permission.

These underlying beliefs permeate all aspects of the culture in a truly inclusive school. Although some teachers may not be able to articulate or consciously acknowledge the way these beliefs guide their practices, these beliefs can be seen in patterns of interactions, verbal and nonverbal language, arrangements of the classroom's physical environment, and approaches to teaching and learning. These patterns will reveal the hidden, primary levels of classroom culture that reflect deeply held beliefs in the value of each child's contribution to the classroom community (Hall, 1983).

Certainly, inclusive schools present unique challenges to both teachers and students. How can a teacher be expected to meet every child's needs in the face of such diversity, given the current political climate calling for accountability? To do this requires embracing an evolutionary model of curriculum and instruction that is designed to support the diversity found in American elementary schools. This will not be found in any one, new, quick-fix solution but rather requires a continually evolving approach to curriculum and instruction that integrates knowledge about how children learn into the ways teachers teach.

Table 1.3.   Elements of a pedagogy of success

The range of appropriate teaching/learning approaches is wide and flexible.

Practices reflect learner-centered concepts of education that are intentionally designed to be responsive to the diversity of children's concerns and potentials.

Appropriate, culturally and socially sensitive, and sufficient learning materials are available for all children and classrooms.

AMERICAN SCHOOLS IN THE 21st CENTURY

Powerful reforms have taken place in American public education throughout the 20th century. Controversy continues regarding which instructional methodologies are most effective and what should be taught. Although some of this controversy emanates from educators, at least as much comes from political arenas. Furthermore, in this era of espousing and promoting inclusion, there is considerable evidence of two themes that have persisted in Western society for more than 2000 years, "the consignment of children to the care of others, and disposal of those who are rejected" (Safford & Safford, 1996, p. 4). If our society truly believes in inclusion, we cannot continue segregating children who are challenging or "undesirable" or sending them away to be educated. Accepting the premise that all children belong in general public schools alongside every other child in their community calls for elimination of these practices of rejection.

Unfortunately, rigid adherence to particular models of curriculum and instruction has supported the belief that a general public school might not be "appropriate" for some children. *Curriculum* is generally used to describe what is being taught, whereas *instruction* is used to describe how it is taught. We believe that this distinction ignores the "hidden curriculum" of schooling that communicates and reinforces societal attitudes, values, and beliefs about diversity and inclusion (Apple, 1979). A lack of attention to the messages teachers communicate to their students through their teaching methods has interfered with the successful development of inclusive schools and classrooms. The approaches presented throughout this book reflect each contributor's understanding of the ways in which the process of instruction is inseparable from the content of the curriculum.

The movement toward providing inclusive education is also understood as the most recent phase in an evolution of responses to children who have presented challenges to the traditional education system. This evolution parallels other movements or "interactive phases" (McIntosh, 1983, 1990) that have prompted new developments in curriculum throughout the history of American education. Understanding the progression toward an inclusive curriculum as evolving through interactive phases rather than discrete stages of development can counteract the kinds of either/or debates that have promoted a pendulum approach to reforms in American public education (Dewey, 1938; Tyack & Cuban, 1995). Different phases of curriculum development have always existed simultaneously. New ideas often emerge from old practices without rejecting all that came before.

Rather, the best of the old becomes integrated into new concepts and practices. Examining the evolution of the current phases of contemporary education demonstrates how an interactive phase model can be used to develop a pedagogy of success for all children.

SO HOW DID WE GET HERE?
A BRIEF HISTORY OF EDUCATION

Education is a formalized arm of the socialization process. It differs from the kind of informal socialization processes that take place within families and communities. Its institutions (i.e., schools) operate with the explicit goal of developing specific knowledge, skills, and dispositions that adults in positions of power and authorities in the larger society believe to be important. This process is as old as civilization. There have always been debates about the purposes of education, whom should be educated, what should be taught, and how it should be taught. For many centuries and in many cultures, the standard mode of education was rote memorization and recitation. When students did not have ready access to printed materials, this approach ensured the transmission of cultural knowledge and religious doctrine. As print became widely available in western nations, the emphasis on rote memorization and recitation declined. As McIntosh (1990) suggested, however, it did not disappear but rather became integrated into later developments.

During the 18th century, sometimes called the Age of Reason or the Age of Enlightenment, European philosophers such as Rousseau, Pestolozzi, and Froebel introduced new ideas that are now associated with modern "progressive education." These men believed children were innately moral and gifted, and that education should be designed to release those gifts. They believed the more traditional methods of memorization and recitation would damage children's creativity and psyches. Children should have opportunities to explore and interact with their environment, especially the natural world, and discover principles themselves. These ideas would have a significant impact on the development of education in the United States and later, in the 20th century, would be reflected in the progressive education movement.

In contrast to Rousseau, the British philosopher John Locke believed that knowledge was not innate, and that knowledge must be imparted onto the blank slates (*tabula rasa*) of children's minds through experience and guided observation. Locke had a significant influence on the French physician Itard, who spent 5 years teaching Victor, the child described as "the wild boy of Aveyron." Itard determined that Victor had severely limited cognition, language, social, motor, and self-care skills. Because Victor had not developed "intellect" through natural means, Itard meticulously identified the rudimentary skills that Victor would need to learn and devised precise strategies to teach new skills by carefully arranging the environment and tapping into all sensory modalities (Lane, 1976).

Thus, Itard became the father of special education, building a "functional curriculum" for Victor through the use of instructional strategies that utilized formalizing notions about developmental sequences, norm-referenced assessment, instructional objectives, systematic instruction, multisensory instruction, and naturalistic observation that are still used today. A closer examination of Itard's approach to educating Victor also reveals his application of principles that today might be identified as progressive, constructivist, and humanistic. Itard began working with Victor by first understanding the social context of Victor's past and present life experiences and designing instructional activities that connected Victor's learning to real-life, meaningful experiences. New experiences were built on successful earlier events. Itard became increasingly aware of the importance of social interaction, personal relationships, and affective components to Victor's learning and development. Throughout their time together, he held on to an unconditional belief in Victor's humanity and ability to learn. In 1907, a century after Itard began his work with Victor, Maria Montessori opened her first schools in Italy, extending Itard's methods to young children who were living in poverty (Lane, 1976).

These aspects of European education would influence American schools during the 19th and 20th centuries. In the 17th century, however, the *first* schools in America were designed to prepare the sons of Puritan immigrants for entrance into the first college that was to become the elite Harvard University. From a 17th century perspective, the development of schools for Puritan men was "progressive," in that it represented movement away from the belief that education was only for landed aristocracy and that religion was the only appropriate subject to be taught. Radical ideals such as individual freedom and pursuit of happiness would later be introduced, fueling both the American and French Revolutions. Intertwined with these ideals was the growing advocacy among the radical elite for public education, thus openly introducing a political agenda into children's education.

Soon after the American colonies won independence in 1776, Thomas Jefferson began advocating for free schools to prepare U.S. citizens to participate in the new democracy. His definition of "citizenry" was, however, neither inclusive nor democratic, but rather referred only to able-bodied, white males. Although he did advocate for young girls to attend elementary schools, their schooling was designed to ensure that they would become supportive wives and better mothers. The content of the curriculum for boys gradually expanded to include general knowledge as well as moral and nonsectarian religious guidance. Instructional methods continued to be centered on the recitation of memorized materials, however, and failure to remember designated material led to corporal punishment or expulsion (Henson, 1995).

Although schools in the United States were not initially developed as inclusive or democratic institutions, they continually moved in that direction. By 1860, half of the nation's children were in school. These students still did not represent a sample of the general population. The majority of children in school remained English-speaking, white males, who were not needed for labor by their families. Still, curriculum and instruction continued to expand and included more content and processes related generally to secular life.

In 1852, Massachusetts passed the first compulsory school attendance laws in the United States. Influenced by European and American progressive ideals, Francis Parker established a school in Quincy, Massachusetts, in 1875. This school was designed to create a natural learning environment in which instruction was characterized by playing, singing, drawing, reading, and counting objects. Games and puzzles replaced recitation and memorization. Children were given real-life problems to solve and from which to develop rules and generalizations about life (Henson, 1995).

By 1918, all states had laws requiring children to attend elementary school (Safford & Safford, 1996). The late 19th and early 20th century had brought unprecedented new waves of poor and uneducated immigrants to the United States. Some advocates of public education had deep concerns for meeting the needs of these children and of others from all backgrounds and social classes. Some educators and political figures feared that immigrants and others of the underclass would become a burden on society. Many of these reformers viewed the primary purpose of public education as the socializing agent that could prepare poor, unskilled, and landless laborers to become workers for the factories and coal mines that were fueling the newly developing industrial society. In response to these concerns, Horace Mann and others advocated "common schools" that would be publicly funded, follow a common curriculum, and establish a common language, culture, and morality among poor and immigrant children.

During the same period, other reformers focused less on the role of education as a means of developing workers. Their attention was directed at education primarily as the vehicle for creating the kind of enlightened populace needed to ensure a democratic society. They proposed a "progressive" approach to curriculum and instruction that promoted the development of the intellect, problem-solving capacities, creativity, and an appreciation for the arts. Thus began the polarization between the positions of the progressives and the traditionalists. This dichotomy would become increasingly politicized throughout the 20th century and continue into the 21st. The educational traditions that grew out of these two opposing positions are presented in the following sections. The problems and possibilities offered by both are examined. Following an interactive model, we propose a perspective that moves beyond this polarization by integrating both. This integration will enable educators to develop approaches that reflect the values and beliefs of an inclusive school culture.

THE PROGRESSIVE TRADITION AND CONSTRUCTIVISM

At the turn of the 20th century, progressive educators promoted the idea that schools should be environments in which learning occurs naturally (Archambault, 1964, 1966; Henson, 1995). These schools would be places in which children could develop their learning capacities more fully and, as a consequence, be prepared to be effective citizens in a democracy. Teachers and children would actively engage in educative experiences (i.e., activities designed to ensure the continued growth and development of the child) (Dewey, 1938, 1964/1902). To demonstrate how this might be done and to refine his ideas, Dewey established a school at the University of Chicago that he directed from 1896–1904. Although there is no evidence to indicate that children with disabilities were included in Dewey's school, many children were sent there by parents because they were unsuccessful in more traditional schools (Dewey, 1938).

Dewey's work in education grew out of the philosophical traditions of pragmatism. He believed that knowledge was acquired through the active participation of the individual in the physical and social world. Individuals were driven by their nature to arrive at solutions to problems that were of interest and concern to their lives. Therefore, the role of education was to provide experiences for individuals through which they would develop their problem-solving capacities. The teacher's role was to create opportunities and guide students through their experiences in ways that promoted growth were and, therefore, educative (Dewey, 1938).

Basic to pragmatism was the notion that no one theory could appropriately explain all of human behavior (Henson, 1995). William James, the philosopher and a colleague of Dewey identified as one of the founders of American pragmatism, expressed these ideas in 1907 in his lecture, "What Pragmatism Means." His metaphor of the "hotel" can also be applied to an inclusive school.

> Pragmatism unstiffens all our theories, limbers them up and sets each one at work. Being nothing essentially new, it harmonizes with many ancient philosophical tendencies.... Against rationalism as a pretension and a method, pragmatism is fully armed and militant.... It has no dogmas and no doctrines save its methods.... It lies in the midst of our theories, like a corridor in a hotel. Innumerable chambers open out on it. In one you may find a man writing an aesthetic volume; in the next someone on his knees praying for faith and strength; in a third a chemist investigating a body's properties; in a fourth a system of idealist metaphysics is being excogitated; in a fifth the impossibility of metaphysics is being shown. But they all own a corridor, and all must pass through if they want a practicable way of getting into or out of their respective rooms. (James, 1907/1992, cited in Miller, 1991, p. 571)

In an inclusive school, as in this hotel, many things are going on at once; everyone is learning different things in different ways, according to their interests, abilities, and needs. Similarly, the classrooms described in this book have opened their doors to many possibilities by embracing a variety of instructional processes that promote the learning and development of the diverse populations of students they serve.

Support for the pragmatist philosophy of education emerged later in the 20th century with Piaget's work in cognitive psychology. Like Dewey, Piaget believed and went on to demonstrate that learning occurred when children were actively engaged in interactions with their environments. These experiences were then assimilated with prior knowledge in developmentally appropriate ways that shaped the development of cognitive structures within the child. Children were seen as self-regulating learners, intrinsically motivated to construct deeper and richer understandings of previous knowledge. This "natural" process of development required no external rewards or structures but unfolded when the child was provided appropriate learning environments with which to interact.

Piagetian theory provided the theoretical framework for educational approaches that became identified as constructivist. Although there is no single constructivist approach, most share beliefs that are also associated with progressive education. These shared beliefs are listed in Table 1.4.

Harris and Graham (1994) explored different models of constructivist teaching and identified the strengths and weaknesses of each in working with children who were identified as having special educational needs. Citing Moshman (1982), the first of these models, called *endogenous constructivism*, supports the use of practices most associated with Piaget. Its emphasis is on the child's construction of new knowledge from old, through child-determined explorations and guided discovery rather than guided teaching. Teaching approaches following from this model focus more on process than content, are often identified as child centered, and embrace the concept of developmentally appropriate practice (Bredekamp & Copple, 1997). Rigid adherence to these kinds of approaches has, however, been found ineffective for some children.

The teacher-directed approaches required by some students with physical disabilities and/or those identified as having developmental, learning, and/or emotional disabilities conflict with the conceptual framework underlying this kind of constructivist approach. When these children do not respond in ways that are considered developmentally appropriate, recommendations for their exclusion from these child-centered classrooms may follow (Mallory & New, 1996). The assumption that typical cognitive and psychological development fol-

Table 1.4.   Shared principles of progressive and constructivist pedagogy

Learning is a social experience.

Individuals solve problems in interaction with their physical and social environments.

Learning should be linked to the real-life experiences to have meaning, purpose, and be long lasting.

Active exploration and creation should include the arts.

Linguistic and mathematical literacy develop naturally as the outcome of children's physical and intellectual development in concert with their experiences.

There is a continuity to experience, with each new development in learning growing out of previous learning.

Conscious reflection on experience is essential for learning.

Social control and rules emerge out of the inherent nature of experiences.

Sources: Archambault, 1964, 1966; Dewey, 1938; Phillips & Soltis, 1991.

lows predetermined and biologically structured sequential patterns also pathologizes children from non–middle class families and/or non-dominant cultures, and others whose learning styles may be at variance with developmental expectations.

Child-centeredness of this kind has therefore been criticized as culturally inappropriate for some children. This variation of constructivist practice reflects white, middle-class child-rearing practices and is supported by middle- and upper-class ideologies (Burman, 1994; Grumet, 1998; Walkerdine, 1984). The mismatch between teachers' non-directive interactions with children and the more directive approaches of many parents from lower socioeconomic and/or non-European American backgrounds frequently places children from non-dominant cultures at a disadvantage in classrooms operating under this model (Delpit, 1995, 1998; Ladson-Billings, 1994).

The examples offered in this book recognize these limitations. Each author offers his or her critique of traditional constructivism and provides alternative approaches. The practices presented in the following chapters instead reflect what Harris and Graham (1994) identified as exogenous constructivism and dialectical constructivism. What differentiates these from endogenous constructivism is the more active role of the teacher in structuring the environments and experiences of children. Exogenous constructivism integrates social learning and information processing theories. The teacher provides direct instruction through modeling, discussions, and explanations; offers deliberate and systematically organized inputs; and develops active learning experiences in natural environments specifically designed to address students' strengths, interests, and concerns.

Vygotsky's (1962, 1978) theories of cognitive development are reflected in dialectical constructivism. Although this instructional approach shares features of both endogenous and exogenous constructivism, it differs in the attention that the teacher gives to the social contexts of student learning. Active learning, interaction, and the construction of understanding remain central features of this kind of constructivist practice. The teacher is actively engaged in creating contexts that engage the child in his or her *zone of proximal development* (Berk & Winsler, 1995). The zone of proximal development is the dynamic developmental state that lies just beyond the competencies the child has already mastered. The teacher is directly responsible for scaffolded instructional experiences at a variety of levels of explicitness, depending on the concerns and abilities of the child. Specificity of instruction is determined by the individual child's responses to the learning contexts provided. The teacher focuses on creating reciprocal interactions between the child and the social and physical environments that provide the context for the learning experience. Instructional approaches include strategy instruction, reciprocal teaching and cooperative learning, guided discovery, and modeling.

Constructivism is clearly more than any one thing. The differences found between classrooms that describe themselves as "constructivist" reflect the social contexts created by the group of students, the perspectives of teachers, and the culture of their schools (Brooks & Brooks, 1994). Although there is neither one definition nor a single constructivist pedagogy, knowledge and understanding are conveyed to learners in every constructivist classroom in three distinct ways. These three attributes of constructivism, listed in Table 1.5, are evident in all of the approaches described throughout this book.

THE BEHAVIORIST TRADITION AND SYSTEMATIC INSTRUCTION

Americans have long been enamored with technology and efficiency. Throughout the 20th century we enjoyed the benefits of the Industrial Revolution's mass production and of revolutionary inventions such as the automobile and airplane. At the beginning of the 20th century, many believed that all problems, including social problems, could be solved by careful application of the scientific method (Thorndike, 1910). The belief that an emphasis on the scientific method could also help improve student performance encouraged school systems to model themselves on the bureaucratic administrative structures and the assembly-line strategies of the factory model. These "factory-model" schools were designed to provide an efficient, inexpensive, and unified system of public education. Their mission was to teach basic skills to students who had never before had an education available to them, while instilling discipline, conformity, neatness, and dependency. Public schools would also teach a common language to

Table 1.5. Three ways knowledge and understanding are conveyed to learners in constructivist classrooms

In constructivist classrooms, knowledge and understanding are

1. Actively acquired by interactions with materials and ideas
2. Social constructions developed through interactions and dialogue with others
3. Created through discovery, creative activities and experimentation

From Perkins, D. (1999). The many faces of constructivism. *Educational Leadership, 57*(3); reprinted by permission.

large numbers of immigrant children who were to be America's new future citizens (Katz, 1971).

At the same time, many in the emerging field of psychology began turning toward developing scientific methods of understanding human behavior. Moving away from the influence of Freudian theory, which had concerned itself with human emotion, academic psychology shifted its attention toward understanding the physiology of emotion and cause–effect relationships in behavior (Cole, 1996). This movement would evolve into what became known as "behavioral psychology." Behavioral psychologists such as Watson, Hull, and Skinner demonstrated how laboratory animals could learn simple tasks, such as discriminating between two shapes, when their correct responses were followed immediately by reinforcing events. When the dimensions of tasks were carefully controlled and systematically manipulated, simple responses could then be chained together to teach more complex responses, such as running through mazes of increasing difficulty. If the carefully presented stimuli and tangible reinforcement of conditioning could be used to train pigeons and mice, many of these psychologists believed this powerful learning technology could certainly improve the instruction of children.

Several trends in the 1950s and 1960s began bringing behavioral psychology into the mainstream of American educational thought. In 1957, Russia became the first nation to successfully launch a satellite into orbit, which launched a massive school improvement campaign in the United States so that it could surpass Russia's space program and secure first place in the "space race." Interactions among the fields of behavioral psychology, education, the military, and business and industry in the United States led to the adoption of a systems approach to staff development and supervision of adult employees. Systems scientists believed organizations and the behavior of the people in them could be analyzed, predicted, and then reshaped through clearly defined objectives and precise instruction. These same principles were applied to design and evaluation of education for children in the late 1960s and 1970s (Mager & Pipe, 1970). Enthusiasts of programmed instruction promoted education based on behavioral objectives, and the U.S. Office of Education started requiring clear statements of objectives for funded projects (Popham, 1973b). Thus, the accountability movement was born.

Critics argued that this kind of systems approach would dehumanize, and the precise statements of outcomes reduce, education to the most superficial (and easily defined) achievements. In one of the first textbooks describing systematic instruction, Popham and Baker (1970) observed that teachers determined the curriculum individually, with haphazard results. (Clearly this was an era before state standards!) They advocated Tyler's (1950) framework for basing curricula on three sources of data: the learner, society, and subject-matter discipline. Particularly within the third area, teachers were advised to ensure scaffolding for key concepts rather than objectives that required retention of great quantities of minute detail (Popham & Baker, 1970). Popham (1973a) acknowledged that it may be easier to define trivial outcomes but warned that seemingly profound and worthwhile goal statements could mask instruction and assessment that is equally trivial. For example, the goal "to demonstrate democratic ideals" suggests preparation of learners to become responsible citizens in U.S. society; good instruction would involve the higher order thinking skills of analysis, synthesis, application, and evaluation. A less thoughtful teacher might address this goal through objectives such as "list five characteristics of a democracy," which requires only rote memorization and recitation and does not imply action related to civic participation. Furthermore, Popham asserted that the focus on behavioral objectives did not imply the use of a behavioral teaching strategy.

Other critics charged that the stimulus-response learning paradigm was too simplistic to be applied to humans, and the use of contingent reinforcement was coercive. Skinner (1971) disagreed and asserted that, far from being coercive, behavioral psychology offered opportunities for children who were in danger of failing to succeed and for average students to excel. Discoveries from laboratory studies with animals had demonstrated how environmental influences could have both positive and negative effects. One phenomenon with profound implications for humans was what Maier and Seligman (1976) termed *learned helplessness*. It was discovered that when animals could not escape from electric shock, eventually they just lay down and accepted the shocks; later, when an escape route was presented, the animals still lay motionless and just accepted the aversive stimuli. The same sort of learned helplessness was observed among children and adults who had been unable to escape from aversive experiences, such as ongoing academic failure or physical abuse. Seligman (1990), however, went on to demonstrate that children and adults can be taught to interpret life events differently to reduce perceptions of helplessness, to learn optimism, and to experience success.

A central principle of behavioral psychology is that providing a reward immediately after a correct response will increase the rate of correct responding (Skinner, 1968). This became translated into teachers' awareness of how praise, tokens, edibles, and other tangible rewards could be effective motivators. Skinner believed the most powerful reinforcement for learning was to provide students with immediate feedback about the accuracy of their responses. He devised materials that would allow students to answer a question, immediately check for accuracy, make corrections if needed, experience success, and go on to the next question. The principles of programmed instruction formed the basis for self-paced learning materials that are still used throughout education. Skinner also developed "teaching machines" to support these ideas. These machines promised to revolutionize education, and, although not sophisticated enough to realize that promise, they were clearly the forerunners of today's computer-mediated instruction.

In the 1960s, behavioral psychologists became interested in the power of operant conditioning, or behavior modification, to teach people with mental retardation who lived in state institutions. By determining the specific sequence of steps for any given task, providing carefully selected cues or prompts, and reinforcing small improvements in performance, psychologists were able to teach self-care and academic skills to people who had been considered unteachable, proving their humanity and capabilities and paving the way for the deinstitutionalization movement of the 1970s. In some respects this was a revival of some of Itard's work, but with a more solid foundation in learning theory and a growing valuation of and emphasis on human rights. The new ideas of behavioral psychology were becoming integrated into social movements identified as humanistic and progressive.

Thus, behaviorism became incorporated into a new "interactive phase," leading to the development of a new field of research known as applied behavior analysis. The three dimensions of applied behavior analysis, listed in Table 1.6, show that it was not enough to train someone to perform complex but pointless tasks in a laboratory. Like their constructivist counterparts, behavioral psychologists recognized the importance of connecting the content of learning to the real-life experiences of the learner. Although this perspective represented a concern for social contexts, in the early stages of this movement, decisions about what was socially important were made by professionals, with little consideration for the interests of family members, much less the social context of the learner. The only conditions used to control the

Table 1.6.   Three dimensions of applied behavioral analysis

1. Precise description and measurement of the behavior under study

2. Careful analysis and demonstration of the conditions that control the behavior

3. Application to socially important behaviors in their usual social settings

Source: Baer, Wolf, & Risley, 1968.

behavior were the cues or prompts and the consequences given by the instructor. These antecedents and consequences were used to exert control over the person. Little consideration was given to the meaning of the events to the person or the person's physical condition, the impact of environmental factors (e.g., heat, noise, crowds), or qualities of the task and prompts (e.g., relevance, challenge, learning style). Consequences were defined in terms of the instructor giving and withdrawing tangible reinforcement or punishment; the person's motivation to control his or her environment was not considered. Too often, the emphasis was on internal validity (i.e., procedures that demonstrate experimental control) rather than ecological validity (i.e., what works for this child and family in their day-to-day activities and environment) (Carr, 1997).

Although these applications of behavioral psychology to the treatment of individuals with cognition and emotional impairments were coercive, they need not be. Integrating behavioral principles within the principles of cognitive psychology while maintaining the values and beliefs of progressivism can lead to "a more active process of learning, and a greater ability to see the dominant modes of thought and behavior which we wish to challenge or change" (McIntosh, 1983, p. 2). Because applied behavior analysis requires careful study of the conditions that "control" behavior, psychologists and special educators have developed a much greater understanding of and respect for the impact of environmental and personal factors on behavior (Nichols, 2000; Vaughn, Dunlap, Fox, Clarke, & Bucy, 1997). Although many researchers and practitioners advocate for forms of applied behavior analysis that are coercive and not concerned with the social context of children's lives (including those who practice the ABA currently popular to train children with autism), another branch of applied behavior analysis has evolved into what is known as positive behavioral support.

Carr identified four distinguishing dimensions of positive behavioral support: 1) consumers are collaborators, not helpers; 2) practices must work for consumers in their everyday activities and settings; 3) "success" is defined by greater inclusion in community-based activities; and 4) the individual with disabilities is viewed as "only one participant in a complex, interactive system" (1997, p. 209). These defining characteristics elaborate on Baer, Wolf, and Risley's (1968) guideline to address socially important behaviors in their typical social settings. Furthermore, these researchers and practitioners have moved from a belief in scientific laws that control human behavior (and a focus on the person with an impairment or excess behavior as a problem to be corrected) to a commitment to carefully investigate the myriad influences that handicap a person. An important goal of intervention is to find ways to reduce or eliminate barriers to successful inclusion, which may lie outside the person more than within (Gallagher, 1998; Trent, Artiles, & Englert, 1998).

Another application of behavioral psychology is Direct Instruction (DI), formerly known as DISTAR (Direct Instruction Strategies for Teaching Arithmetic and Reading). DI is based on analyses of the subject matter, including the important concepts, the relationship between concepts, and how the concepts form the whole; the communication that will effectively convey the concepts and relationships among concepts; and the methods by which teachers can deliver the lessons most effectively and efficiently (Engelmann & Carnine, 1982; Tarver, 1996). Although critics of DI have raised concerns that the scripted lessons may be dry, any type of lesson can be presented in a dry style of delivery. If delivered well, DI lessons can be exuberant, giving children a context in which they are encouraged to move and shout as a legitimate part of learning. Furthermore, the "call and response" format provides a familiar culture of participation for many children. Because the rules of participation and the rules for constructing new understandings are explicit and consistent, DI teaches children from nondominant cultures how to succeed in school, thus gaining access to the "culture of power" from which they are too often excluded in more child-centered, constructivist classrooms (Delpit, 1998).

This chapter has identified numerous characteristics of behavioral approaches and demonstrates that there is no single behavioral approach. In this text, we will use the term *systematic instruction* to refer to a selection of behavioral strategies. The features of systematic instruction embedded in the practices described in this book are listed Table 1.7.

THE SEARCH FOR A PEDAGOGY OF SUCCESS

Educators now know a good deal about how children learn. Many approaches grounded in behaviorist theory have clearly provided opportunities for children whose abilities and talents may have otherwise languished. The development of special education instructional technology has provided opportunities for many children who, in the past, would have been excluded from public schools and community life. In spite of the positive impact of systematic instruction, dangers also exist. As discussed previously, instructional methods can become separate from the curriculum; isolated skills may be taught in a part–whole, reductionist approach; instruction may focus on chil-

Table 1.7.   Features of systematic instruction

Instruction is individualized. This does not require individual instruction, which is provided only one to one. Individualization can also occur within whole-class or small-group instruction.

Curriculum content and instructional processes are subjected to task or concept analysis. This does not imply that parts are taught separately from or prior to the whole. Rather, they have been explicated to ensure that they receive intentional and, when needed by individual students, more intensive instruction.

Observable and measurable objectives are established for curriculum, units and/or lessons comprising the curriculum and, when necessary and appropriate, for individual children.

Specific cues or prompts are used to promote initial performance or successive approximations toward desired objectives; and to guide practice or independent performance that is "accurate."

Active engagement and participation becomes a prerequisite to learning. In keeping with the principle of individualization, active engagement may "look" different for each child.

Specific correction procedures are applied to prevent failure. Correction procedures are neither punitive nor substitutes for problem solving, discovery learning, or self-correction.

Reinforcement is provided for appropriate responses to increase the likelihood that they will be repeated and to motivate students toward greater challenges. Although tangible rewards may be helpful to engage a student who has experienced little success, the most powerful rewards are usually those that foster a sense of belonging, a sense of control over one's situation (e.g., succeeding at challenging work), or joy in the work itself (Glasser, 1992; Kunc, 2000).

Maintenance and generalization procedures are used to ensure a range of applications for knowledge and skills, demonstrated over time (Stokes & Baer, 1977).

Ongoing assessments are put in place to ensure that learning is occurring continuously.

dren's impairments and overlook their strengths; and remediation may take precedence over enrichment. Similarly, rigid adherence to constructivist practices built on Piagetian models of cognitive development can fail to provide positive learning experiences for all students. The differing concerns and abilities found among children in an inclusive classroom require teachers to provide individualization and differentiated instruction. Curricular, instructional, and environmental adaptations need to be made in response to differences in students' temperaments, learning styles, interests, and abilities within the specific context of their classroom communities. Children's failure to be self-directed, active learners may reflect sociocultural expectations, developmental idiosyncrasies, and/or specific disabilities. To be successful, some of these children may need more direct instruction and external guidance from adults than what may be conceived as developmentally appropriate.

These critiques are not intended to diminish the significant achievements that have resulted from the application of either behavioral or cognitive psychology in schools. Rather, we are interested in developing a rationale for the blending of systematic and constructivist approaches to create approaches that can enable all children to participate as active members of learning communities in ways that enrich their lives, expand their experiences, promote their independence, and develop their capacities. The contributors to this text hope that by applying their understanding of cognitive theory, culture and learning, behaviorism, and instructional technology with Dewey's (1938, 1964/1902) notion of progressive education, teachers will gain knowledge of both theoretical understandings and practical approaches to instruction that can be applied in diverse environments. The examples offered in the following chapters are effective instructional approaches for all children in ordinary elementary schools and classrooms. These examples reflect Dewey's belief that the role of education is to provide experiences through which students can develop their problem-solving capacities. Although they represent an eclectic application of a variety of methodologies, what the examples all have in common is an understanding that knowledge is the consequence of individuals participating actively in their physical and social worlds, and that individuals are driven to arrive at solutions to problems that are of interest and concern to their lives. The teacher's role is to create opportunities and guide students through these experiences in ways that are growth promoting and, therefore, "educative" (Dewey, 1938). This is what we define as a pedagogy of success.

REFERENCES

Apple, M. (1979). *Ideology and curriculum.* Boston: Routledge & Kegan.

Archambault, R.D. (Ed.). (1964). *John Dewey on education.* University of Chicago Press.

Archambault, R.D. (Ed.). (1966). *John Dewey on education: Appraisals.* New York: Random House.

Baer, D.M., Wolf, M.M., & Risley, T.R. (1968). Some current dimensions of applied behavior analysis. *Journal of Applied Behavior Analysis, 1*(1), 91–97.

Berk, L., & Winsler, A. (1995). *Scaffolding children's learning: Vygotsky and early childhood education.* Washington, DC: National Association for the Education of Young Children.

Bredekamp, S., & Copple, C. (Eds.) (1997). *Developmentally appropriate practices in early childhood programs.* (Rev. ed.). Washington, DC: National Association for the Education of Young Children.

Brooks, J.G., & Brooks, M.G. (1994). *The case for the constructivist classroom.* Alexandria, VA: Association for Supervision and Curriculum Development.

Burman, S. (1994). *Deconstructing developmental psychology.* New York: Routledge.

Carr, E.G. (1997). The evolution of applied behavior analysis into positive behavior support. *Journal of The Association for Persons with Severe Handicaps, 22*(4), 208–209.

Cole, M. (1996). *Cultural psychology: A once and future discipline.* Cambridge, MA: Belknap Press of Harvard University Press.

Delpit, L.D. (1995). *Other people's children: Culture conflict in the classroom.* New York: New Press.

Delpit, L.D. (1998). The silenced dialogue: Power and pedagogy in educating other people's children. *Harvard Educational Review, 58*(3), 280–298.

Dewey, J. (1938). *Experience and education.* New York: Macmillan.

Dewey, J. (1964). The child and the curriculum. In R. D. Archambault (Ed.), *John Dewey on education* (pp. 339–358). Chicago: University of Chicago Press. (Original work published 1902.)

Engelmann, S., & Carnine, D. (1982). *Theory of instruction: Principles and applications.* New York: Irvington Publishers.

Gallagher, D.J. (1998). The scientific knowledge base of special education: Do we know what we think we know? *Exceptional Children, 64*(4), 493–502.

Glasser, W. (1992). *The quality school.* New York: Harper Perennial Library.

Grumet, M. (1998). *Bitter milk: Women and teaching.* Amherst: University of Massachusetts Press.

Hall, E.T. (1983). *The dance of life: The other dimension of time.* New York: Doubleday.

Harris, K.R., & Graham, S. (1994). Constructivism: Principles, paradigms, and integration. *Journal of Special Education, 28*(3), 233–247.

Henson, K.T. (1995). *Curriculum development for educational reform.* New York: HarperCollins College Publishers.

James, W. (1991). What pragmatism means (Lecture No. 2). In J.E. Miller, Jr. (Ed.), *Heritage of American literature: Civil war to the present, volume II* (pp. 569–571). New York: Harcourt Brace Jovanovich College Publishers. (Original work published 1907).

Katz, M. (1971). *Class, bureaucracy and change: The illusion of educational change in America.* New York: Praeger.

Kunc, N. (2000). Rediscovering the right to belong. In R.A. Villa & J.S. Thousand (Eds.), *Restructuring for caring and effective education: Piecing the puzzle together* (2nd ed., pp. 77–92). Baltimore: Paul H. Brookes Publishing Co.

Ladson-Billings, G. (1994). *The dreamkeepers: Successful teachers of African American children.* Cambridge, MA: Harvard University Press.

Lane, H. (1976). *The wild boy of Aveyron.* Cambridge, MA: Harvard University Press.

McIntosh, P. (1983). *Interactive phases of curricular re-vision: A feminist perspective* (Working Paper No. 124). Wellesley, MA: Wellesley College, Center for Research on Women.

McIntosh, P. (1990). *Interactive phases of curricular and personal re-vision with regard to race* (Working Paper No. 219). Wellesley, MA: Wellesley College, Center for Research on Women.

Mager, R.F., & Pipe, P. (1970). *Analyzing performance problems.* Belmont, CA: Fearon-Pitman Publishers, Inc.

Maier, S.F., & Seligman, M. (1976). Learned helplessness: Theory and evidence. *Journal of Experimental Psychology, 105,* 3–46.

Mallory, B., & New, R. (1996). *Diversity and developmentally appropriate practice.* New York: Teachers College Press.

Maslow, A.H. (1987). *Motivation and personality* (3rd ed.). New York: HarperCollins.

Moshman, D. (1982). Exogenous, endogenous, and dialectical constructivism. *Developmental Review, 2,* 371–384.

Nichols, P. (2000). The role of cognition and affect in a functional behavior analysis. *Exceptional Children, 66*(3), 393–402.

Perkins, D. (1999). The many faces of constructivism. *Educational Leadership, 57*(3), 6–11.

Phillips, D.C., & Soltis, J.F. (1991). *Perspectives on learning.* New York: Teachers College Press.

Popham, W.J. (1973a). *Criterion referenced instruction.* Belmont, CA: Fearon Publishers.

Popham, W.J. (1973b). *The uses of instructional objectives: A personal perspective.* Belmont, CA: Fearon Publishers.

Popham, W.J., & Baker, E.L. (1970). *Systematic instruction.* Englewood Cliffs, NJ: Prentice Hall.

Safford, P.L., & Safford, E.J. (1996). *A history of childhood and disability.* New York: Teachers College Press.

Seligman, M.E.P. (1990). *Learned optimism.* New York: Alfred A. Knopf.

Skinner, B.F. (1968). *The technology of teaching.* New York: Appleton-Century-Crofts.

Skinner, B.F. (1971). *Beyond freedom and dignity.* New York: Alfred A. Knopf.

Stokes, T., & Baer, D. (1977). An implicit technology of generalization. *Journal of Applied Behavior Analysis, 10,* 349–367.

Tarver, S.G. (1996). Direct instruction. In W. Stainback & S. Stainback (Eds.), *Controversial issues confronting special education: Divergent perspectives* (pp. 143–165). Needham Heights, MA: Allyn & Bacon.

Thorndike, E.L. (1910). The contribution of psychology to education. *Journal of Educational Psychology, 1,* 5–12.

Trent, S.C., Artiles, A.J., & Englert, C.S. (1998). From deficit thinking to social constructivism: A review of theory, research, and practice in special education. *Review of Research in Special Education, 23,* 277–307.

Tyack, D., & Cuban, L. (1995). *Tinkering toward utopia: A century of public school reform.* Cambridge, MA: Harvard University Press.

Tyler, R.W. (1950). *Basic principles of curriculum and instruction.* Chicago: University of Illinois Press.

UNESCO. (1997). *Inclusive schools and community support programs.* Report 1996, First Phase 1997. Paris: Author.

UNESCO. (2000). *Inclusive education and education for all: A challenge and a vision.* Paris: Author, Section for Special Needs Education.

Vaughn, B.J., Dunlap, G., Fox, L., Clarke, S., & Bucy, M. (1997). Parent–professional partnership in behavioral support: A case study of community-based intervention. *Journal of The Association for Persons with Severe Handicaps, 22*(4), 186–197.

Vygotsky, L.S. (1962). *Language and thought.* Cambridge, MA: MIT Press.

Vygotsky, L.S. (1978). *Mind and society.* Cambridge, MA: Harvard University Press.

Walkerdine, V. (1984). Developmental psychology and the child-centered pedagogy: The insertion of Piaget into early education. In J. Henriques, W. Hollyway, C. Urwin, C. Venn, & V. Walkerdine (Eds.), *Changing the subject: Psychology, social regulation and subjectivity* (pp. 152–202). London: Methuen.

CHAPTER TWO

Addressing Issues of Cultural and Linguistic Diversity in the Early Childhood Classroom

MONICA MILLER MARSH

During the mid-1980s, the National Association for the Education of Young Children (NAEYC), the largest professional organization in the field of early childhood education, published a set of guidelines defining developmentally appropriate practices (DAP) for programs serving children from birth to age 8 (Bredekamp, 1987). The guidelines were developed in response to the conservative backlash during the Reagan era that placed a renewed emphasis on the measurement of the abilities of young children and the accountability of teachers. The 1987 DAP guidelines provided a pedagogical framework for early childhood educators to follow as they developed curricula and drew on instructional strategies. The guidelines specified teaching practices that were considered appropriate for young children and contrasted them with practices that were considered inappropriate. The designated appropriate practices were considered by the NAEYC to be best practices for all young children.

This chapter discusses the controversy among early childhood educators provoked by the 1987 publication of the DAP guidelines and illustrates how the notion of best practices has shifted over time. Following this discussion, a day in the life of a first-grade classroom is

---

Portions of this chapter also appear in Miller Marsh, M. (2003). *The social fashioning of teacher identities*. New York: Peter Lang Publishing, Inc.

chronicled through the use of quotations, stories, and vignettes. Emphasis is placed on the diverse array of teaching strategies this teacher uses as she works toward best practices for all of the children in her care.

THE EVOLUTION OF BEST PRACTICES

The original version of the DAP guidelines is built on a Piagetian theoretical foundation that is child centered and constructivist in nature. From a Piagetian perspective, each child is conceptualized as a unique being that possesses an inner potential. According to Piaget (1971), children experience universal, linear stages of development across a variety of dimensions (e.g., social, emotional, cognitive). Children are believed to be continuously in the process of actively constructing their intellectual capabilities as they move toward becoming independent abstract thinkers. Early childhood teachers take on the role of facilitators as they carefully observe a child's level of ability and interest and present learning experiences and activities to that child when he or she is developmentally ready. From this perspective, race, class, gender, cognitive ability, and physical ableness are perceived as individual characteristics located within the child.

A number of critiques written by scholars in the field of early childhood education emerged in response to the DAP publication (see Kessler & Swadener, 1992; Mallory & New, 1994). These scholars argued that the underlying assumption of the DAP guidelines was that all children in all classrooms could benefit from the same educational experiences. Furthermore, they contended that what they perceived as the white middle-class standards advocated in the DAP guidelines maintain social inequities by hierarchically organizing knowledge and discouraging the development of alternative methods of teaching that may better meet the concerns of non-dominant cultural groups of children (Lubeck, 1994; Mallory & New, 1994). If the instruction in schools is based on white, middle-class norms, then children who are white and middle-class enter the classroom as successful communicators because the language and communication patterns used by their teachers are already familiar to them. For children who are not members of the dominant culture, however, a mismatch occurs between home and school when they enter the classroom (Berk & Winsler, 1995). This places children from nondominant cultures at a disadvantage, because from the time they enter school they must focus their efforts on acquiring the "language of schooling" in which their Caucasian, middle-class peers are already well versed.

The NAEYC responded to these critiques by publishing *Developmentally Appropriate Practice in Early Childhood Programs* (Bredekamp & Copple, 1997), a revised edition of the 1987 document. Among other things, the revised DAP document acknowledges that teachers need to develop an understanding of the social and cultural contexts of children and families. It incorporates the work of Russian psychologist Vygotsky and others who promote an approach to learning and teaching that places greater emphasis on the social, cultural, and historical aspects of a child's life. More specifically, Vygotskian theory emphasizes the social origins of language and its influence on the development of individual thought (Vygotsky, 1978). For this reason, the work of Vygotsky has been referred to as social constructionist as well as constructivist.

Rather than conceiving of learning as taking place inside the child, from a Vygotskian perspective, learning happens outside the child in relation with others. An individual's development depends on her or his interactions with others, and the role of the teacher is to support and assist that child's cognitive functions, which are already in the process of developing (Berk & Winsler, 1995; Tharp & Gallimore, 1988). Teachers provide students with experiences that are challenging yet can successfully be accomplished with the guidance of adults and more capable peers. The high priority given to language and the emphasis on co-construction of knowledge means that the most effective type of instruction occurs when teachers work individually with students or when students are given opportunities to work collaboratively. Parents, siblings, and other caregivers are called on as resources to work in collaboration with school personnel.

Although still firmly rooted in Piagetian theory, the revised DAP document acknowledges that best practices can differ across early childhood contexts. Aspects of constructivism, social constructionism, behaviorism, and social learning theory can be considered appropriate practices, especially when incorporated into an inclusive early childhood classroom (Powell, 2000).

ENGLISH LANGUAGE LEARNERS

Inclusive early childhood classrooms are comprised of children with varying physical, emotional, and intellectual abilities as well as diverse cultural, socioeconomic, and linguistic backgrounds. Teaching English Language Learners (ELL) in the early childhood classroom is an area that is receiving increased attention. The number of children in the

United States who speak English as a second language is growing. During the 1993–1994 academic year, 2.1 million students in public schools in the United States were speaking English as a second language (Kushner & Ortiz, 2000). More than 200 languages were represented, with Spanish predominating (Kushner & Ortiz, 2000). According to Wong-Fillmore (1991), children who are considered ELL fall into two distinct categories: 1) children born to recent immigrants or who immigrated to this country at a very early age and 2) children born in the United States but immersed in home environments that use the linguistic, social, and cultural norms of their first language. The Bilingual Education Provision of the Improving America's Schools Act of 1994 (PL 103–382) requires that non–English-speaking children be provided with school services that help them to acquire English as a second language. Services range from programs that provide language instruction in a child's native language to full immersion in English-only programs.

According to the National Institute on Early Childhood and Development, ELL should be provided with opportunities to develop high levels of English proficiency that complement their first language skills (Kushner & Ortiz, 2000). Instruction in the primary language can result in cognitive advantages and development of the personal, linguistic, and cultural competence that is necessary for academic and social success in school (Hamayan & Damico, 1991). Children should be provided with opportunities to express in English what they already know in their native language and to build on their knowledge and cognitive skills. Even after students are able to receive all of their instruction in English, providing opportunities to "refine their native language skills" will allow them to "become fully bilingual and biliterate" (Kushner & Ortiz, 2000, p. 129).

Although the DAP guidelines provide little specific direction for early childhood teachers who have ELL enrolled in their classrooms, they do refer the reader to the NAEYC position statement, *Responding to Linguistic and Cultural Diversity—Recommendations for Effective Early Childhood Education* (1995), which addresses this issue. The NAEYC advised that early childhood teachers provide "multiple learning alternatives" and suggested that teachers use a range of formal and informal assessments, observations, and samples of children's work to identify a student's English language abilities and the areas that need to be strengthened. Teachers are also encouraged to arrange activity schedules; facilitate cooperative learning opportunities; and modify, adapt, and create materials for ELL when needed (Kushner & Ortiz, 2000). Early childhood teachers are encouraged to pay special attention to the differences between the home and school culture and work to negotiate between the two contexts. For example, curriculum and instruction should accept and respect parental expectations while simultaneously preparing children to be socially and academically successful in the school culture (NAEYC, 1995).

THE FIRST-GRADE
CLASSROOM OF MS. GONZALES

Ms. Gonzales, a bilingual teacher who is Latina, can occasionally be heard speaking or reading in Spanish to the first-graders in her classroom. This is one of many teaching strategies Ms. Gonzales uses to meet the needs of the diverse population of children in her care. The teaching strategies that Ms. Gonzales employs as she strives to create an inclusive and socially just early childhood classroom reflect how she incorporates some of the previously discussed theories into her daily practice.

Ms. Gonzales' first-grade classroom is large, stimulating, and full of activity. Every shelf and countertop seems to be covered with science artifacts, math manipulatives, books, or writing materials. Colorful posters relating to the topics the children have been studying in class line the walls. Artwork, including tissue paper cutouts that the children created to celebrate Día de los Los Muertos, hang from a clothesline that is strung across the room. Learning centers for math and writing and a "book nook," complete with overstuffed pillows and a rocking chair, are positioned around the perimeter of the room. Six child-sized tables and chairs are positioned on one side of the room.

There are 26 first graders in Ms. Gonzales' class. Demographically, the class consists of 4 African American children (3 girls, 1 boy), 3 Southeast Asian children (1 girl, 2 boys), 1 East Asian female, 3 Latino children (2 girls, 1 boy) and 15 Caucasian children (7 boys, 8 girls). Seven children attend the English as a Second Language (ESL) Program, three of whom are Spanish speakers. Mirroring the socioeconomic makeup of the elementary school in which the first grade is housed, half of Ms. Gonzales class is considered middle-class to upper-middle class whereas the other half is considered low-income.

Hidden Numbers

The first-graders and Ms. Gonzales are sitting in a circle on the floor. Ms. Gonzales picks up the large plastic bag sitting in front of her that is filled with num-

ber boards and number tiles. She takes a number board and a container of tiles out of the bag and dumps the tiles on the number board. She looks at John who is sitting next to her and asks, "John, will you play with me today?" A huge smile spreads across John's face as he says, "Yes."

Ms. Gonzales explains that the name of this game is Hidden Numbers. She looks down at the pile of tiles then back up at the faces around the group, "What do you think John and I should do first?" "Turn the numbers down!" says Charlie. Ms. Gonzales says, "That's a good guess, but actually we need to turn all of the numbers up!" She and John quickly turn all of the tiles face up. She looks back at the group, "Okay, what do you think we should do now?" There is some chatting among the children and several of them put their hands in the air, indicating that they have an answer. Ms. Gonzales calls on Charlene, who explains that they should put the numbers in the correct order on the board.

"That's right! John and I are only going to put the numbers 1 to 20 on the board for right now. When you play, I would like for you to put all 100 numbers on the number board." Ms. Gonzales and John finish placing the number tiles in their correct spots and Ms. Gonzales says, "We are now ready to play the game. I am going to ask John to cover his eyes with his hands. I am then going to pick up one square, turn it over, and ask him to open his eyes and see if he can guess what number it is." She smiles at John who turns his head to the side and covers his eyes with his hands.

Ms. Gonzales picks up the tile with number 16 written on it, puts her finger over her lips gesturing for the children to remain silent, and shows the tile to the class before turning it face down and replacing it on the number board. She then tells John that he can look. It takes a few seconds before John shouts out "16!" The children and Ms. Gonzales clap. John and Ms. Gonzales switch roles and demonstrate one more time how this game is played.

Ms. Gonzales then explains to the children that they will continue to work with the partner assigned to them 2 days ago. Some children look a bit disappointed, while others look across the circle and flash their partner a big smile. Ms. Gonzales directs the children to pick up a container of number tiles and a number board and to find a spot that will be comfortable for them to play the game.

Ms. Gonzales heads over to Dionne and Grace first and says, "I challenge this team to put the numbers 1 through 20 on the board and to name each number in order." Dionne smiles and replies, "Okay!" Grace, looking puzzled, stares down at the number board. Ms. Gonzales translates the direction that she has just given in English into Spanish. Grace looks at Ms. Gonzales and smiles. Then she turns to Dionne, and still smiling, she nods her head and says, "Okay."

As Ms. Gonzales is talking with Grace and Dionne, some giggling is heard across the room. Ivan and John are moving each other's tiles around on their boards and laughing. Their partners, Charlie and Lynn, are also laughing. Ms. Gonzales makes eye contact with Ivan and shakes her head. He quickly averts his eyes and begins to rearrange the tiles on his own board. Ms. Gonzales finishes her conversation with Grace and Dionne and moves toward the giggling foursome.

Pete and Trevor are placing their numbers on the number board. "How's your number board going?" asks Ms. Gonzales as she walks by. Trevor puts the number 81 on the 18. Pete looks at him and says, "That is 81—not 18!" Together they search for the correct number tile. ✓

At that moment a number tile is heard bouncing off of the heater. Ms. Gonzales looks at Ivan and John who are tossing the tiles, and their two partners, who are laughing. Without saying a word she walks up to the chalkboard and writes Ivan's initials and then John's initials in a box that has a BB (Beware Box, explained later in this chapter) written above it. She then walks back to the four children. Looking directly at Lynn and Charlie, Ms. Gonzales says, "Part of your job right now is to help Ivan and John focus on the math game. The tiles need to be placed on the board in order for the game to be played. If you need to move to a different spot so that you are not distracted by one another, I will help you carry your board. Would you like me to help you move or do you want to stay here and play the game?" The children say that they want to continue sitting next to one another. Ms. Gonzales says, "Fine. I trust that you will do your work." She then walks over to the carpet on which Paul and Doug are sitting.

Paul turns over a 10 and a 20 as Doug covers his eyes. Paul indicates to Doug that it is okay to look and Doug opens his eyes. Ms. Gonzales says to Doug, "There are two tiles missing that are together. Can you figure out where they are?" Doug answers that 10 and 20 are missing. Ms. Gonzales asks him how he knew. At first he shrugs his shoulders but after some encouragement he tells Ms. Gonzales that he knows because they are in the same line with 30, 40, 50, and so forth. He uses these numbers when he counts by 10's. Paul, in halting English, explains that this is a pattern. Ms. Gonzales tells Paul that he is absolutely right. She then challenges them to turn three tiles over for the next play to see if they can discover another pattern.

In this vignette, Ms. Gonzales presents a mathematical activity, *Hidden Numbers* in which children are asked to sharpen their counting skills, practice number identification, and discover numerical patterns. She has thought very carefully about not only the mathematical abilities of the children that she has placed in each partnership but also about the linguistic and social abilities of each child.

Consider the partnership of Dionne and Grace. Grace, the newest student in the class, has just arrived from Mexico. She speaks very little English, though her number recognition skills are quite good. Ms. Gonzales says Dionne, an African American female, is in need of special education services. Although Dionne had been referred for special education services, she did not meet school district criteria for any specific type of disability, so she was considered ineligible. Ms. Gonzales modifies and adapts Dionne's assignments in ways that allow her to build on her abilities. Ms. Gonzales explains how she adapts spelling assignments for Dionne:

> In spelling, you're supposed to write a sentence for each word and Dionne doesn't write on her own yet. She's getting there..... I have Dionne dictate a sentence to an adult; they write it down and she copies it. I still expect her to do the spelling sentences. I expect her to be able to manipulate the spelling words into language and to recognize that her sentences have meaning in the same way that I would do for the other students.

Rather than expecting less of Dionne, Ms. Gonzales modifies lessons and activities for her that accommodate and stretch her intellectual abilities. Dionne is working on identifying the numbers 1 through 20. She has number recognition skills, but she cannot always put numerals in the correct order. Grace, however, can recognize the numbers, but she cannot always correctly identify them in the English language. In this activity these two students work together to share and build on the knowledge that each brings to the partnership.

Pete is also an ELL; he has been in the classroom since the beginning of the school year and his English has improved greatly. Pete and Trevor, like Dionne and Grace, assist one another in this particular learning activity through the challenges that they provide for one another and by correcting one another's mistakes.

Ms. Gonzales does her best to accommodate the concerns of Pete, Grace, and the other ELLs in her classroom, thereby increasing the impact of the ESL classes they all attend. She accomplishes this in a variety of ways. She gives directions in Spanish as well as English when she is introducing new activities. She provides picture books in a variety of languages in the "book nook" and occasionally she will read a story in both Spanish and English. For example, she read the Spanish version of the *Paper Bag Princess* by Robert Munsch (1992) to the class by reading each page in Spanish first and then translating it into English. As a result, many of the children in the classroom have come to appreciate the Spanish language. On one occasion, an English-speaking child requested that a book be read in Spanish and English. Ms. Gonzales turned the request over to the children and asked them to make the decision by casting a vote in favor of reading in Spanish and English, which resulted in a tie. Ms. Gonzales responded by saying, "I think that because we had those extra 20 minutes of math and I have so many special things that I wanted to do this afternoon, today I'm just going to read in English. But, at some point, maybe during quiet time, for those people who are interested, I will read it only in Spanish." She did make time available later in the day to read the book in Spanish, and more than half the class listened to the story a second time.

By drawing on her own bilingualism in the classroom, Ms. Gonzales illustrates to the children that multiple languages can be used to communicate knowledge. Ms. Gonzales also validates the languages of the Hmong and Korean children as she illustrates that language diversity is a positive attribute that children bring into the classroom.

Ms. Gonzales draws on all types of children's literature to provide opportunities for all of her students, not just those who are ELLs, to see themselves in the curriculum. She does this by choosing children's books that represent children and families from diverse racial, ethnic, socioeconomic, and religious backgrounds as well as varying levels of physical and cognitive abilities. For example, the children were formally introduced to issues of ethnicity and class when they engaged in an author study of Vera B. Williams.

Although Williams is Caucasian, she writes about children and families who are members of nondominant cultures. The class read six of Williams' books, including *A Chair for My Mama, Something Special For Me,* and *Music, Music for Everyone.* These three books feature a young Latina named Rosa whose family experiences economic hardship. Through reading and discussing such stories, Ms. Gonzales presents the children in her class with representations of life experiences within an ethnic community. Furthermore, she legitimizes the lives of the students and families who are members of nondominant cultures by providing them with representations of their communities and experiences within the school curriculum.

At times, Ms. Gonzales uses literature to work actively against stereotypes and prejudices that are exhibited by the children. One of the chapter books that Ms. Gonzales reads to the children is *Justin and the Best Biscuits in the World.* Although the topic of this book is African

American cowboys in the United States, Ms. Gonzales uses the text as an opportunity to also address the issue of gender. Consider the quotation made by one of the cowboys in the book and the following exchange that was recorded in Ms. Gonzales' classroom.

> "Women's work! I hate it!" Ms. Gonzales stops reading and says, "I bet some people other than women wash dishes and make beds. What do you think?" Several children begin to speak at once. Ms. Gonzales asks for children to raise their hands. She calls on Janice, who shares that her father puts the dishes in the dishwasher every night and that he also does the laundry. Charlie states that he thinks it is women's work because his mom does all of the housework. Other children share what happens in their homes. Ms. Gonzales explains that both she and her husband share the tasks at home. She then asks the children to think about how they share the responsibilities for keeping the classroom neat and describes how both boys and girls carry out the tasks of sweeping the floor, scrubbing the tables, and organizing things around the room.

By acknowledging and questioning the sexist quote in the book, Ms. Gonzales disrupts stereotypical representations of women in children's texts. By asking the children to examine the sexist passage in the book, she also invites them to think more critically about the gendered roles that are traditionally upheld in society. She then asks the children to reflect on their own roles in the classroom, pointing out that gender is not a factor in terms of who does the sweeping, cleaning, and scrubbing in their first-grade classroom. By asking children to question stereotypical representations of gender, by organizing situations such as classroom cleanup in which children work across gender lines, and by continually presenting children with examples that run counter to rigidly defined notions of gender, Ms. Gonzales disrupts the gender stereotypes that young children often bring with them to school.

In a later conversation, Ms. Gonzales commented on this discussion and her attempts to dispel the stereotypes that exist around issues of gender. She specifically mentioned Charlie as one of the children who had difficulty moving beyond gender stereotypes:

> Charlie has a lot of typically male/female gender lines, and he brings them up all of the time. So whenever he comes

up with one of these comments, I try to ask a follow-up question such as, "I wonder, Charlie, could you do that, too?" And then someone from the other side of the room would go, "Yeah, I do that all the time."

Ms. Gonzales acknowledges that gender discrimination exists. She attempts to disrupt examples of gender discrimination that she encounters in the classroom or in the comments made by the children so that it becomes more difficult for them to maintain stereotypes and prejudices.

In some classrooms prejudice also arises when children from varied backgrounds don't follow codes of acceptable behavior at school. Therefore, Ms. Gonzales makes it a priority to explicitly teach "school culture" to the children in her classroom. From the very beginning of the school year, Ms. Gonzales makes it clear that in her first-grade classroom, everyone is responsible for helping everyone else to be successful. She does this through her chosen teaching strategies and through modeling and verbalizing her expectations for behavior. Modeling is not only used to introduce the idea of a "school culture." Ms. Gonzales uses this modeling technique to introduce many of the new ideas, projects, and even objects used in the classroom.

In *Hidden Numbers*, Ms. Gonzales organizes the math activity so that children work in pairs to co-construct knowledge. Prior to pairing children in lessons such as this, Ms. Gonzales introduces the various math manipulatives, and she models ways to share these materials. First, she provides time for the children to play with the manipulatives. She then makes the distinction between playing and using the materials to solve problems. Each time she introduces a new activity to the group, she chooses one child to help her model how the activity should be carried out.

Another example of this type of modeling occurred one day after the children had a particularly difficult time focusing on their work with their reading buddies. Ms. Gonzales asked a child to role-play with her what a good reading buddy would look like. As the child attempted to interact with Ms. Gonzales, she played with her hair, bit her nails, and acted as if she was trying to get another child's attention across the room. Of course, the children found this role-play to be extremely humorous. When the role-play was completed, Ms. Gonzales asked the children if she had been a helpful reading buddy for her partner. The unanimous answer was "No!" The children were then asked to brainstorm the characteristics of a helpful reading buddy. Two children were then called on to role-play some of the things on the list that the children had generated.

Ms. Gonzales recognizes that even though she explicitly models her expectations for behavior in the classroom, some of the children find it more challenging than others to meet these expectations, especially when they are paired with particular children. Just as Ms. Gonzales intentionally groups children with certain resources together, she also purposefully separates children. For example, she noted that she did not place Paul and Rick, two white males, at the same table. She went on to explain that this was because they were always acting out by giggling, touching, poking, and talking continuously when they were together. She shared the thinking behind the way that she grouped certain children together at the tables where they carried out much of their academic work:

> I made sure that Paul and Rick weren't together, and I know that's a relationship that I'm conscious of. I just place them in separate places almost immediately. There are a couple of groups of kids that I try to spread out, and, at the same time, I try to make sure that there's a couple of strong readers and not so strong readers at every table so that if we had to do a group activity, there would be someone who would kind of take charge if there's any reading that needs to happen. And then other people that can kind of be more general community members have different roles, basically.

Purposefully organizing seating arrangements is another way that Ms. Gonzales helps children to be successful in the classroom. In spite of the best planning, there are occasions when children's actions interfere with their learning or the learning of other students. When these types of situations arise, Ms. Gonzales first attempts to redirect the child's behavior by making eye contact, gently touching the child on the arm or shoulder, or physically positioning herself next to the child. For example, when Alejandro was attempting to entertain the other children at his table by making faces and talking during a literature lesson, Ms. Gonzales simply stopped what she was doing in front of the classroom, looked directly at Alejandro, and put her finger up to her lips. She then walked over to his table, stood beside him, and spent the next several minutes teaching the lesson from this position. Through her actions, Ms. Gonzales refocused Alejandro's attention and the attention of his tablemates without saying a word.

Ms. Gonzales' methods of redirecting a child's actions were not always successful, however. On those occasions, she turned to a more systematic method of classroom management, one that revolved around the use of what Ms. Gonzales referred to as the Beware Box (BB). In *Hidden Numbers,* she used this technique when John and Ivan were tossing their tiles around the room. Ms. Gonzales had unsuccessfully attempted to redirect the behavior of the boys and their partners earlier in the lesson. When this first attempt at redirection failed, Ms. Gonzales walked up to the front of the room and wrote the initials of both boys in the square marked BB on the chalkboard. Ms. Gonzales explained:

> This is my Beware Box. It's like a warning system, so that when I have given a verbal warning to someone already then the second time their name goes into the beware box and that says "Warning! You're about to lose a privilege." If their name would go up for the second time, if they would either get a second warning, or they would continue doing the same thing, I would erase their name out of that box and they would miss their recess. It's like a three-strikes-and-you're-out system.

Through the use of the BB, Ms. Gonzales provides individual students with a clear response to their misbehavior. Yet, rather than simply using this as a strategy to single out individual children, she uses the initials to signal to the class that they are now responsible for assisting that child by not providing an audience for her or his actions. For Ms. Gonzales, misbehavior was something that occurred within a community rather than simply being the disruptive actions of one individual. Signaling to children in this way that they need to be aware of their actions and asking other children to participate in helping individuals redirect their actions are ways that Ms. Gonzales ensures that the social identities of individual children will not be constructed in a negative manner. When individual children take on negative social identities, they tend to become isolated and are set apart from the rest of the group. In Ms. Gonzales' classroom, nobody is excluded from the group as a result of his or her behavior. All of the children are valued and respected as community members.

Ms. Gonzales reinforces this notion of helping one another to be socially successful through the use of another systematic strategy. She rewarded collective behavior through the use of Terrific Table (TT) points. Drawn on the chalkboard next to the BB is a square on the chalkboard with the letters TT above it. In her words:

A table will get Terrific Table points if they seem like they are really working well together. I usually don't focus on just one table—I try to focus on the whole class. If they are really focused on what they are doing then every table will get one point. They are working up to 100 table points... Right now they're working toward a little art project. Our last one was a game day.

Again, Ms. Gonzales turns to an explicit and systematic strategy to support the building of classroom community and collaboration. Ms. Gonzales believes that every child wants to be a successful member of the classroom community and that working together through a point system motivates them to work at behaviors and relationships that are very challenging for some children. It is fitting that they all celebrate their collective success through a special project.

Ms. Gonzales intentionally organizes learning activities so that children have opportunities to work with partners and in both small and large groups. She also provides the children with opportunities to choose to work collaboratively or individually in learning centers. She uses both a teacher-directed and a student-centered approach in the classroom.

The following vignette, titled *Volcanoes,* presents another example of Ms. Gonzales' pedagogy illustrating how she integrates a variety of subject areas and teaching strategies as she presents a science lesson.

Volcanoes

Ms. Gonzales is perched on a stool in the front of the class. "Who can read what we have written on these two sheets of paper?" Ms. Gonzales points to the two sentences and calls on Takisha to read. Takisha reads, "What do you know about volcanoes?" and "What do you want to know about volcanoes?" Ms. Gonzales praises her strong reading skills and explains that she is going to give the children 5 minutes to talk at their tables to see if they can answer the questions that she has written on the paper. Ms. Gonzales explains that after they talk in groups, they will share what they have discussed and she will write the questions on the chart paper.

For the next 5 minutes, the children chat with one another about volcanoes. Ms. Gonzales gives a 2-minute warning and says, "Boys and girls, you

need to finish your conversation. I want to find out what you talked about with the people at your table. If you have something that you would like me to print on one of our charts, please raise your hand." Ms. Gonzales points to the first piece of chart paper and says, "What do you know about volcanoes, Grace?"

Grace responds, "Volcanoes blow up."

"All right," says Ms. Gonzales as she writes the sentence on the chart paper. She asks the children, "What do I need at the end of this sentence?"

Several students shout, "A period!"

"Right," says Ms. Gonzales, "because this is a statement and not a question. Charlie, do you have something to add to one of these posters?"

He points to the second poster and says, "Volcanoes are by houses."

"Hmm," says Ms. Gonzales, "so you want to find out if volcanoes are near houses?" "Yeah," says Charlie.

Ms. Gonzales writes, "Are volcanoes near houses? Can anyone tell me what I need at the end of this sentence?"

A child yells out, "Question mark!"

"A question mark," says Ms. Gonzales. "We need a question mark because we just asked a question."

This type of dialogue continues for about 10 minutes. Children share that they know that volcanoes are hot, that they produce a substance called lava, and that there are volcanoes all over the world. They ask questions about why volcanoes blow up and how hot the rocks are when they blow out of the volcano.

Ms. Gonzales then explains, "Today you will be working at four volcano learning centers. I am not going to pair you with someone, but you can work together if you choose. The first center is a word search. You need to challenge yourself to find some of the words, such as lava *and* volcano, *which we have been using in our discussion today. The second center consists of different types of rocks such as pumice, cinder, and volcanic ash. Descriptions of the rocks are written on these small cards. I want you to use these hand-held magnifying glasses to examine these rocks and then I would like you to draw and write your observations on the sheets of paper that I have put out for you. The third center is a worksheet that has a series of pictures that illustrate the steps of a volcano erupting. I would like you to color the pictures, cut them out, then staple them in the correct order from beginning to end." As Ms. Gonzales describes the steps that need to be done at the third learning center, a tense look crosses over Charlie's face. Charlie asks, "You'll need to cut and staple? What if you don't know how to do it? I'm not so good at cutting and stapling." Ms. Gonzales smiles and says, "You'll need to staple and cut and that's why I'm giving you practice. It is okay to ask someone for help if you need it."*

Ms. Gonzales points to the fourth center and explains that they will be drawing and labeling volcano posters with her, "I will give you more detailed directions when you come to this center to work with me. If you finish a center early, you can look at the books on volcanoes that I have spread out on the carpet for you."

For 1 hour and 15 minutes the children work on the activities at the centers. Some children are working in dyads or triads whereas others are working individually. Charlie calls for Ms. Gonzales to come over to help him work with Alejandro, who is attempting to do the crossword puzzle. "How do you say, 'That is the word that means the volcano blows up' in Spanish?" asks Charlie. Ms. Gonzales asks him to say it in English to Alejandro first, which Charlie does. She then repeats the sentence in Spanish to Charlie who repeats it in Spanish to Alejandro.

After 20 minutes, Ms. Gonzales reminds the children to finish up what they are doing at one center and move on to the next. Dionne, who has been working by herself, begins to cry. "I'm not finished," she sobs. Ms. Gonzales walks over to Dionne, lightly touches her on the arm and says loud enough for only Dionne to hear, "Take your time and finish, Dionne. When you are done you can move to center two. Don't worry about going to center four today. You and I can work together on the poster tomorrow morning." Dionne looks relieved as she wipes her eyes and continues to staple the volcano squares into a sequence.

In this lesson, Ms. Gonzales puts several strategies into practice. First, she begins the lesson by making a K-W-L chart, which allows children to express what they know (K) about the topic of volcanoes and to articulate what they want to learn (W) about volcanoes. Later they will record what they actually learned (L). Ms. Gonzales and the children use the K-W-L chart as both an assessment and a curriculum development tool. It allows Ms. Gonzales to assess the background knowledge that the children possess about this particular topic and helps her to develop curriculum that presents new information that can be used to support what the children already know. The children help to shape the curriculum through the questions that they ask. Ms. Gonzales incorporates these questions into the lessons and activities that she plans for the first graders.

The learning center concept being used in this particular science lesson accommodates the concerns of the diverse academic, language, and fine motor abilities of her students. Students such as Dionne, who are not able to complete the work at a particular center, are given more time to complete the centers that address their greatest concerns.

Ms. Gonzales organizes the centers so that students who are ELLs are able to seek the help of others in the class who are English speakers. Furthermore, children such as Charlie, who have difficulty with fine motor skills, are encouraged to try cutting and stapling on their own first but are encouraged to seek help if these tasks become too frustrating. Ms. Gonzales described Charlie in the following manner:

> Charlie is not very good at physical manipulation. He doesn't cut very well, he doesn't fold very well—things such as that. But I would rather have him do it and practice doing it so that if there were an emergency he could cut himself out!

Even though Charlie has difficulty with his fine motor skills, Ms. Gonzales insists that he can successfully complete the same types of activities as the rest of the class. She often provides him with extra opportunities to practice his fine motor skills, such as cutting strings of yarn with another student that the class will use at a later time to make solar system mobiles. These extra opportunities help Charlie feel more confident in his use of these skills and provide him with practice that will allow him to become more competent.

Ms. Gonzales acknowledges and builds on the resources of each child and helps him or her become more competent in those areas in which he or she is not as skilled. She does not deny the disparate skills and abilities among the children, but rather, she structures learning situations that challenge and build on each child's ability to learn. In addition, she does not deny their frustration and concerns about failing; she affirms their feelings and offers ideas for how they can succeed. Ms. Gonzales provides each child with the opportunity to find a place as a successful person in the classroom.

SUMMARY

Ms. Gonzales draws on a number of instructional strategies to support and sustain an inclusive and equitable classroom community as she attempts to meet the social, emotional, cognitive, and language diversity that this group of first-graders brings with them to school. Ms. Gonzales perceives the diversity among the children in her classroom as a resource and acknowledges the differences in cognitive ability, physical ability, language, race, class, and gender. She explicitly draws on these differences to help children develop deeper understandings of themselves and one another.

Elements of Vygotskian theory are reflected in Ms. Gonzales' pedagogy in the way that she takes an active role in organizing shared learning experiences with and for the children. She intentionally pairs students who can intellectually support and assist one another as they work jointly toward solving a problem. These pairings provide individual children with experiences that challenge their emerging cognitive skills. Ms. Gonzales provides a similar learning experience when she works with individuals or with small groups in a learning center format. For Ms. Gonzales, the creation of knowledge is a shared event.

In addition to teaching practices rooted in Vygotskian theory, Ms. Gonzales draws on intentional and systematic strategies to promote social practices that work against notions of individualism and competitiveness by encouraging members to be responsible for one another (Ladson-Billings, 1994). When a member or members of the group are experiencing difficulty controlling their actions, Ms. Gonzales calls on the rest of the community to support and assist that child. By signaling to children that they need to be aware of their actions and by asking other children to participate in helping individuals redirect their actions, Ms. Gonzales ensures that the social identities of individual children will not be constructed in a negative manner. In this first-grade classroom, no child is excluded from the group as a result of her or his behavior.

This chapter provides an example of how one teacher uses multiple instructional strategies to carry out what she considers to be best practices for young children. Ms. Gonzales creates opportunities for each of the children in her care to craft positive social and academic identities while positioning them as valued and respected members of their first-grade community.

REFERENCES

Berk, L.E., & Winsler, A. (1995). *Scaffolding children's learning: Vygotsky and early childhood education.* Washington, DC: National Association for the Education of Young Children.

Bredekamp, S. (Ed.). (1987). *Developmentally appropriate practice in early childhood programs serving children from birth through age 8.* Washington, DC: National Association for the Education of Young Children.

Bredekamp, S., & Copple, C. (Eds.). (1997). *Developmentally appropriate practice in early childhood programs* (Rev. ed.). Washington, DC: National Association for the Education of Young Children.

Hamayan, E.V., & Damico, J.S. (1991). Developing and using a second language. In E.V. Hamayan & J.S. Damico (Eds.). *Limiting bias in the assessment of bilingual students* (pp. 40–73). Austin, TX: PRO-ED.

Improving America's Schools Act of 1994, PL 103-382, 20 U.S.C. §§ 630 *et seq.*

Kessler, S., & Swadener, E.B. (Eds.). (1992). *Reconceptualizing the early childhood curriculum: Beginning the dialogue.* New York: Teachers College Press.

Kushner, M., & Ortiz, A. (2000). The preparation of early childhood education teachers to serve English language learners. In *New teachers for a new century: The future of early childhood professional preparation* (pp. 125–154). Washington, DC: National Institute on Early Childhood Development and Education, U.S. Department of Education.

Ladson-Billings, G. (1994). *The dreamkeepers: Successful teachers of African American children.* San Francisco: Jossey-Bass.

Lubeck, S. (1994). The politics of developmentally appropriate practice: Exploring issues of culture, class, and curriculum. In B.L. Mallory & R.S. New (Eds.), *Diversity & developmentally appropriate practices: Challenges for early childhood education.* New York: Teachers College Press.

Mallory, B.L., & New, R.S. (Eds.). (1994). *Diversity and developmentally appropriate practices: Challenges for early childhood education.* New York: Teachers College Press.

National Association for the Education of Young Children (NAEYC). (1995). NAEYC's position statement: Responding to linguistic and cultural diversity —recommendations for effective early childhood education. *Young Children, 51*(2), 4–12.

Piaget, J. (1971). *Psychology and epistemology.* Harmondsworth, England: Penguin.

Powell, D. (2000). Preparing early childhood professionals to work with families. In *New teachers for a new century: The future of early childhood professional preparation* (pp. 61–87). Washington, DC: National Institute on Early Childhood Development and Education, U.S. Department of Education.

Tharp, R.G., & Gallimore, R. (1988). *Rousing minds to life.* New York: Cambridge University Press.

Vygotsky, L.S. (1978). *Mind in society: The development of higher psychological processes.* Cambridge, MA: Harvard University Press.

Wong-Fillmore, L. (1991). Language and cultural issues in early education. In S.L. Kagan (Ed.), The care and education of America's young children: Obstacles and opportunities. *Ninetieth yearbook of the National Society for the Study of Education* (pp. 30–49). Chicago: National Society for the Study of Education.

CHAPTER THREE

Project-Based Instruction

JUDY W. KUGELMASS

Project-based instruction (PBI) is a teaching approach that requires systematic planning of activities and careful guidance and promotes productive dialogue and interaction among children. PBI provides a framework for creating the kind of balance between systematic instruction and constructivist practice that can ensure the success of every child in an inclusive elementary classroom. In this chapter, PBI and related concepts are defined, their history explored, and theoretical and research bases examined. The roles of teachers and support personnel in inclusive classrooms implementing PBI are also described and the phases teachers move through as they develop projects with students are presented. The "Foxfire approach" is offered to illustrate how teachers can create a classroom culture that supports the effective application of PBI in heterogeneous classrooms. Two examples of PBI demonstrate why teachers become committed to using projects in their classrooms. The chapter concludes with a discussion of the implications of teachers' work for the development of inclusive classrooms.

PROJECT-BASED INSTRUCTION

In describing the approach to teaching presented in this chapter, the author carefully chose the term *project-based instruction* (PBI) rather than either of the more commonly used *project method* or *project approach*. Although each designation signifies instructional methods in which classroom investigations are central, PBI differs from the others in that projects are intentionally designed by teachers and students to address specific learning objectives. PBI emphasizes key terms: *Instruction* is *based* on the activities that take place within the context of classroom *projects.* The objectives addressed by these projects may include those prescribed by mandated curriculum objectives, state or school district learning standards, and/or individualized learning objectives, such as those found in a student's individualized education program (IEP). In PBI, teachers intentionally facilitate activities designed to develop knowledge, skills, and/or dispositions while reinforcing and applying children's existing cognitive, linguistic, and social skills in novel situations. This approach deepens and expands on what children already know, and motivates them to learn even more (Katz & Chard, 2000).

Before examining some of the ways in which projects can become an important feature of inclusive classrooms, it is important to define several key concepts. The term *project* refers to an in-depth study of a particular topic, usually undertaken by a whole class working on subtopics in small groups, sometimes by a small group of children within a class, and occasionally by an individual child. The key feature of a project is that it is an investigation—a piece of research that involves children in seeking answers to questions they have formulated by themselves or in cooperation with their teacher and that arise as the investigation proceeds (Katz & Chard, 2000).

The projects developed in PBI are designed to promote student inquiry and research into a topic that is related to the general curricula and/or students' interests. The activities in which children become engaged lead to the creation of products and/or performances that demonstrate their learning (Blumenfeld et al., 1991). Although the processes and outcomes are unique to each group of children, all project work shares the characteristics listed in Table 3.1.

THEORETICAL BASE AND RELATED RESEARCH

The features that characterize project work reflect constructivist principles that emerged from the work of Dewey (1902/1964, 1938), Piaget (1959, 1962), and Vygotsky (1962, 1978). Table 3.2 summarizes the beliefs central to these principles.

A strong theoretical rationale, based in cognitive and developmental psychology, exists for encouraging students' explorations and investigations and applying learning to real-life situations. Unfor-

Table 3.1. Characteristics of project work

The project is directed at examining one or more subject areas, general themes, and/or children's concerns.

Activities are developed that engage students in experiences that promote their cognitive, linguistic, and social-emotional development.

Children are encouraged and supported in their use of multiple learning modalities and intelligences.

Opportunities are provided to apply previous learning and academic skills in new situations.

Children are actively engaged with one another in designing, developing, and assessing their work.

Student learning is demonstrated by a culminating product or performance.

tunately, empirical research that clearly demonstrates the learning outcomes of PBI and related practices is limited. After reviewing studies investigating the outcomes of project-based learning (PBL), Stites (1998) concluded that empirical research was limited for the following reasons:

1. It is difficult to isolate the effects of project-based learning because it is generally implemented as a component of more comprehensive reforms.

2. It is difficult to compare the outcomes of PBL across settings because it is implemented differently in different contexts.

3. Standardized achievement tests may not be the best or most accurate measure of what students learn in classrooms in which PBL and other constructivist practices are implemented (p. 1).

The research base supporting PBI is built on what is known about promoting children's cognitive, linguistic, and social development, and the kinds of dispositions that support lifelong learning (Blumenfeld

Table 3.2. Beliefs underlying constructivist practices

Learning is a social experience.

Individuals solve problems in interaction with their physical and social environments.

Learning should be linked to real-life experiences to have meaning and purpose and to be long-lasting.

Children's active explorations and creations should include use of the arts.

Linguistic and mathematical literacy develop as outcomes of children's physical and intellectual development in concert with their experiences.

Each new development in learning growing out of previous experiences.

Time is spent on conscious reflection.

Social control and rules emerge as natural consequences of the learning experience.

Source: Archambault, 1964; 1966; Dewey, 1938; Phillips & Soltis, 1991

et al., 1991). PBI is designed to provide opportunities for students to apply and deepen knowledge and skills they have already acquired or are just beginning to acquire. It has its greatest impact on what Katz and Chard identified as the "dynamic" dimension of development (2000, p. 22). This aspect of development recognizes the delayed impact and cumulative effect of experiences on the ways children change and grow. The impact of PBI on these dynamic aspects is difficult to demonstrate and has not been adequately examined. Rather, most research on the efficacy of educational practices has relied on assessing their impact on children's normative development or educational performance.

Although it has been difficult to measure the success of PBI by itself, researchers have identified positive outcomes in early childhood and elementary education programs that use project approaches. For example, Stites (1998) cited research by Au and Carroll (1997) and Tharp and Gallimore (1998) who examined the Kamehamea Elementary Education Program (KEEP) in Hawaii, California, and Arizona. This early education program, in which PBI was an integral component, demonstrated positive learning outcomes among diverse groups of young children (Stites, 1998). Reviews of research on outcomes related to the use of PBL in other contexts have also revealed that, although students may do neither better nor worse on conventional assessments of knowledge, they are more skilled at applying their knowledge in new situations than more traditionally educated students (Stites, 1998). Research examining the impact of problem-based learning on the clinical problem-solving skills of medical students has shown, for example, that physicians who received training on resolving the actual problems of people exhibited superior clinical skills as compared with other doctors whose education did not include these kinds of experiences (Albanese & Mitchell, 1993; Vernon & Blake, 1993). Generalizing findings from studies using adult participants to the learning outcomes of young children is certainly questionable. This kind of research has raised questions, however, regarding the reliability and validity of research and evaluation studies that rely only on standardized tests of academic achievement to assess the long-term impact of PBI and other constructivist practices.

STOPPING THE PENDULUM AND FINDING A BALANCE

Projects are not new to early childhood and elementary education. They have been used in progressively oriented educational programs in the United States since the early 20th century (Dewey, 1902/1964).

Beginning in the 1920s, projects became a central feature of many British schools (Katz & Chard, 2000). The use of projects declined in American public schools as progressive education fell out of fashion, however. The intense pressure for academic achievement that emerged during the late 1940s and 1950s pushed American public education even further away from instructional models that included concerns for the social, emotional, and aesthetic development of children that are frequently addressed by PBI. At the same time, nurseries and early elementary schools were being created in the United Kingdom representing what became known as "open education." Based on Piagetian theory and progressive ideology, these "British Infant Schools" promoted children's decision-making capacities. Teachers provided minimal intervention. Instead, adults' roles focused on creating stimulating learning environments and encouraging children to actively pursue their individual interests (Smith, 1997).

In the early 1960s, interest in these schools began to grow among American educators. That interest supported the re-emergence of progressive education in the United States (Helm & Katz, 2001). Teachers were trying to break away from what they believed to be rigid instructional methods reflecting outdated social mores of the 1940s and 1950s. During the 1960s and 1970s, student-generated projects became a central feature of a new progressive educational movement in the United States. Projects would, however, fall out of fashion once again in the 1990s, as the socio-political pendulum of American education swung back, embracing more skills-based, teacher-directed, and behaviorally based methodologies.

Katz and Chard (2000) demonstrated how the rise and fall of what they referred to as "the project approach" represents an over-correction of mistaken applications of constructivist and progressive practices that did not include systematic instruction or assessment of children's performance. They recommended the use of projects to "complement and enhance what children learn through other parts of the curriculum" (p. 12) and emphasized the need to use a balanced approach to instruction. They pointed to the evolution of the project approach at Bank Street (Hyson, 1994) in the United States and Reggio Emilia (Fraser & Gestwicki, 2000) in northern Italy as examples of how an ongoing commitment by a school system to the central role of projects in the education of young children has led to these kinds of important refinements. Although the project approach used at Bank Street and Reggio Emelia differ somewhat from the approaches presented in this chapter, each uses projects to integrate students' interests and abilities with the academic curriculum while promoting cognitive, linguistic, aesthetic, and social-emotional development.

The 21st century focus on accountability in public education relies on evaluating school performance by examining student performance on standardized tests of academic achievement. Despite research findings that demonstrate the inappropriateness of these kinds of measures as evidence of the efficacy of PBI and related approaches, and the dynamic developmental gains these kinds of learning experiences offer, many experienced teachers feel pressure to abandon constructivist instructional methodologies. Standardized testing programs serve as a disincentive for new teachers who might otherwise be interested in including PBI and related approaches in their classrooms. Well aware that their teaching will be judged by students' performance on mandated tests, many revert to "teaching to the test." Also, both experienced and new teachers are reluctant to try PBI because of inadequate preparation in their teacher education and/or in-service training programs.

In order to continue to teach in ways that promote children's overall development and still conform to demands for accountability, the teachers whose work is presented in this chapter and their colleagues have developed assessment rubrics that document achievement of state-mandated learning standards as well as the goals and objectives in students' IEPs. By doing this, neither teacher has had to abandon an approach to instruction that enhances children's skills and heightens motivation. Rather, they have stopped the pendulum and entered a new phase in their teaching that supports both the normative and dynamic aspects of children's development and learning.

ROLES OF THE TEACHER
IN PROJECT-BASED INSTRUCTION

The information presented in Table 3.3, adapted from the work of Katz and Chard (2000, p. 13), illustrates the multiple roles that teachers play during both direct instruction and PBI. These roles do not oppose one another, but rather support one another. Teachers can and should integrate direct instruction with PBI to help children develop skills and motivation, make choices, demonstrate their expertise, and assure accountability. Although direct instruction may be the most efficient way to introduce new skills and information to children, projects provide children with opportunities to apply newly acquired information and abilities, make authentic choices (Kohn, 1993), demonstrate expertise, and become accountable for their own learning.

Table 3.3.   The teacher's roles in providing a systematic approach to project-based instruction

	Systematic instruction	Project-based instruction
Developing skills	Teacher assists students in acquiring new skills.	Teacher provides opportunities for applying existing and/or newly emerging skills.
Promoting motivation	Teacher provides extrinsic motivation for student achievement.	Teacher promotes intrinsic motivation by supporting projects built on student interests.
Facilitating choice	Teacher selects activities and materials and sets parameters for student work.	Teacher serves as guide for students' choice of topics, levels of challenge, roles, activities and materials.
Providing expertise	Teacher possesses knowledge and experience regarding the content and process of student learning.	Teacher capitalizes on students' proficiency and knowledge related to the content and processes needed for the success of the project. Students share their expertise with one another.
Assuring accountability	Teacher is responsible for monitoring and assessing children's learning and development.	Teacher shares responsibility with students for monitoring and assessing learning and achievement during and at the completion of a project.

Engaging Children's Minds by L.G. Katz & S.C. Chard. Copyright © (1989) by Ablex Publishing. Reproduced with permission of Greenwood Publishing Group, Inc., Westport, CT.

Teachers in inclusive classrooms need a wide repertoire of teaching strategies. Some children have the ability to acquire new skills with minimal teacher direction, whereas others need direct instruction and may even need to have a complex task broken down into discreet parts, with each component taught separately. Some children need praise and acknowledgment from an adult in order to persist at difficult tasks, whereas challenging activities may intrinsically motivate other students. Some can make reasonable and appropriate decisions on their own, whereas others need a good deal of adult guidance. What matters most is that every child experiences success while expanding his or her capacities. This goal calls on teachers to carefully consider the ways in which projects and other constructivist practices are introduced into their classrooms. The following sections of this chapter explore ways of addressing these issues.

THE PHASES OF PROJECT-BASED INSTRUCTION

Three phases are generally identified as essential for the successful instructional use of classroom projects (Chard, 1998a/1998b; Helm & Katz, 2001; Katz & Chard, 2000). Chard (1998b, p. 6) called these

- Phase I: Getting Started
- Phase II: Developing the Project Work
- Phase III: Concluding the Project

Although these phases are often described as distinct from one another, the examples of PBI presented in this chapter demonstrate that projects do not always follow distinct and linear steps. Rather, these steps run together. Project work is a recursive process, with periodic returns to earlier phases.

The three-phase model proposed by Chard and others reflects the assumption that most children have developed the prerequisite dispositions, abilities, and skills needed for independent group work before coming to school. This belief represents a middle-class bias that has been shown to put some children at a disadvantage (Delpit, 1995; Heath, 1983; Ladson-Billings, 1994; Walkerdine, 1984). The diversity found among students in heterogeneous classrooms requires that teachers engage in preliminary steps that include assessing and preparing students before they get started. Classroom teachers, working in collaboration with special education teachers, teachers of English as a second language, speech-language pathologists, and/or other related service providers, need to assess the abilities and needs of each student as part of an instructional team (Rainforth & York-Barr, 1997). This assessment can be accomplished by observing and documenting children's participation and performance in group activities or miniprojects. In combination with other information about individual students, teachers and support personnel can determine the nature and degree of direct support that might be needed by individual children and/or an entire class. Some students will need support throughout a project.

Related service providers can assist teachers to identify appropriate objectives for individual children. Some students might need direct instruction in specific skills as preparation for their successful participation in a particular project. Ideally, this kind of instruction would be offered within the context of other activities or lessons occurring in class. Although pre-instruction increases the success of PBI, prerequisite skills cannot become a hurdle to participation. Historically, teaching prerequisites has relegated some students to perpetual practice on isolated skills. As Barbara Regenspan explains in Chapter 7, however, "practice for" *must always* be connected with "the real thing." This kind of connected teaching often requires additional and ongoing instructional support from related service providers working in collaboration with the teacher and one another. Table 3.4 offers an expanded view of the phases of PBI that includes consideration of both preparation and the provision of on-going support for students.

The phases identified in Table 3.4 go beyond the three suggested by Chard and others (Chard, 1998a, 1998b; Katz & Chard, 2000). They include the need to establish a classroom culture that encourages inquiry and supports diversity. This kind of collaborative learning com-

Table 3.4.   Phases of a systematic approach to project-based instruction

Phase 1 – Laying the Groundwork
1. Establish a classroom culture that promotes collaboration and caring.
2. Assess children's skills related to group work (e.g., cooperative learning, conflict resolution).
3. Assess children's skills related to inquiry-based learning (e.g., brainstorming, problem solving strategies).
4. Provide preliminary experiences (mini-projects) and direct instruction to develop skills needed for group work and inquiry-based teaching.
5. Identify student needs for modified expectations, continuing instruction, and support from peers and/or adults.

Phase 2 – Designing the Project
1. Establish norms and/or rules of behavior with children and agree on a process to address future problems and resolve conflicts.
2. Present the curriculum areas, themes, or issues to be investigated.
3. Identify which children already know related topics, themes, or issues.
4. Brainstorm ideas for a project.
5. Develop questions with students to guide their inquiries.
6. Select ideas to be used for the project.
7. Develop assessment rubrics.
8. Arange for supports, embedded instruction, and adaptations for students whose prerequisite skills remain weak.

Phase 3 – Carrying Out the Project
1. Teacher and/or students select individuals to work on different aspects of the project as groups or pairs.
2. Teacher and/or students determine activities and roles of participants.
3. Teacher and/or students identify needed resources.
4. Teachers and related service providers ensure supports, instruction, and adaptations needed for all students' participation in the project in valued roles.
5. Teacher provides ongoing monitoring and assessment.
6. Students report to one another and their teacher regarding progress and any needed assistance.

Phase 4 – Concluding and Assessing the Project
1. Students present their findings to the teacher, classmates, and others.
2. Students and teachers reflect on the experience (e.g., what worked well, what should have been done differently, what they would like to do next, and so forth).
3. Students and teachers assess the degree to which they met the objectives of the project as identified on the assessment rubric.

munity provides the foundation for addressing the diverse concerns of children in inclusive classrooms. It also gives attention to the ongoing supports and systematic instruction that some students will need to participate in PBI. The activities suggested in Table 3.4 have been applied successfully in heterogeneous classrooms such as those described in this chapter. Again, although these "phases" are presented here as a list, the activities described do not necessarily proceed in the linear order implied by Table 3.4. In some instances, students and teachers may skip steps or return to earlier phases to revise their plans. Revisions may be needed because of individual student concerns, poor planning, or unanticipated events that emerge in spite of well-developed planning.

The problems that children confront while carrying out projects may or may not be anticipated by their teacher. Deciding whether to make students aware of potential pitfalls rests on the teacher's assessment of the specific situation. Should he or she let the children face the consequences and solve a problem on their own, ask the kinds of questions that will guide students in discovering the flaw, or intervene directly and point out the need to revise their plan? Whatever the decision, the strategies used should be designed intentionally to benefit every student. Assisting children in understanding the need to make revisions or allowing them to solve their own problems can become an educative experience once students have the necessary knowledge, skills, and dispositions to address the problems they face. Mistakes can then become opportunities for new learning rather than evidence of incompetence.

THE "FOXFIRE APPROACH"

The Foxfire approach is a comprehensive instructional model that incorporates both systematic and constructivist practices into the development of classroom projects. Foxfire began as a high school English course to develop literacy skills and preserve local cultural traditions among rural Appalachian youth. The first Foxfire students initiated the project through investigations of the lives of older people in their community. The information they gathered led to the creation of a magazine focused on Appalachian life and traditions. Articles from this student-generated magazine were later compiled into *The Foxfire Book* (Wigginton, 1971). Its commercial success led to the publication of 12 more books based on the work of subsequent generations of students. The Foxfire approach emerged from applying and refining, in U.S.

public school K–12 classrooms the approach that led to the creation of these books (Foxfire Fund, 1991).

What evolved was neither a curriculum, nor a specific instructional method, nor a technique. Rather, a framework for teaching developed, guided by a set of Core Practices that reflected many of the same principles characterizing constructivist teaching. These Core Practices, however, called for balancing learner-centered activities with teacher direction. Summarized in Table 3.5, they are neither a formula nor a prescription for teaching. Rather, these Core Practices are a guide for creating classrooms that balance the needs of the child with the curriculum. These guidelines help assure the academic integrity of students' work while making explicit connections to children's interests and experiences. The Core Practices also help establish the kind of classroom culture essential to the application of PBI in an inclusive classroom.

No two classrooms look the same. Children and teacher(s) continually shape classroom life through their ongoing negotiations. Classrooms that reflect the Foxfire approach do share certain characteristics, however. Students are actively engaged with one another, their teachers, and instructional materials, and help shape the curriculum (Core Practice 4). They talk openly and knowingly about what they are learning and reflect on why and how it is being learned (Core

Table 3.5. Foxfire core practices

1. The work teachers and learners do together is infused from the beginning with learner choice, design, and revision.
2. The role of the teacher is that of facilitator and collaborator.
3. The academic integrity of the work teachers and learners do together is clear.
4. The work is characterized by active learning.
5. Peer teaching, small group work, and teamwork are all consistent features of classroom activities.
6. Connections between the classroom work, the surrounding communities, and the world beyond the community are clear.
7. There is an audience beyond the teacher for learner work.
8. New activities spiral gracefully, out of the old, incorporating lessons learned from past experiences, building on skills and understandings that can now be amplified.
9. Imagination and creativity are encouraged in the completion of learning activities.
10. Reflection is an essential activity that takes place at key points throughout the work.
11. The work teachers and learners do together includes rigorous, ongoing assessment and evaluation.

The Foxfire Fund, Inc. (2002). *From Thinking to Doing: The Foxfire Core Practices*, p. iv; reprinted with permission.

Practice 10). Much of their work is done in groups (Core Practice 5), with a good deal of peer interaction. Children's lives and experiences in the world outside the classroom, including their communities and families, are actively and consciously integrated with rigorous academic work (Core Practices 3 & 6), as are the arts and aesthetic considerations (Core Practice 9). Assessment is ongoing and integral to instruction, frequently including performance and/or portfolio assessments (Core Practice 11). As a component of this process, children are continually asked to reflect on and evaluate their own learning (Core Practice 10) (Kugelmass, 1991).

When applied in classrooms that include students who have been traditionally viewed as having special educational needs, the Core Practices assist teachers in providing educational experiences that address subject-area "givens" while simultaneously addressing individual academic, social, and functional skills. This is achieved by first engaging students in the creation of a developmentally and age-appropriate learning community, in which diversity is valued and all children are provided with opportunities to develop their talents (Kugelmass, 1995). The Foxfire approach begins by engaging students in establishing guidelines for behavior and classroom norms. This is often done through "Memorable Experiences" and "Good Teachers/Good Students" activities.

In the "Memorable Experiences" activity, students are asked to remember and describe a time, either in or out of school, when they enjoyed learning something new. Each child describes the experience to the class. The teacher then guides a discussion directed at discovering the features these experiences shared with one another. These features are listed on chart paper and hung in a visible place in the classroom. The list is used to provide a framework for establishing the criteria for learning activities that will take place throughout the year.

The "Good Teachers/Good Students" activity follows a similar process. It is used to develop class norms for behavior during projects and other group activities. Students are asked to identify a person they believe to be a good teacher. This person need not hold the formal position of a teacher, but could be anyone who ever taught them something. Once again, after the students share stories, the teacher facilitates a discussion and leads students to create a list of features that were common to many of these good teachers. Students are then asked to consider the ways in which this list also reflects the characteristics of a good student, and then to generate a second list that describes the characteristics of a good student. The two lists are used to establish a set of guidelines for behavior. The entire class (including the teacher) participates in developing class rules or norms that emerge out of what students see as essential to being both a good teacher and student. These are hung in the room and referred to throughout the year and are revised as needed.

These group activities require the involvement of every student. Through facilitation of active participation in decision making and encouragement and support for those who had difficulty with the task, the teacher begins to model a classroom culture in which students' personal experiences are valued. The collective set of classroom norms consider everyone's experiences, thus laying the groundwork for establishing the kind of learning community essential for successful group projects. Clearly, many preliminary skills are necessary for a group of children to accomplish the kinds of tasks just described. As in all instructional activities, the teacher's judgment is required to assess the abilities, interests, and concerns of the group and to make necessary modifications that enable the successful inclusion of every student.

The specific activities just described may not, in fact, be appropriate for every group of children. Indeed, the teachers in the classrooms that are described next designed their own strategies to establish the kind of classroom community in which students take ownership of their own learning, and support one another. These two examples demonstrate how teachers can respond to these demands. The teachers, whose work with students are described in the following sections, have had the advantage of participating in a teacher education program whose inclusive focus prepared general and special education teachers to develop approaches to curriculum that promote the dynamic development of their students. One, an experienced special educator and speech-language therapist has been using PBI for 5 years. The other was a student teacher in elementary education throughout the project she describes. She worked in a fourth-grade classroom with a general education teacher with 25 years' experience, who has been using projects throughout her career. Both have had to respond to a political climate that demands accountability.

"WATCH OUT FOR BIRDS:"
A KINDERGARTEN BIRD HABITAT PROJECT

Once a teacher experiences the positive impact of PBI in an inclusive classroom, it is difficult to return to using only traditional modes of teaching. Mary Gell, a speech-language therapist and special education teacher, has experienced this. The positive outcomes she has seen in students has led to her active promotion of the Foxfire approach in the inclusive classrooms she supports. Last year, in an attempt to bring this approach to the six kindergarten teachers with whom she collaborates, Mary helped secure a mini-grant through the Catskill Regional Teachers Center to support a project on bird habitats. The following statement offers the rationale for this project, as presented by Mary in the grant application:

> The Greene Primary School embraces an inclusion philoso-
> phy at all grade levels: kindergarten, first, and second.
> Special education teachers co-teach with regular education
> teachers and share responsibility for all students within the
> classroom. As a result, all students benefit from the experi-
> ence and teaching styles of two teachers. It is within this at-
> mosphere that I feel the Foxfire approach would best suc-
> ceed. With team teaching to support all students, the
> Foxfire approach will help all students meet the outcomes
> of the New York State Learning Standards.

The money from the grant was used to pay for a trip to a zoo in a city 70 miles from the small rural community of Greene, New York, where her school is located. The field trip spiraled into a project in which the children in each of six kindergarten classes created imagi-nary birds and built habitats for them, with the assistance of a local artist. Each classroom habitat and its respective birds was then put on display for the entire school and surrounding community.

The idea for this project and many of its associated activities did not originate from children's questions, nor reflect children's particu-lar interest in birds. Rather, the trip to the zoo emerged from teachers' concerns regarding the limited experiences of many children in this small rural community, and the consequences of these limitations on school achievement. Although the 116 children in six kindergarten classrooms appeared to represent a homogeneous group of European-American 5-year-olds, the classrooms were characterized by consider-able developmental and socioeconomic diversity. Approximately 35% of the students came from families eligible to receive free and/or re-duced price lunch, many received additional academic supports and related services, and four received special education services. The processes used for preparing students and designing, carrying out and assessing the bird habitat project are described in the following sec-tions. Each corresponds to one of four phases of PBI outlined previ-ously in Table 3.4.

Phase 1—Laying the Groundwork

Mary understood that a culture of inclusion needed to be developed before the children in these four kindergarten classrooms could work successfully on a complex project. Working with the classroom teachers to incorporate the Foxfire approach, she helped design activities early in the school year that promoted children's cooperation with one another. In the following statement, she describes some of the ways this was achieved.

> We would do cooperative groups throughout the year, in the early part of the year. [This included] the open circle discussions we had in which they would take turns. We would talk about really respecting each member no matter what. This little boy, Troy, who has Down syndrome, became as vocal and as participatory as any other member and the kids respected that, and we laid that groundwork before we began the project by doing a lot of interactive circle work. And Troy's work is always included; he's never pulled aside or sent to a different room; whatever project we would do as a class, he was always a part of it…
>
> Another thing we really tried to do a lot was reflection in the classroom. So, we would do a theme or a small project or talk about fire safety and ask the kids to reflect on something that they learned or that they would like. Somehow there was always a reflection piece and a lot of that became a classroom book. We made a lot of classroom books that allowed the kids to illustrate a picture. We might have a sentence starter and some kids would write… usually using phonetic spelling, but they would write complete sentences with their feelings and their thoughts and then illustrate it. It became a wonderful addition to the book area and they could read through it at any time. It was part of the groundwork, really showing respect for one another and that everybody participated.
>
> So that was part of the groundwork for the big project. The other part was a lot of circle work with children holding an object that was sometimes related to a theme, but we would also do a lot of sharing and interaction and that really tied into the IEPs for the students who struggled to express themselves verbally. They were allowed that time. And people would respect the person holding whatever the

object was. It helped prepare us because there was a lot of interaction in this project. It helped us problem solve together and cooperatively come up with an idea.

Phase 2 – Designing the Project

Mary and the six other teachers prepared for the project before it was formally introduced to the children. They met to identify how they would address New York State Learning Standards for kindergarten; meet the unique concerns of individual children; and also incorporate an active, hands-on, and collaborative approach to teaching. To accomplish this, they developed a "Kindergarten Lesson Plan with Core Practices" (see Figure 3.1.), listing state learning standards for kindergarteners in the areas of English-language arts (ELA), mathematics, social studies, and science. They also listed the Foxfire Core Practices that would guide their instructional practice. This checklist and the accompanying lesson plans provided an ongoing assessment of the project. It was used to both identify the learning standards addressed during different activities and to monitor the application of the Core Practices. Although the example provided in Figure 3.1. addresses "The Life Cycle of a Bird," its goals and objectives were focused on English and language arts. The checklist and accompanying lesson plan helped teachers organize classroom activities specifically directed at facilitating children's ability to listen to a story in a large group, speak in complete sentences, and contribute to the class discussion. The lesson plan also helped the teachers identify and gather needed resources and materials, review teaching procedures, and establish objectives for assessing the outcome of the lesson.

Although the children were given many opportunities to choose activities earlier in the year, their teachers felt that to successfully develop and implement an ongoing project of this size and scope, kindergarteners needed direct guidance. As a way of balancing the use of activities that promoted students' active engagement with the need to achieve specific outcomes, the teachers began the project by engaging the children in a "KWL" process. This approach first explored what children already Knew (K), then identified what they Wanted (W) to learn, and, finally, the children and their teachers explored and described how they would demonstrate what they Learned (L). This information was then used to develop observation guidelines and questions for future lessons and guide children in their explorations and eventual assessment of their own learning. The children would

Teacher(s):	Kindergarten	**Date:**	TBA

Collaborative Staff:	Paraprofessionals Teaching Assistants	**Time(s):** TBA	

Lesson Name:	Life Cycle of a Bird	**Lesson Plan:** 5	

Goals/Objectives

English/Language Arts

X To listen to a story in a large group
X To speak clearly in complete sentences
X To contribute to class discussion
__To identify upper case letters
__To associate sounds and letters
__To predict outcomes of pictures
__To recognize reading & writing as left–right
__To write upper and lower case letters
__To write phrases with phonetic spelling

__To follow 3-step directions successfully
__To express ideas well with growing vocabulary
__To restate information when necessary
__To identify lower case letters
X To develop comprehension skills
X To sequence a story using 3 pictures
__To write first and last name
__To write words with phonetic spelling
__To write sentences with phonetic spelling

Math

__To count to 20
__To identify and write numbers to 20
__To identify half of an object
__To add 2 sets of objects
__To add to patterns
__To read a simple graph

__To count 1:1 to 20
__To sequence numbers to 20
__To use measurement language
__To separate sets of objects
__To make new patterns
__To identify basic colors and shapes

Social Studies

__To learn about myself
__To learn about school
__To learn about human wants/needs
__To learn symbols of citizenship
__To learn about making rules

__To learn about my family and others
__To learn about my neighborhood
__To learn about how others meet needs
__To learn about rights and responsibilities
__To learn about safety and health rules

Science

__To be able to think and talk about science
__To know about common plants
__To know about earth

__To know five senses
X To know about common animals
__To know land, water, seasons, and weather

(continued)

Figure 3.1. *(continued)*

Approach

Core Practices
1. The role of teacher must be that of collaborator, team leader, and guide.
2. The academic integrity of the work must be absolutely clear.
3. The work is characterized by student action, not passive receipt of information.
4. A constant feature of the process is its emphasis on peer teaching.
5. Connections between the classroom work and surrounding communities and real world are clear.
6. There must be an audience beyond the teacher for student work.

Literature Base: S.J.Calder, *If You Were a Bird*

Materials Needed: Puppet and nest with eggs, chicks, and mother bird

Life Cycle of chicken (4-part display puzzle)

Life Stages of a Bird (mini-book)

Lesson Procedure

1. Introduction: Where do birds come from? Discussion with whole group
2. Read book *If You Were a Bird*
3. Use puppets to retell sequence of a bird's life
4. Explain life cycle of a chicken with display puzzle. Similarities? Differences?
5. Students complete Life Stages of a Bird mini-book independently at table.
6. Partner read with peer when mini-book is complete
7. Parent Connection: students read mini-book with parent then explore home environment to find birds at various stages.

Student Outcomes

Class Objective	Level 3	Level 2	Level 1
Listen and attend to story in large group.	All students attend to story.	Some students attend to story.	Few students attend to story.
Understand life cycle of bird.	All students complete mini-book and identify different stages.	Some students complete mini-book and identify different stages.	Few students complete mini-book and identify different stages.
Students partner read with peers.	All students attempt to read with peer independently.	Some students attempt to read with peer independently.	Few students attempt to read with peer independently.

Figure 3.1.   Mary Gell and six other teachers developed this "Kindergarten Lesson Plan with Core Practices," listing state learning standards for kindergarteners in the areas of English language arts, mathematics, social studies, and science. The form shown here is filled out for the classroom described in this chapter.

demonstrate what they learned (L) about birds and their habitats by presenting their individual and group projects.

Phase 3 – Carrying out the Project

Although the teachers designed and developed a good deal of this project, children were provided numerous opportunities to develop and apply new knowledge and skills, make authentic choices, demonstrate expertise, and become accountable for their own learning. This was done in ways that were developmentally and individually appropriate for every student. Mary Gell's description of the processes used in carrying out the project illustrates how this balance was achieved, blending both teacher-directed and constructivist practices.

> Each kindergarten classroom had a different habitat: There was the rain forest, northern forest, backyard, arctic, desert, and wetlands. So, they [the children] selected a habitat for their classroom, and they would also have to include birds that would correspond to that habitat. One of the classrooms that I was in most of the day did the desert. The teacher and I would check out all the books on deserts and the kids would essentially do the research and look at what elements were in a desert, which was one of the lessons. We would introduce the habitat, but the kids would research and talk about that as a class, in small groups, or in pairs. They would just get a book and kind of go through it, and we would talk about it and chart different parts of that habitat. I'd say," Let's see. What is a habitat?" They would discuss it, read about it, and we would talk about it.
>
> We also tied in the five senses so that it would be a little more concrete for the kindergarten level. "What would you hear if you were in the desert? What would you see? What would you smell?" and that kind of thing . . . I think we helped them a lot more than if they were older. But the kids did most of the work. We would just roll out this big, gigantic piece of paper, and then they would start adding the different elements you would see there. And these were all things that they had found in their research through books. After we did that, then they would build the habitat and an imaginary bird that could live there. Everybody contributed to building the habitat in someway.

Phase 4 – Concluding and Assessing the Project

Assessment was an ongoing process throughout this project. Students were continually engaged in self-assessment as their teachers reminded them to look in their books and be certain that they had included the correct features of the habitat and the birds that would live there. When they discovered this wasn't the case, children would revise their own work, with the assistance of peers and teachers. These kindergartners also evaluated the success of their individual and/or class projects by returning to the original questions they had generated during the KWL process. In doing this, they not only assessed their work but also found that they had been able to learn what they set out to discover. Because the teachers had prepared rubrics to guide the assessment of student participation and achievement during key activities, they were also able to determine whether or not each student's work addressed state learning standards. The truly authentic assessment of what had been learned would, however, become evident when children were called on to explain their habitats and birds to other children and adults who came to see the display of their habitats and the imaginary birds who lived there.

Some children needed more assistance than others and could only explain minimal details, but each could show what he or she had contributed to the class project. Although all students did not achieve complete understanding of the academic content, the social skill development of every child was enhanced. The children with special educational concerns were provided opportunities to develop the social and emotional skills identified as specific objectives on their IEPs. Mary reported that every child with an IEP made considerable gains in these areas. Every student demonstrated an increased capacity to work cooperatively. Some special educators and parents did, however, express concerns regarding whether children's academic, cognitive, and developmental needs were addressed as well as they might have been using more intensive, one-to-one direct instruction. Mary responded to these concerns in discussing the child with Down syndrome:

> **JWK:** As a special educator, did you feel that the goals you had for him were met in this kind of way?
> **MG:** I did, I absolutely did.
> **JWK:** That is a question people have, especially when they believe a child needs direct one-to-one teaching.
> **MG:** No one person was assigned to him as a specific one-to-one aide during the project . . . This is my own personal

philosophy. He should not always be with the same person; sometimes it would be the general education teacher, sometimes it would be myself, sometimes it would be the one-to-one person who was assigned to him; but we would all take turns to support him. So, he would always have support within whatever group situation he was in, but it was never the same person. And we all knew his IEP goals and objectives. We had very good communication on his capabilities, our expectations, and where we were pushing him in that whole zone of proximal development. We knew where he was and we knew where we wanted him to go, but we just found that the counting, the colors, all the basic IEP goals that he had, could be met. And for him, one of the big speech goals was improving his mean length of utterances [MLUs]. He went from approximately a 2 to a 3.5 by the end of the year. He's speaking in full sentences. He's using verbs now, and I really think that it was due to so much exposure to the vocabulary. That and the peer interaction, and the whole setting up the kids to be respectful of everyone, not just the teacher, and not just the general education kids; it was everybody's doing. I saw it work.

FOURTH-GRADERS EXAMINE THE LIVES OF HOMELESS CHILDREN

Visiting schools and classrooms in the days and weeks following the September 11 tragedy confirmed what I already knew about young children in America: Although many feel physically safe and secure in their own homes, most are aware that this is not the case for all children. Television, movies, and the Internet have exposed children to realities far beyond their own homes and neighborhoods. Of course, many children in American schools have experienced poverty, war, and hunger directly. Regardless of their personal situations, once children become aware of hardships facing other children, they become motivated to help. The project presented next emerged from these kinds of concerns among one group of fourth graders. It demonstrates how PBI can be more than an effective pedagogical tool for developing academic skills. Projects of this kind also provide opportunities for children to explore issues that reach beyond the confines of their classrooms.

The description of the processes used to develop and implement this project demonstrates how systematic and developmentally appropriate attention to students' awareness of social inequities can enhance skills and dispositions that empower effective social action, while also addressing specific academic objectives. The community and school in which this project took place resembles Mary's locale in many ways. Both are located in rural communities adjacent to a medium-sized urban community housing, a large university, and several technology-based industries. Great extremes exist in economic conditions among students, with some coming from affluent, professional families, whereas others live in abject poverty. Some live in homes without electricity, central heating, or running water. Their parent(s) may not be able to read, are frequently unemployed, and receive public assistance. Other kinds of diversity are also reflected in differences in family structures: Two-parent families, blended families, single parents, foster parents and same-sex partners are all raising children. Five children in the class in which the following project was implemented were receiving special education services.

Phase 1– Laying the Groundwork

Although this project began in February, the foundation for the cooperation and collaboration needed for its success was established early in the school year. This was accomplished by developing class rules with students and providing them with an understanding of the importance of respect in the classroom. Laying a foundation of respectful interactions supported the emphasis on group problem solving central to the instructional processes used in this project. Deb a student teacher who worked in the classroom during the semester this project was initiated, describes the classroom teacher's approach to creating the kind of collaborative classroom community that made the project possible:

> She does a lot of different activities that talk about respecting each other, that ask, "Why do we do it?" But she doesn't just give the students answers, the kids have to come up with reasons of why respect is important. When any kind of problems surface, so many teachers I've seen send the kids to the office and it becomes a major problem. She doesn't handle it that way. She calls a class meeting, or if the student identifies a problem, the student can call the class meeting. And then everyone gets together and they start talking over the problem: "How do you see it?"; "How did you see it?"

At least 1 day per week, students had lunch in the classroom with their teacher. These luncheon meetings provided opportunities for informal conversations and frequently offered insights into children's interests and concerns. Deb's following remarks explain how the class project on homelessness began in just that way.

> A couple of kids were talking about taking a trip to New York City and seeing people living on the street. They were saying, "We are lucky because we don't have that around here." So that triggered something and we (the teachers) wanted to make sure that the kids knew that homelessness is everywhere. It may not be visible here, but we have it.... They were all telling stories about lots of things and I said, "You guys are great. We should write a book!" And a week later they came up to me and said, "We thought about what you said and we want to write a book. We want to raise money to help the homeless."
>
> So, from that, I found a web site for the National Coalition for the Homeless [http://www.nationalhomeless.org] and found out about the book *Fly Away Home* [Bunting, 1991] and got some written material called *America's Homeless Children: A Reader for Elementary School Students* [National Coalition for the Homeless, 2001]. So, we started discussing homelessness with the children by reading *Fly Away Home*. It's about a boy who is homeless and lives in an airport.

Phase 2 – Designing the Project

Once the classroom teachers became aware of the children's concerns about homelessness from these lunch talks, more systematically designed discussions were organized. The classroom teacher began by pairing each child in the class with a partner to talk about what he or she knew about homelessness. The following questions were given to the students to guide their discussions:

1. What causes people to become homeless?
2. Why don't we see many homeless people in our community?
3. Why might it be difficult for a homeless person to get a job?

After these initial conversations, students were provided with materials from local service organizations and the National Coalition for the Homeless (2001). They were then divided into four groups, with each group responsible for examining a specific section of the materials everyone received. Students were then asked to compare their initial beliefs about homelessness with the information examined by their group. Each group then created a web-shaped graphic organizer to represent what they now knew about homelessness. After these were presented to the class, each group web became included into a whole class graphic organizer. From this exercise, students learned that most homeless people were not the lazy, shiftless, drug addicts they had initially imagined. Rather, many homeless people were children, living in families that had lost their homes because an adult breadwinner had lost a job. In some cases, one parent may have become ill, abandoned the family, or died. The children were also surprised to learn that, although less visible than in big cities, homelessness existed in their own community. Locally, there were people living in vacant buildings in small towns, or in abandoned trailers and cars in more remote rural areas. The few shelters that did exist were in places they had never visited. The following day, each group was asked to create a Venn diagram, comparing what they knew about children who were and were not homeless. After comparing what each group had written, they discovered that homeless and non-homeless children had a good deal in common.

The children wanted to do something to help. After several brainstorming sessions, they decided that they would do a class project that would have two distinct, yet complimentary components: 1) Create a class book containing poems they would write and 2) sell the book to raise money to assist homeless children. The children knew they would be learning about and creating several types of poetry: haiku, lyric, narrative, free verse, and limericks. This poetry unit was designed to meet the required learning standards to be assessed on the fourth-grade, statewide examination in English and language arts. For the class book, each student would select his or her best poem. As their teacher pointed out, however, before they could sell the book to raise money, they needed their principal's permission. And, before that could happen, they needed to develop a clear plan to present for his approval. She explained that they needed to present the rationale for their ideas, what they would include in their poetry book, and how it would be created.

Lengthy discussions followed. The teacher's skillful facilitation led the children to recognize the complexity of the project. They realized that they would, therefore, need to work in small groups, or committees, to complete different aspects of the project. With her guidance, committees were formed that would be responsible for 1) meeting with the principal, 2) binding the books, 3) taking and delivering orders, 4) recording finances, 5) writing a cover page that explained the project, and 6) illustrating and designing gift bags for the books. The committee that would meet with the principal became known as the "Idea Committee." Their job required gathering the following information:

- Who is involved in the project and who will benefit from the book sales?
- What will the class be doing?
- Where will they be working in this?
- When will they begin and end?
- Why are they doing the project?
- How will they be doing the project?

The answers to these questions then provided direction for carrying out the project by the entire class.

Phase 3 – Carrying Out the Project

Portraying the phases of any project as independent from one another is inaccurate. Project work is always a recursive process, with each phase containing aspects of others or requiring periodic returns to earlier phases. During this project, while the Idea Committee was deciding what to present to the principal, other students were creating poetry. One or more examples of each form of poetry had been presented to the class by the teacher, the features of each form defined, and specific examples examined. The entire class then created a class poem to illustrate the form under study. Each child would then write a rough draft of his or her own poem, to be edited by the teacher and corrected by the child for a final draft. This process would be modified and adapted to address the special concerns of individual students. Some needed more assistance and had more revisions than others. Every child could contribute at least one poem to the class book. The following examples of two "I am . . ." poems illustrate the range of complexity of children's poetry included in the class book.

> Barbara
> funny, nice, brave.
> Child of Betty.
> Who is friends with Keisha, Shay and Ben.
> Who feels happy about having friends.
> Who needs a pet, family and friends.
> Who gives money, CDs and games.

Who fears heights, stalkers and earthquakes
Who'd like to see Larry B.
Who dreams of the city
A student of this school.
Gem.

Joseph
Funny, cool
loving, helping, caring
working, popular, smart, cute
Kid

Once the Idea Committee received the principal's approval for the project, and while students worked on the poetry unit, additional committees were formed. To ensure the successful participation of every child, assignments to committees were based on student interests and on the skills and concerns of individuals in each group. After discussing the purpose of these committees with the class and reaching consensus about their responsibilities, the teacher prepared written materials to help guide student work. For example, the Writing Committee was given a list to guide the explanation page they were to develop. The group needed to tell readers 1) where the donation was going, 2) why the class had chosen to support a child's attendance at the annual "Kid's Day" on Capitol Hill in Washington, D.C., 3) what the class had learned about homelessness from reading *Fly Away Home*, and 4) what the class had learned about poetry.

A less verbally complex, but equally important assignment was given to the Order Form Committee. They were to design a usable order form that included identifying information about the purchaser, cost, and quantity. The Book Order Committee would be responsible for using these forms and filling orders when the books arrived. This group would need to work cooperatively with the Finance Committee that was responsible for collecting, counting, and recording money in the ledger book on a daily basis. The Book Binding Committee would also need to be kept informed, to assure that they made enough copies in a timely manner.

Phase 4 – Concluding and Assessing the Project

The outcomes of this project were assessed in several ways and at several levels. At the academic level, every student successfully completed the unit on poetry and demonstrated the ability to create at least one poem in each required form. Every student also successfully completed a short-answer test at the conclusion of the poetry unit, demonstrating an understanding of the vocabulary and terminology used in poetry. In addition to successfully achieving these academic goals, the class completed the poetry book and sold enough copies to send a child to Washington, D.C., to participate in "Kid's Day" on Capitol Hill, sponsored by the National Coalition for the Homeless. These were not the only desired outcomes, however. The teacher was also interested in promoting children's social skills and problem-solving abilities. To assess these, she monitored each child's contribution to assigned committee work and during whole-class discussions. Every child participated as an active and cooperating member.

The teacher also hoped to promote her students' understanding of complex societal problems and their role as citizens in a democracy. These outcomes were more difficult to assess. It is impossible to measure the absolute impact of this kind of experience on a child's growth and development. The children clearly became inspired by the project, and planned to enlarge their efforts the next year. They hoped to raise enough money to go to Washington and lobby on behalf of homeless children. This certainly indicates the success of this project in the short term. The true assessment of what these fourth graders have learned will, however, require their continued commitment to promoting social justice through collective action.

CONCLUSION

When students become disruptive or are unresponsive to active methods of instruction, it is often assumed that they need more teacher direction in a more highly structured environment. Some critics of project methods believe that there are some children who cannot benefit from active, learner-centered educational experiences. This response is neither completely inappropriate nor unfounded. In fact, disruptive behavior or non-responsiveness by students may be a sign of a mismatch between how the teacher is teaching and what students need. When students consistently fail to respond appropriately to a given teaching approach, however, teachers and support personnel need to engage in a comprehensive assessment of the situation rather than assuming these students cannot benefit from participation in activities such as those described in this chapter. This kind of ecological assessment must include a critical examination of instructional methods and the contexts within which problems occur. The outcome of such an examination will lead to suggesting modifications in instruction and/or adding supports to assure a student's success, rather than removing a child from a classroom.

Unfortunately, what more typically occurs is that an unresponsive or unruly child is seen as the sole source of the problem. The student's impairments are identified and remediation in the form of teacher-directed, one-to-one, or small-group instruction in discreet skills is recommended (Poplin, 1988; Skrtic, 1991). If the child is found to need more structure, then he or she may be removed from the general education classroom while classmates continue to be involved in more experiential activities. The exclusion of some students from constructivist activities may initially appear to meet the needs of the child. What is not being acknowledged, however, is that removing some students from the general education classroom or withdrawing interactive learning experiences reduces the opportunity for engaging in the kinds of activities all children need in order to become more independent and self-directed learners. Being included in interactive learning experiences within the general education classroom provides opportunities for every child to interact with peers who can serve as appropriate models and provide achievement motivation. Each child is also offered an opportunity to discover the talents and unique perspectives that classmates with different experiences, lifestyles, cultures, languages, and abilities bring to a task.

When some teachers who identified themselves as progressive began calling for the exclusion of unruly and/or unresponsive children from their very active classrooms, John Dewey noted that "Exclusion is perhaps the only available measure at a given juncture, but it is no solution"(Dewey, 1938, p. 57). He suggested that rather than removing these children, teachers adopt a more "common sense solution and modify instruction" (p. 57). To do this, they would need to alter the conditions in their classrooms.

> [The teacher] must survey the capacities and concerns of the particular set of individuals with whom he is dealing and must at the same time arrange the conditions that provide the subject-matter or content for experiences that satisfy these needs and develop these capacities. (Dewey, 1938, p. 58)

In offering this advice, Dewey was encouraging classroom teachers to move beyond the ideological box they had built for themselves. He recognized that by not adapting or modifying instructional approaches to meet the needs of certain children, some "progressive" educators might, in fact, be withholding the kinds of educative experiences they believed to be essential for all children. Suggesting that they use common sense to reach children who were not responding to progressive educational approaches was neither a call for abandoning these instructional methods nor a rationale for teachers to lower their expectations for some students. Rather, Dewey was asking teachers to become more actively involved in guiding students' learning.

REFERENCES

Albanese, M.A., & Mitchell, S. (1993). Problem-based learning: A review of the literature on its outcomes and implementation issues. *Academic Medicine, 68*(1), 52–81.

Archambault, R.D. (Ed.). (1964). *John Dewey on education.* Chicago: University of Chicago Press.

Archambault, R.D. (Ed.). (1966). *John Dewey on education: Appraisals.* New York: Random House.

Au, K., & Carroll, J.H. (1997). Improving literacy achievement through a constructivist approach: The KEEP demonstration classroom project. *Elementary School Journal, 97,* 203–231.

Blumenfeld, P.C., Soloway, E., Marx, R.W., Krajcik, J.S., Guzdial, M., & Palincsar, A. (1991). Motivating project-based learning: Sustaining the doing, supporting the learning. *Educational Psychologist, 26*(3), 369–398.

Bunting, E. (1991). *Fly away home.* New York: Clarion Books.

Chard, S.C. (1998a). *The project approach: Making curriculum come alive.* New York: Scholastic.

Chard, S.C. (1998b). *The project approach: Managing successful projects.* New York: Scholastic.

Delpit, L.D. (1995). *Other people's children: Culture conflict in the classroom.* New York: New Press.

Dewey, J. (1938). Experience and education. New York: Macmillan.

Dewey, J. (1964). The child and the curriculum. In R. Archaumbault (Ed.), *John Dewey on education.* (pp. 339–358) Chicago: University of Chicago Press. (Originally published in 1902).

Foxfire Fund (1991). The Foxfire approach: Perspectives and core practices. Hands-On: *A Journal for Teachers, 41,* 3–4.

Fraser, S., & Gestwicki, C. (2000). *Authentic childhood: Exploring Reggio Emilia in the classroom.* Albany, NY: Delmar.

Garbarino, J. (1992). *Children and families in the social environment* (2nd ed.). New York: Aldine de Gruyter.

Heath, S.B. (1983). *Ways with words: Language, life and work in communities.* Cambridge, England: Cambridge University Press.

Helm, J.H., & Katz, L. (2001). *Young investigators: The project approach in the early years.* New York: Teachers College Press.

Hyson, M. (1994). *The emotional development of young children: Building an emotion-centered curriculum.* New York: Teachers College Press.

Katz, L.G., & Chard, S.C. (2000). *Engaging children's minds: The project approach* (2nd ed.). Stamford, CT: Ablex.

Kohn, A. (1993). *Punished by rewards: The trouble with gold stars, incentive plans, A's, praise, and other bribes.* Boston: Houghton Mifflin.

Kugelmass, J.W. (1991). The ecology of the Foxfire approach. *Hands-On: A Journal for Teachers, 42,* 14–20.

Kugelmass, J.W. (1995). Educating children with learning disabilities in Foxfire classrooms. *Journal of Learning Disabilities, 28,* 245–253.

Ladson-Billings, G. (1994). *The dreamkeepers: Successful teachers of African American children.* Cambridge, MA: Harvard University Press.

McCullers, J.C., Fabes, R.A., & Moran, J.D. (1987). Does intrinsic motivation theory explain the adverse effects of rewards on immediate performance? *Journal of Personality and Social Psychology, 52*(5), 1027–1033.

National Coalition for the Homeless (2001). *America's homeless children: An educational reader for elementary school students.* Retrieved December 14, 2002, from http://www.nationalhomeless.com

Phillips, D.C., & Soltis, J.F. (1991). *Perspectives on learning.* New York: Teachers College Press.

Piaget, J. (1959). *Language and thought of the child.* London: Routledge and Kegan Paul.

Piaget, J. (1962). *Play, dreams and imitation in childhood.* New York: Norton.

Poplin, M.S. (1988). The reductionistic fallacy in learning disabilities: Replicating the past by reducing the present. *Journal of Learning Disabilities, 21,* 401–416.

Rainforth, B., & York-Barr, J. (1997). *Collaborative teams for students with severe disabilities: Integrating therapy and educational services* (2nd ed.). Baltimore: Paul H. Brookes Publishing Co.

Skrtic, T. (1991). *Behind special education: A critical analysis of professional culture and school organization.* Denver: Love.

Smith, L.A.H. (1997). "Open education" revisited: Promise and problems in American educational reform. *Teachers College Record, 99*(2), 371–415.

Stites, R. (San Mateo County Office of Education). (1998). *What does research say about outcomes from project-based learning? Evaluation of project-based learning.* Retrieved December 14, 2002, from http://pblmm.k12.ca.us/PBLGuide/pblresch.html

Tharp, R.G., & Gallimore, R. (1988). *Rousing minds to life: Teaching, learning, and schooling in social context.* New York: Cambridge University Press.

Vernon, D.T.A., & Blake, R.L. (1993). Does problem-based learning work? A meta-analysis of evaluation research. *Academic Medicine, 68*(7), 550–563.

Vygotsky, L.S. (1962). *Language and thought.* Cambridge, MA: MIT Press.

Vygotsky, L.S. (1978). *Mind and society.* Cambridge, MA: Harvard University Press.

Walkerdine, V. (1984). Developmental psychology and the child-centered pedagogy: The insertion of Piaget into early education. In J. Henriques, W. Hollyway, C. Urwin, C. Venn, & V. Walkerdine (Eds.), *Changing the subject: Psychology, social regulation and subjectivity* (pp. 152–202). London: Methuen.

Wigginton, E. (Ed.) (1971). *The Foxfire book.* New York: Doubleday.

Curriculum and Instruction in Schools for All Children

The chapters in Section Two deepen and extend the principles established in Section One. Chapter 3, on project-based instruction, illustrates how instruction from many different content areas can be integrated, while also developing human capacities too often neglected in the "core curriculum." Chapters 4 through 7 focus on the content areas of literacy, mathematics, technology, and the arts. These chapters resonate with Chapter 3 in that they show holistic concerns for children, and, although focusing on a particular area of the curriculum, they also illustrate how different areas of the curriculum may overlap, either by chance or by design.

Readers will notice that these chapters are written in a variety of styles. The editors made a conscious decision not to try to homogenize these diverse writing styles; rather, we wanted each author's voice to be heard and their unique personalities to be seen. These authors are parts of the fabric of the school in which we work; they give it texture and strength. Some readers will enjoy the variety; other readers will enjoy one chapter and struggle with another. These different styles, as well as each reader's reactions to them, provide readers with opportunities to learn something more about education because this collection of authors represents the array of both teachers and students in every school. It is because of these diverse personalities and styles that we advocate the use of both systematic and constructivist approaches.

By nature some teachers are drawn to more constructivist approaches whereas others easily adopt systematic approaches. Within their classrooms, however, are children who will benefit from varied combinations of these approaches. The chapters in this section model for teachers strategies to teach essential content while blending constructivist and systematic approaches in ways that meet the concerns of diverse groups of students.

CHAPTER FOUR

Finding the Middle Ground in Literacy Instruction

KAREN BROMLEY

n the 1990s, whole language practices and constructivism in the United States were blamed, in part, for poor scores on achievement tests. Whole language is criticized for providing too much constructivist instruction and too little systematic instruction in basic skills. With the adoption of standards and standardized assessments, there is pressure at local, state, and national levels for teachers to replace constructivist, whole language practices with systematic and direct phonics instruction. Demands for heavy phonics skills teaching are based on a narrow view of literacy, however, and assume, erroneously, that direct skill instruction will overcome inequities among learners such as those resulting from poverty and ensure later literacy success (Coles, 2000). A focus on early and systematic phonics instruction may cause teachers to minimize or ignore critical factors related to literacy learning, including prior knowledge, motivation, interest, metacognition, purpose, relevancy, peer interactions, and so forth; a focus on constructivist instruction may leave students with inadequate literacy skills, such as the ability to decode words by sounding them out, that are prerequisites to becoming successful readers and writers.

A CLOSER LOOK AT "BALANCE"

Today, as in past decades, in New Zealand schools, a balanced approach includes characteristics of both systematic instruction and constructivism, specifically, "issues of environmental design, assessment, modeling, guidance, interactivity, independence, practice, oral language acquisition, writing and reading processes, community building, and motivation" (Reutzel, 1999, p. 322). U.S. scholars, researchers, and practitioners labeled these practices whole language (Anderson, Hiebert, Scott, & Wilkinson, 1985). They were never, however, fully implemented in the United States. In reality, whole language has been defined and implemented in a variety of lesser ways in the United States. Many educators ignored balance and adopted only the constructivist practices that were part of the original concept of whole language. But, New Zealand's balanced approach is really a complex set of practices that reflect both systematic, teacher-directed instruction, and constructivist, teacher-guided instruction. Systematic (or direct) literacy instruction is based on the notion that there is specific knowledge about reading and writing that the teacher systematically passes on to the learner without any active participation on the part of the learner. Constructivist instruction is based on the notion that the learner draws on prior knowledge and text information to make inferences and actively participates in constructing personal meanings through reading and writing.

Whole language has been defined and implemented in a variety of lesser ways in the United States. Many educators ignore balance and adopt only the constructivist practices that were part of the original concept of whole language. Today, in the United States, the pendulum seems to be swinging in the direction of systematic and explicit instruction in basic skills. This shift limits opportunities for learners to have the meaningful interactions with text and each other that build literacy beyond basic skills. Balanced literacy instruction is, however, based on a broader view of literacy that includes these opportunities and the critical factors just mentioned. It is both systematic (or teacher-directed) and constructivist (or teacher-guided). Balanced literacy instruction has four essential conditions (Cambourne, 1999). It is:

1. *Explicit*: Teachers deliberately demonstrate and make learners aware of the processes and skills they need to become literate.
2. *Systematic*: Teachers base instruction on proactive, rational planning that includes formal planning documents (e.g., lessons, activities, assessment tools).
3. *Mindful*: Teachers aim for metacognitive awareness by knowing that the way a learner takes in information or learns literacy skills determines how he or she uses both later (Langer, 1997).
4. *Contextualized*: Teachers focus learning on what makes sense to the learner by creating meaningful purposes and activities for learning.

Balanced literacy instruction begins with what the learner knows, but does not leave it up to him or her to figure everything out for him- or herself. It is intentional and can be articulated from assessment data. It is characterized by careful decision making by the teacher and is not random, unplanned, or without explanation. It uses modeling, demonstration, and guided practice and provides opportunities for application. Balanced instruction is thoughtful, active, meaningful, and includes engagement and interactions with others, such as reading and writing that is guided, shared, and independent (Reutzel, 1999). Balanced instruction is based on a set of beliefs about what children should know and a flexible program of how it can be learned that grows from a comprehensive view of literacy (Fitzgerald, 1999). Balanced instruction that optimally develops literacy blends Cambourne's (1999) four conditions in varying degrees for each individual student.

In fact, balanced instruction could be called thoughtful eclecticism, a term that describes teachers who adapt and use a creative combination of methods determined by the concerns of students (Duffy & Hoffman, 1999). No single best method has been found simply because "different students require different methods at different times" (p. 13). The most effective teachers analyze, adapt, and integrate various programs, materials, and methods as the situation demands. They know there is no one best method of literacy instruction (Allington & Cunningham, 2002). As seen in the vignette that follows, Mrs. Silbur's challenge as a principal is to help teachers better understand the balance between systematic instruction and constructivism in order to provide the best literacy practices for all students.

MRS. SILBUR'S SCHOOL

The school in which Mrs. Silbur and her K–6 teachers work is located in a diverse urban neighborhood that includes many immigrant families from around the world, most with Asian, Hispanic, and African roots, as well as second- and third-generation European families. It is a Title I school with 70% of students receiving free or reduced price lunches and 15% of students receiving special education services. About 8% of students receive English as a second language (ESL) instruction.

The school follows inclusive practices and provides instruction for struggling readers and students with special concerns in classrooms with heterogeneously grouped regular education students. Most classrooms have more than one adult working with students at the same time. In a typical day, many people might work together in one classroom, including the classroom teacher, paraprofessionals, a reading specialist, a special education teacher, an ESL teacher, and a speech-language pathologist, as well as volunteer grandparents and student teachers from a nearby university. Individuals and small groups of children receive intense, supportive instruction outside the classroom for only small periods of time. The following classroom vignettes show how many teachers in this school demonstrate a thoughtfully eclectic approach that blends both systematic and constructivist teaching.

Some of Mrs. Silbur's teachers feel the tug of direct and systematic skill instruction as a remedy for low test scores and a way to right the wrongs attributed to whole language instruction. Mrs. Silbur, however, views literacy on a continuum with direct and systematic skill instruction at one extreme and constructivism and holistic processes at the other. She calls the literacy program balanced because it combines a whole language philosophy with phonics instruction. She tells teachers that, historically, beliefs about how to teach literacy have followed the sweep of a clock's pendulum with shifts occurring regularly between a direct, systematic, or skills approach and a holistic or constructivist approach.

> I've read a lot recently about balanced literacy instruction as an antidote to mandated phonics instruction that excludes whole language practices. However, I don't believe you can separate early word learning skills from holistic teaching, and balanced instruction is what I see in the classrooms of my best teachers. They don't exclude one approach in favor of the other. In fact, they blend the two, but in different ways, depending on the individual concerns of students. On the one hand, every child requires some basic phonics skills as one strategy for making sense out of print. Some children, with just a little phonics knowledge, seem to understand intuitively how words work, whereas others need more phonics instruction and guidance to read fluently. On the other hand, we know that all children need to be immersed in stories and texts that are meaningful to them so they can apply their growing repertoire of phonics and sense-making skills, and we know that all children don't need the rote skill practice of phonics workbooks. It's a continuing challenge for some of my teachers to maintain balance in their literacy teaching, though, because of the pressure they feel from the state tests that are used to compare them and their students' performances.

The following vignettes illustrate a balanced approach to literacy instruction in selected K–6 classrooms.

EMERGENT LITERACY: MISS DAVIS' KINDERGARTEN CLASS

Miss Davis knows how the environment in her kindergarten classroom can encourage children to step into the world of school-based literacy (Morrow, 1989). She promotes emergent literacy and social interaction by providing opportunities to communicate using print, scribbles, drawings, and play. She arranges the room with children's desks in groups of two and three so they can work together. She has a rug area for whole group instruction and several centers in corners and along the walls. She changes the focus and/or activities at each center regularly to challenge children with new opportunities and tasks. At any one time there may be a restaurant center, reading and writing center, math center, post office center, blocks center, listening center, painting center, or science center where small groups of children work and play together.

In these centers, Miss Davis encourages reading and writing behaviors by including paper, pens, pencils, books, and other literacy tools that invite children to practice literate behavior together. For example, in the restaurant center she puts large, glossy menus discarded by a local restaurant chain, pencils and small pads of paper for taking orders, colored pictures of various meals posted on the wall with appropriate printed words such as *hamburger, pizza,* and *milk,* a newspaper, a cookbook, empty boxes of food in the kitchen area (e.g., cereal, cake mix, macaroni and cheese, muffins), and so forth. She includes a small cash register with play money, a chef's hat, apron, pots, plates, silverware, tablecloth, and a desk with two chairs.

The first time Miss Davis introduces the restaurant center, she participates with three children as the rest of the class watches. She knows that taking a role, joining in the play, and modeling the desired play behavior helps her children have meaningful literacy engagements in the center (Christie, 1990). Miss Davis plays the role of a patron and models appropriate behavior, nudging the three to act out their roles of cook, waiter, and patron by making statements and asking appropriate questions, such as, "What looks good to you? What do you think you'll order?" "We've read the menu. Will you take our orders now?" "The recipe for brownies might be in the cookbook." "Could you give us our check now?" "How much do we owe you?" "How much tip should we leave?" "The food was great! Thank you!"

By participating, she helps the children think about and rehearse what happens in a real restaurant. Miss Davis has found that being involved in the play at first and modeling literacy for children results in more meaningful interactions and literacy use than assuming they will know what to do and not showing them how to role play.

A peek at this center in use reveals four children role-playing what happens in a restaurant as they talk with each other and "pretend" to read and write. Two patrons order their food after looking at menus, then read a newspaper or magazine as they await their food; a chef reads a cookbook and box directions to prepare food; a waiter or waitress writes orders and checks, serves food, adds numbers, and uses the cash register. In a center such as this one, children learn to imitate and practice literate behavior as they work together in a situation that is much like the real world. Of course, most of these children are not yet fluent readers or writers, but, as seen in Figures 4.1 and 4.2, they can become aware of literacy in their environment and begin to approximate literate behavior.

In addition to designing the classroom to promote literacy development, Miss Davis demonstrates literacy daily for her children with oral reading and shared reading. Sometimes, she introduces a picture

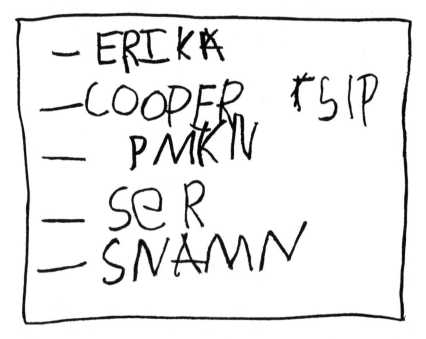

Figure 4.1.   As "chef" in the restaurant center, Erika lists the ingredients she will use to make pumpkin pie: "pumpkin, sugar, cinnamon, salt and pepper."

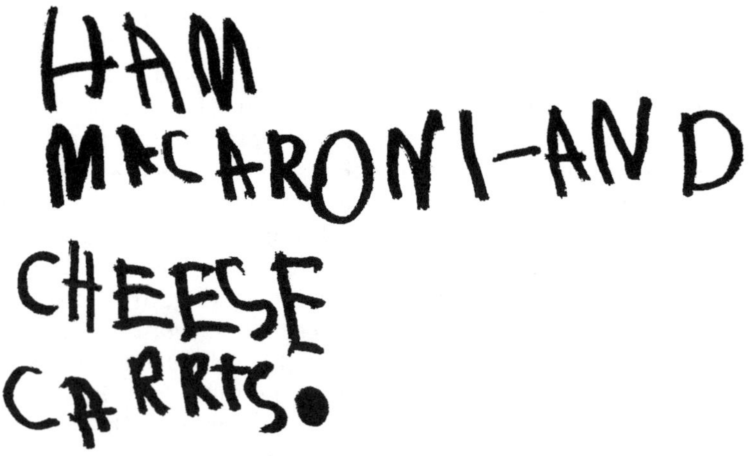

HAM
MACARONI-AND
CHEESE
CARRTS.

Figure 4.2. As "waiter" in the restaurant center, Joshua writes a customer's order by copying words from food boxes in the center.

book and reads it orally to the class, stopping here and there to share pictures, ask for interpretations, clarify what is happening, or predict what might happen next. Often, she does a shared reading lesson with her class in which they read together from a "big book," one that is large enough for everyone to see (e.g., 24" x 30") and has a predictable story line. Miss Davis might read the story to her class first using the same techniques she does for oral reading. During a second reading she points to each word as she reads to reinforce the idea of one-to-one correspondence between speech and print. She stops at appropriate places and asks children to fill in a word or phrase that rhymes with a previous word. As children become familiar with the concepts, repetitive language patterns, rhymes, and refrains of the predictable story, they can often repeat entire lines. After they have read a predictable story several times, they enjoy reading it chorally as she points to the print. Miss Davis then leaves several smaller copies of the "big book" at the reading center so children can reread it there.

Reading to children and engaging in shared reading has several benefits. Children learn left to right progression, add words to their sight vocabulary, see and hear fluent reading being modeled for them, develop comprehension and prediction skills, and share in a pleasurable experience with the teacher and each other.

Miss Davis wants her children to be able to recognize and name the upper and lower case letters of the alphabet and she also teaches letter-sound correspondence, but clearly not to the exclusion of other practices that build literacy skills and a love of reading. Knowing that ames are among the first words they will recognize, ns the school year by focusing on the consonants that students' names. During their morning sharing time, en teaches a brief letter lesson. For example, she calls chiiu.. ention to the letter "B" that begins the names Brad, Bobby, Brittany, and Beth. Then, she writes the upper- and lowercase "Bb" at the top of a piece of chart paper and begin a list of "B" words by writing these four names first and underlining the capital "B" in each. She pronounces each name carefully and has the class repeat each name as she points to it. She asks the children to look at several objects she has gathered (pencil, battery, book, eraser, facial tissue, apple, and so forth) to see which begin with "B," and adds these to the list. Then she asks them to look around the room for other words to add to the list. And, for homework she asks them to have a family member help them find a "B" word at home and bring it to school to add to the list. She also extends the word hunt by rereading a book the class just finished and asking the students to find "Bb" words in it.

As the list grows and the children "read" it together each day, Miss Davis takes the opportunity to point out that some "B" words are short and others are long, and "We can tap or clap out the parts of longer words such as *'boom-er-ang.'*" As the children become familiar with the list of words, Miss Davis has them say each word and clap out the syllables with her. This helps develop children's *phonological awareness,* the knowledge that spoken words are composed of sounds. Identifying syllables in words prepares children for *phonics,* the knowledge that printed words are composed of the sounds in spoken words. Miss Davis knows that children can learn to read and write as they learn to recognize and name letters, however, so she does not make learning letter names a prerequisite for literacy.

This glimpse into Miss Davis' kindergarten classroom shows some ways in which she blends systematic and constructivist instruction to help her children become literate. She shares her insights here:

> I've discovered that I can expect a lot more from my students than I ever realized. I never thought writing was possible in kindergarten, but now we do shared writing together all the time and they're learning to read what we write as well as write on their own. I teach more direct, systematic skills than I ever used to because the children are ready for them. I've also discovered that children often learn as much from each other as they do from me. I tell them we have 23 teachers in this room—that's 22 of them and one of me!

Miss Davis knows what her students need to learn, so she provides both direct instruction in skills and opportunities for them to construct their own knowledge as they engage together in literacy activities. She believes that providing an appropriate context in which skills can be used and practiced is more effective than rote practice of skills in isolation from meaningful learning.

CONCEPTS ABOUT WORDS: MR. FERRARO'S FIRST-GRADE CLASS

Mr. Ferraro's first-grade classroom and the strategies he uses reflect a focus on children creating their own knowledge and understanding through active participation and interaction. At a science center, children observe and document in their learning logs the life cycle of a caterpillar as it spins its chrysalis and later becomes a Monarch butterfly. At a literacy center, children select books to read alone or with a partner. At a writing center, a variety of writing tools including pencils, colored pens, paper, glue, magazines, scissors, staplers, and crayons are available so children can make their own books and dictionaries. These opportunities for self-directed, constructivist student learning suggest Mr. Ferraro views participation and interaction as important for his 26 first-graders.

Mr. Ferraro says that his students' concepts about words vary greatly. When asked to define their understanding of what a word is, his students provided a variety of responses, for example:

"A word is a sentence, a letter." (Shannon)

"It's something in a book. It's like a letter." (Vanessa)

"It's something you can write. Something you can say like I am saying a whole bunch of words now. Sometimes cartoons say words. Well, most of the time they do." (Joshua)

"Something you can spell and you can read it and if you don't know it you can skip it an go on to another word." (Clara)

Shannon and Vanessa don't seem to understand what a word is yet. Joshua and Clara possess more sophisticated and multidimensional concepts of a word, a goal that Mr. Ferraro has for all of his students. To teach them about words, letters, and sounds as well as rhyming words and word families, Mr. Ferraro uses the children's names. One of the ways he builds the concept that a name is a word is by giving children individual mailboxes labeled with their names in which to receive and send mail—letters to families, notes to each other, and class work. Mr. Ferraro also posts a jobs chart on which children change the names and jobs weekly, and he plays Names Bingo and Words I Know Bingo regularly with them. To play these games, Mr. Ferraro prints each child's name or a word chosen by the child on a paper card and has the children use game chips, candy or cereal, to cover each letter as he calls it out. When a child covers all the letters in his or her name or word, the child eats the snacks and says the word. As children begin to recognize words, Mr. Ferraro builds knowledge of letter sequence by printing each letter of the chosen word on a separate card, mixing the cards up, and having each child arrange them in the correct order before they play Bingo.

Along with reading poetry and predictable books to his students to help them recognize rhyming words, Mr. Ferraro uses children's names to help them discover sound–letter relationships and patterns. For example, he shows his students how to make a whole "family" of words that rhyme with the name Pat. By reciting the alphabet and changing the first letter of Pat, they make a list of words containing the "–at" phonogram: *bat, cat, fat, hat, mat, rat, sat, tat* and *vat.* More able children suggest consonant digraph substitutions to make words such as *chat* and blend substitutions to make *brat* and *flat.* Mr. Ferraro also shares the children's book *Andy (That's My Name)* by Tomie dePaola (1973), which depicts characters in the book rearranging the letters in Andy's name and adding letters to make many different words from Andy (see Table 4.1).

Mr. Ferraro also uses a strategy called Making Words that requires students to manipulate the letters in a target word to create other words (Cunningham & Allington, 1999; Cunningham & Cunningham,

Table 4.1. Words that can be created by rearranging and adding to the name Andy.

One syllable	Two syllables
Can	Candy
Dan	Dandy
Fan	Handy
Man	Mandy
Pan	Randy
Ran	Sandy
Tan	
And	
Hand	
Band	
Land	
Sand	
Stand	

Source: DePaola, T. (1973). *Andy (that's my name).* Englewood Cliffs, NJ: Prentice Hall.

Table 4.2. Words that can be created by rearranging and adding to the name Maryann.

One syllable	Two syllables
A	Any
An	Mary
May	Anna
Ray	Army
Ram	Nary
Ran	
Man	
Ann	
Arm	
Yam	
Name	
Yarn	

1992). Mr. Ferraro often introduces this activity by using a child's name. He writes each letter of the name on a separate card and shows children how to rearrange the letters to make words of one letter, two letters, three letters, and so forth. For example, there are many words that can be made from the name Maryann (see Table 4.2).

Next, Mr. Ferraro writes the letters of each child's name on cards and helps individuals and small groups rearrange letters to make words. During this activity, Mr. Ferraro makes lists of the words children make so they can see what they have created, read them together, and return to read them afterwards. Children discover that for short names with one vowel, such as Jan, there are few words to make unless the children substitute initial consonants that let them create word families from names such as *Jim*—dim, him, Kim, rim, Tim, slim, and swim and *Jan*—ban, Dan, fan, man, Nan, pan, ran, tan, and van. But, from longer names they can create more words, such as from *Shirley*—her, his, hire, sire, he, she, and yes, and from *Benjamin*— I, a, an, am, Ben, Jen, men, jam, bam, man, ban, and Jan. Of course, to be successful with Making Words, children need to possess at least a small fund of words they can recognize on sight. But rearranging letters to construct words can give beginning readers a sense of how letters and sounds can go together in different ways to make different words.

Mr. Ferraro also uses names to reinforce basic counting and number concepts. He has each child print his or her name on a strip of paper, count the letters in the name, write the numeral and number name, and then the class makes a bar graph on a bulletin board, as seen in Figure 4.3, by posting names in columns according to their length.

Mr. Ferraro finds that Making Words builds his first graders' letter and word recognition skills, spelling, and decoding abilities. To connect this strategy to a content area, Mr. Ferraro

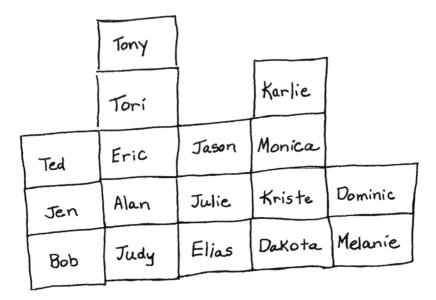

Figure 4.3.   Children focus on the number of letters in familiar words (their names) to make this "bar graph of our names."

1. Chooses a target word from science or social studies with one or two vowels that will make several smaller words when the letters are rearranged (e.g., spider, winter, splash, turtles, carrots, thunder, friends, trunks, spends, gardens, candle)
2. Makes a list of the shorter words that can be made from the target word
3. From this list, chooses several words that include a) words to sort for the pattern(s) he wants to teach, b) both little words and big words, c) words that can be made with the same letters in different places (e.g., arm, ram), d) a proper name(s) that concerns a capital letter(s), and e) words most students have in their listening vocabularies
4. Writes the words on index cards and orders them from shortest to longest
5. Prints large letter cards to use as he models Making Words and prints smaller letter cards for each child, one for each letter in the target word (e.g., *s*p*i*d*e*r*), giving each child an envelope or plastic bag with four consonants (e.g., d, p, r, s) and two vowels (e.g., i, e). He writes uppercase letters on one side and lowercase letters on the other side of each card and prints consonants in black and vowels in red.

6. Using a pocket chart or blackboard tray to hold the large letter cards, makes a two-letter word, such as Ed, explaining that it is a name. He has the children make it on their desks with their letters.

7. Asks children to find the letter r and put it with -ed on their desks to make a color word red and asks a child to make it with the pocket chart cards for the class to see

8. Continues having children make the words pie, pies, dies, rid, sip, ride, side, ripe, rise, pride and drips. He uses each word in context and explains its meaning and has children say the words they make and/or count the letters. Last, he helps them make the target "big" word—spider.

9. Uses a pocket chart to sort the word cards (created in Step 4) according to similarities. For example, he displays three words printed that contain the same pattern (ride, pride, side) and asks how they are the same. Or, he mixes them up and displays all the word cards on the pocket chart and asks children to find three words that end with "S," contain "D," or begin with "R," and so forth.

Making Words and the other activities described here help Mr. Ferraro's students learn that by changing one letter or a sequence of letters, they can make a word into another word. They also learn to recognize letters and sounds, create rhyming words, decode, find patterns, and manipulate the alphabet. Most important, by playing with letters and words in these ways, Mr. Ferraro's students begin to develop their knowledge of language and how it works as they sound words out, build word-recognition skills, and add words to their sight-word vocabularies. Once his children understand how to play Making Words, Mr. Ferraro often puts them in pairs or small groups to do the activity together. To introduce a second-grade teacher to Making Words, Mr. Ferraro combined his class with the second grade class to form mixed-age pairs and modeled a Making Words lesson for them. Then he had his first graders teach the second graders with a new word and in this way he helped a colleague learn a new strategy that is appropriate for decoding, spelling, and word learning well beyond first grade.

In addition to learning about phonemic awareness and phonics through shared reading and activities that focus on words, Mr. Ferraro and his children do lots of shared writing. He often has children dictate to him, and he transcribes their ideas. For example, during a study of Change, in science, Mr. Ferraro's students studied a Monarch butterfly as it emerged from its cocoon. As the children talk about what they see and have learned, Mr. Ferraro transcribes their ideas onto chart paper. As he writes and the children watch, Mr. Ferraro uses this shared writing activity and others like it to focus children's attention on letter sounds, the visual aspects of words, and the form of written language. As he transcribes their words, he often uses prompts such as, "What letter do you think comes next? Where should we put the period? What little word do you see in that big word? How can we say that using school language?"

When they reread these stories together and children have trouble figuring out a word, Mr. Ferraro helps them become strategic readers. He builds the children's metacognitive skills by modeling several fix-up strategies for them (Bromley, 2002). Mr. Ferraro's goal is for his students to be aware of their own comprehension and actively make sense out of print. So, he shows children how to use these strategies by thinking aloud for them the way he might use each strategy when he comes to a word he doesn't know. For example, when Mr. Ferraro reads *Charlotte's Web* by E.B. White (1952), a story about finding friendship in unlikely places, he uses this oral reading event to model strategic reading for his class. When Charlotte the spider used the word *terrific* to describe Wilbur the pig, Mr. Ferraro skips it and reads to the end of the sentence or paragraph saying:

> Oh-oh, that's a word I don't know. (He writes it on the board for the children to see.) Let's see if I can think what makes sense here when I reread the sentence. Gee, I just noticed that in the picture Wilbur has a huge, contented smile on his face. Now, I'd better get my mouth ready. The word begins like Tom—"tuh." Next, it has an "er" that says "rrr" and "if," a word I already know. So, I can sound it out to say "turrif," and maybe the last part "ic," sounds like "ick," to make the word "turrifick." So, looking at Wilbur's smile and sounding the word out makes me think "terrific" probably means "great." These are some clues that might help me figure the word out by using both sounds and sense.

Then, when Mr. Ferraro rereads the sentence, he supplies the unknown word *terrific*. And, he talks with the children about the other strategies on the fix-up list that can help them become more metacognitively aware. He often thinks aloud like this for his students and asks them to help him use the strategies to work out the pronunciation and meaning of new words. Mr. Ferraro also encourages children to share the strategies they use to successfully decode words so they become mindful, independent readers.

The teachers in Mr. Ferraro's school have adopted this list of strategies because they believe the strategies are important for every reader to possess. The teachers have made a schoolwide commitment and they post this chart in every classroom. Many teachers make laminated tag board books of these fix-up strategies, shown in Figure 4.4, for children to use as they read. Some of the first-grade teachers felt their children couldn't read the words on the list, but soon discovered that for younger children and those who cannot yet read, the pictures were enough to remind them of what to do.

Mr. Ferraro also models the thinking–writing process for children with shared writing that demonstrates how oral language can become printed language. When special education teachers, ESL teachers, and reading teachers are scheduled in his room, Mr. Ferraro often divides the class into smaller, heterogeneously mixed groups so he and the reading specialist or special education teacher, for example, can also do shared writing activities. Smaller groups give children more opportunities to contribute and engage actively in the discussion and writing. Mr. Ferraro says shared writing allows all of his students, including

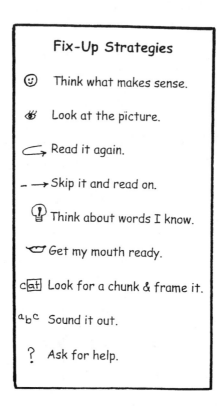

Figure 4.4.   Post these fix-up strategies on a chart in your classroom, or put them on individual bookmarks for students to use as they read.

students who are learning English as a second language, students with learning disabilities, and/or readers who are struggling for other reasons, to contribute as they collaborate to create stories, reports, letters, and so forth. Most important, Mr. Ferraro sees his children transfer these skills into their daily journal writing and other independent writing. Also, he says that as his children learn to use sense-making strategies when they read together, he sees this carry over into their independent reading as well.

Mr. Ferraro's reading and writing practices described here include both systematic instruction and constructivism. The Making Words lessons have specific objectives and require planning and preparation ahead of time. Mr. Ferraro demonstrates what he wants the children to do and then guides them as they practice what he has taught them. As the children create their own words, they discover, among other things, how letter substitutions make new words, word families, and rhyming words, and they learn standard spelling. The shared writing instruction also helps children develop knowledge of the rules of language as they use their own language to construct meaningful stories. When Mr. Ferraro models the use of the fix-up strategies and encourages children to practice them when they come to difficult words, he is also systematically and mindfully guiding them toward metacognitive awareness and independence.

GUIDED READING IN GRADES 1–6: MISS MURRAY'S FOURTH-GRADE CLASS

The faculty of grades 1–6 formed study groups to read and discuss an instructional approach called *guided reading*, which represents a balance between constructivist and systematic instruction (Fountas & Pinnell, 1996). The aim of guided reading is to teach children to use and develop strategies for reading and comprehending increasingly more difficult levels of text independently. This allows children to become independent and self-directed readers and learners. Mrs. Silbur and her group studied this approach carefully, visited schools where it is used, attended workshops and conferences to learn more about it, and now use it with all students, including those who have learning disabilities, those who are learning English as a second language, and those who struggle with literacy for other reasons.

Miss Murray, a fourth-grade teacher, uses guided reading with groups of four to six students (Fountas & Pinnell, 2001). Like Mr. Ferraro and her other colleagues, she wants her students to develop their capacities to think critically and be self-directed learners. Miss Murray's class of 23 students includes 10 students who are reading on grade level, 3 reading above grade level, and 10 reading below grade level. Of those reading below grade level, four receive the services of a special education teacher and the reading specialist supports six others. Whenever she can, Miss Murray takes advantage of these pull-in teachers who come into her room by having them do guided reading lessons. Each teacher works with a small group of students who use similar reading processes and can read the same level of text with support. To teach a guided reading lesson, Miss Murray does the following:

1. Selects a book the children can read easily so the focus is on meaning making but also problem-solving to figure out unknown words.
2. Introduces the story, drawing on children's background knowledge. She often does a "picture walk" through the book by having her students look at the illustrations as she talks about them, using vocabulary that is unique to the story. She encourages children to notice, point out, and comment on things in the pictures.
3. Has children read the story silently or whisper read it. She observes those who seem to have trouble, and where, or sits beside a child to hear him whisper read and notes words/phrases that give him trouble.
4. Interacts briefly with any child who needs help. She encourages him or her to think about the story or use strategies to solve difficult words.
5. Invites talk about the story through personal response and questions that help assess and extend children's understanding. She revisits the story to point out and share word-solving strategies.
6. Occasionally has children do a second reading of the story chorally to encourage fluency, or extend the story through writing, drama, or art.
7. Takes a running record of oral reading miscues with one reader after each silent reading to determine the child's miscues, strategy use, and comprehension.

Guided reading requires Miss Murray to actively engage children before, during, and after reading, as the examples of the essential elements of guided reading approach show in Table 4.3. She observes and assesses individual reading behavior to make decisions about how to interact with the child about the story, what strategies the child needs to learn to use, and what level of story to read next. In a guided reading

Table 4.3.   The essential elements of guided reading

	Before the reading	During the reading	After the reading
Teacher	Selects an appropriate text, one that will be supportive but with a few problems to solve Prepares an introduction to the story Briefly introduces the story, keeping in mind the meaning, language, and visual information in the text, and the knowledge, experience, and skills of the reader Leaves some questions to be answered through reading	"Listens in" Observes the reader's behaviors for evidence of strategy use Confirms children's problem-solving attempts and success Interacts with individuals to assist with problem solving (when appropriate) Makes notes about the strategies of individual readers	Talks about the story with the children Invites personal response Returns to the text for teaching opportunities such as finding evidence or discussing problem solving Assesses children's understanding of what they read Engages the children in the story through activities such as drama, writing, art, or additional reading
Children	Engage in conversation about the story Raise questions Build expectations Notice information in the text	Read the whole text or a unified part to themselves (softly or silently) Request help in problem solving (when needed)	Talk about the story Check predictions and react personally to the story Revisit the text at points of problem solving May reread the story to a partner or independently Engage in activities that extend and respond to the text

lesson, the teacher models, demonstrates, and encourages children to apply strategies to comprehend text with prompts such as those in Table 4.4. In this way, she helps children use meaning cues, syntactic cues, and visual cues to figure out unknown words as they construct meaning.

Miss Murray and her colleagues are trying not to fall into the trap that some schools do with guided reading. Some teachers alter guided reading in ways that weaken its effectiveness and are so dramatic that the practice is guided reading in name only. First, in some schools guided reading has become a whole group practice with children grouped by ability so that lessons are taught to entire classes. Second,

Table 4.4.   Prompts to use during guided reading that encourage children to comprehend and become independent Word Solvers or Word Wizards

Discussion starters	During reading
Was your prediction right	Does that make sense
What did it remind you of	Did you look at the picture
How did it happen	Does it sound right
What would happen if	Skip the word and come back
What did you notice	Can you make a guess
Why did the character	Can you chunk the word
How would you feel if	What does it start with
Why do you think	Can you get your mouth ready
What do you know about	What might fit there
What makes you say that	Do you know a word like that
How did the author	What word could you try
Tell me about	What do you know that might help
	You're almost right, try again
	That is a good way to figure it out

the books or stories chosen for children to read are often at their frustration level and they know fewer than 90% of the words, which makes comprehension extremely difficult. Third, teachers sometimes form ability groups in their classrooms that never change and children don't progress at their own individual rates or work with anyone except those in their group.

Aware of these abuses of guided reading that work against the intent of constructivist practices, Miss Murray still occasionally uses guided reading lessons with her entire class. She wants to provide opportunities for peer interaction in which her students can experience and model higher levels of literacy and provide support for each other's growth. So, a child who may not be able to read a book on his or her own might hear it read by a partner or listen to it on tape and then participate in a discussion of the story as a member of a heterogeneous group. Miss Murray says:

Sometimes I want the whole class to share the experience of a particular book. For example, in social studies we read *Thunder Rolling in the Mountains* by Scott O'Dell and Elizabeth Hall (1992) together. This book helped us experience the flight of the Nez Perce tribe from Oregon to Montana because it was written in the first-person and through the eyes of Swan Necklace, a character who is nearly my students'

age. It is more personal and powerful than reading in a social studies text about our treatment of Native American
tribes in the late 1800s. Reading a book together as a group
also brings the class closer and builds a feeling of community. It gives us all common information and a reading experience to share, but most important it gives everyone
common knowledge so everyone has a voice for discussions.

To use guided reading with a whole class, Miss Murray sometimes
pairs struggling readers with better readers and alternates between
reading to her children while they follow in their books and having
the children read silently. This practice makes reading a difficult book
easier for students and lets Miss Murray model word-solving and comprehension strategies for them as she reads. In guided reading lessons,
discussions and questions focus on helping students know what to do
when they meet an unfamiliar word and what to do when meaning is
unclear. Miss Murray believes small-group work allows all students to
interact, so it takes their thinking to higher levels as they learn from
each other. Group makeup is flexible as Miss Murray changes the membership according to student concerns, interests, and use of strategies.
For her small-group instruction, Miss Murray chooses books written at
each child's instructional reading level, so they can read 90–95% of
the words independently, but need to apply reading strategies to the
remaining unfamiliar words.

When Miss Murray works with a small group, she is able to identify the strategies students are using and give instruction in the strategies they have not yet mastered. For example, listening to several children whisper read one day, Miss Murray noticed they had trouble with
the word *spectator.* So, after the discussion that followed the story, Miss
Murray and the students revisited the pages on which this word appeared to talk about ways to figure it out using context. She also took
the opportunity to teach the group that the root *spec-* comes from
spectare, which means to watch or behold, and invited students to help
her create a Word Square for spec-, as seen in Figure 4.5. A Word
Square is a visual tool for identifying, defining, drawing, and remembering prefixes, suffixes, roots, and whole words. She created it on
chart paper and then students copied it into their response journals as
a model to use in making their own Word Squares.

Miss Murray also asked the students to Web-a-Word with her and
brainstorm all the words they could think of that contain the root
word spec-, as seen in Figure 4.6. As one student added a word such
as *inspection,* another student suddenly thought of *inspector,* and a third
student came up with *spectacle,* which prompted another to add *specta-*

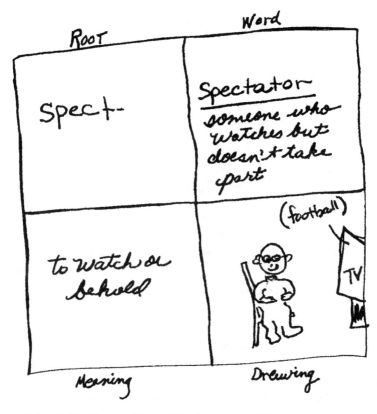

Figure 4.5. A Word Square builds vocabulary by requiring a definition and linking a drawing to the word in a sentence.

tor. Then students went to their dictionaries and found many more new words they hadn't known previously. They began to see relationships among the words and generalize their observations to other words they already knew (e.g., "Hey, spectroscope is like microscope and telescope, and scope- means to spy, look carefully or see"). To extend this learning to other roots and introduce students to new multisyllabic words, Miss Murray had pairs of students use dictionaries to create Word Squares and do Web-a-Word for three other roots: duct-, graph-, and derma-, and then share these with the class.

Miss Murray added a component to her guided reading lessons that she believes is important. She discovered that the running record and miscue analysis do not necessarily give her a full picture of a child's comprehension. A running record is a series of checks (for words read correctly) and transcribed errors (for mispronounced words) that a teacher makes to represent how a child reads orally. A

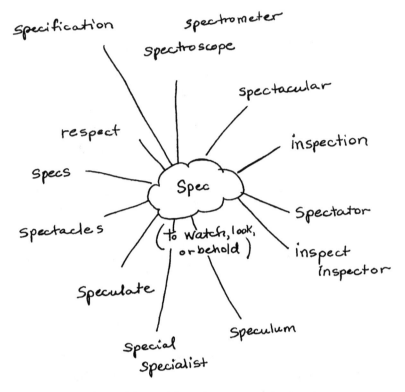

Figure 4.6.   A Web-a-Word for spec helps students see many related words.

miscue analysis is a teacher's interpretation of the meaning of the oral reading miscues or errors a child makes. Miss Murray added a retelling component to guided reading because it gives her important information about a student's comprehension that she doesn't always get from a running record or a miscue analysis.

Miss Murray has a student retell what he remembers from the story, and she prompts with questions to determine his understanding. A miscue is an attempt to represent text using incomplete information and, as such, can reveal a lot about a student's reading process. Miss Murray often finds that a child will make many miscues that do not affect his comprehension. For example, a child might read the printed word *horse* and say *pony;* mispronounce or omit a proper name; omit descriptive words such as *angrily* or *slowly;* omit function words such as *the, and, or,* and *on;* or insert words that are not there such as adding *big* to the phrase "the red truck." Miscues such as these are relatively minor and, because they do not disrupt comprehension, they suggest that the child is reading for comprehension. Giving only a cursory glance at the high number of miscues in the running record without analyzing the miscues carefully might, however, suggest a more severe problem than is there. So, listening to the child retell what he or she has read, as well examining his or her miscues carefully in relation to the text, lets Miss Murray check his or her comprehension so she can decide on future reading materials and strategy instruction.

Guided reading lessons require large classroom libraries and opportunities for students to read a variety of fiction and nonfiction written at their instructional levels. As with other reading approaches, students become fluent readers more quickly if they have a lot of opportunities to read materials they select that are written on their independent reading levels. Therefore, having plenty of books available in your classroom in which students recognize 98% of the words and understand at least 95% of the concepts, as well as giving students time to read, is critical.

When children are not doing guided reading, they can read and write independently or work in collaborative groups at centers in the classroom. They can also write in literature response journals using a combination of teacher-supplied prompts as seen in Figure 4.7, free writing, and questions. Miss Murray often identifies one or two prompts for children to use and has them write freely, too. Combining free responses with prompts lets children connect personally to parts of a story that resonate with them as they think about what they have read. Asking targeted questions lets Miss Murray focus her students' attention on the author's style of writing. For example, when her students are reading *Out of the Dust* by Karen Hesse (1997), a book about a young girl's life in the Oklahoma dustbowl in the late 1800s, she uses this prompt: "How do Billie Jo's short, dated entries in *Out of the Dust* make you feel? Why do you think Karen Hesse used this style of writing for this story?" Or, when they read *Tuck Everlasting* by Natalie Babbitt (1986), a story about an ageless family and a young girl who discovers their secret, Miss Murray prompts them to think about the author's intentional use of setting by asking questions such as, "What is the function of a fence? What does it do? Why do you think Natalie Babbitt puts a fence around Winnie's house in *Tuck Everlasting*?" Miss Murray also varies the format of the journal, see Table 4.5. For example, a favorite format is the diary or character journal in which students become the main character. In Figure 4.8, Melissa, a fourth-grader, became Sound-of-Running-Feet, the main character in *Thunder Rolling in the Mountains*. Prompts, targeted questions, and varied formats such as these let students bring their own meaning to texts and encourage interpretations as long as students can substantiate their opinions.

1. It makes me think of...
2. I felt...
3. It reminds me...
4. I learned...
5. It's about...
6. I noticed...
7. I know...
8. I didn't understand...
9. I drew...
10. A key word is...
11. The main idea is...
12. I think...
13. I predict...
14. I wonder...
15. I agree with...
16. I disagree with...
17. It didn't make sense...
18. If I were..., I would...
19. I changed my prediction because...
20. It wasn't accurate or realistic because...
21. As a reader, I...
22. As a writer, I...
23. The author left out...
24. If the main character was...
25. If the story were told from another perspective...
26. The story was like..., because...
27. The character called..., reminds me of...
28. If I were..., I would...
29. The setting was important becuase...
30. I think...is a symbol for...
31. The author wrote the story to...
32. The author's writing is special because...
33. A question I want to ask is...
34. I want to talk about...
35. Another way to say that is...

Figure 4.7. Teacher-supplied prompts encourage students to respond to what they have read.

In Miss Murray's guided reading lessons, she uses a blend of systematic and constructivist instruction. She has objectives and directs the lesson in explicit and systematic ways. She also takes the lead in deciding on the content and reading levels of the books to read. Miss Murray makes a point of observing and assessing reading to determine

Table 4.5.   Forms that entries in literature response journals can take

Prompts
Questions (and answers)
Predictions
Quotations
Diaries (become the character)
Character descriptions & sketches
Double entries (Book & Me)
Summaries
Notes & free response
Lists (special terms, slang, foreign language, new words)
Glossaries
Interviews
Letters (buddy, teacher, a character, the author, parent)
Sequels
Time lines
New chapter titles
Graphic organizers (Venn diagrams, concept maps, and so forth)
Drawings
Maps
Charts & tables
Log of books read
Self-evaluation of reading
Self-evaluation of writing growth

what strategies to model and teach, directing and extending comprehension, and involving the children in interactions that enrich their understanding and appreciation of the story. Miss Murray also includes elements of constructivism as she strives to have students make meaning from print and learn from the story, each other, and her. She has her fourth graders read and reread stories both alone and together to become fluent readers capable of reading increasingly more difficult print independently. The specific lesson on root words embodies both direct instruction and constructivist practice. Listening to her students' oral reading helped Miss Murray determine that a lesson on roots was appropriate for them. As she taught the lesson, she gave students opportunities to interact with each other in small groups to share their knowledge and learn from each other. As Miss Murray's practice shows, guided reading, done appropriately, can be a thoughtfully eclectic approach to literacy instruction.

I feel heartsick when I hear the howls of coyotes at night. I long to howl with them and keen out my loss to the moon. We buried our dead today. Most were women and children and some had been killed in their sleep. I cannot help but feel sickened. The bluecoats call us a name which means "Nose Piercing" but they can be called savages. They who kill women and children first are certainly worthy of the name.

Sound-of-Running-Feet
(Melissa)

Figure 4.8.   Melissa responds emotionally in her journal as she takes on the persona of Sound-of-Running-Feet, the main character in *Thunder Rolling in the Mountains.*

READING AND WRITING

No discussion of reading instruction is complete without a discussion of writing. In each of the classrooms you have just read about, instruction in reading and writing go hand-in-hand. Miss Davis and Mr. Ferraro regularly show their kindergarten and first-grade children how spoken words can be written down and that what they write can be read aloud. Miss Davis, Mr. Ferraro, and Miss Murray use workbook pages sparingly with their students. They have found that children become better writers, and learn the skills of writing more easily when they craft their own written pieces, rather than spending time filling in blanks on workbook pages. These teachers often have students write in literature response journals about stories and books they have just read, and integrate writing into their science and social studies curricula. They believe students learn to organize their thoughts, express themselves effectively, use appropriate punctuation, and try invented spelling as they move toward standard spelling when they write and revise their own fiction and nonfiction and share it with an audience. These teachers review what their students have written in their journals to identify progress and specific problems students are having, and to determine if and how students are representing sounds with print and making connections among reading and writing.

Many teachers find that giving students choices among the writing products and projects they complete creates motivated writers. Miss Murray believes students can and should write all sorts of things, and she found that her fourth-graders write with enthusiasm when they have choices. She integrates writing into science and social studies teaching because she knows it is a good way to reinforce content area learning. Some of the writing options she offers include book reports; learning logs; buddy journals; advertisements; poetry; character biographies; travel brochures; lab reports; essays; plays; observations; ABC books; and letters to people such as politicians, business people, authors, and publishers.

Miss Murray believes "viewing" is one of the language arts, and one of the ways she builds skills is in observing, analyzing, and interpreting the pictures and graphic displays embedded in electronic media. She has a technology center in a corner of her classroom with a list posted above the computer (see Table 4.6). Miss Murray and the class add to and change the list regularly. Miss Murray also encourages students to use the computer alone or in pairs to do research for their writing. To extend students' understanding, for every story or topic the class reads or studies, Miss Murray assigns a pair of students to find and report on interesting background information or related information.

Her students use the computer and those in the school's computer lab to write, revise, and publish their stories and science or social studies projects. She encourages collaborative research projects and urges students to share their knowledge and skills with each other. For project work, she uses flexible groups, sometimes grouping students according to friendship patterns or common interests, other times by ability, and often mixing them randomly. Miss Murray believes that

Table 4.6. The sign posted above the computer in the technology center of Miss Murray's classroom

Helpful and Interesting Web Sites
http://www.askanexpert.com
http://www.maps.com
http://www.puzzlemaker.com
http://www.wordsmith.org/awad/index.html
http://www.encyclopedia.com

both weaker writers and proficient writers have resources they can share as they work together and learn from one another. Miss Murray knows that using the computer builds reading, writing, and viewing skills as students search and view web sites; learn better keyboarding skills; cut and paste text to revise with a word processor; and insert clip art, tables, and photographs, among other things.

Mr. Ferraro, Miss Murray, Mr. Ducet, a fifth-grade teacher, and several other colleagues incorporate the writing process into their classrooms. Mr. Ducet is experimenting with what he and his students call classroom workshop (Daniels & Bizar, 1998), a 45- to 60-minute (or longer) time block set aside at least 3 days a week when everyone is involved in the writing process. In their classroom workshop, students work on writing projects from language arts, science, or social studies. Sometimes the entire class is involved in different kinds of research and writing on one topic, a social studies unit for example. Other times, students work on a variety of projects. Mr. Ducet has a pocket chart posted on a bulletin board with a tag board pocket for each part of the writing process and his students' names printed on tag board strips, as seen in Figure 4.9. Each day, students put their name in the pocket that shows where they are in the writing process. Then,

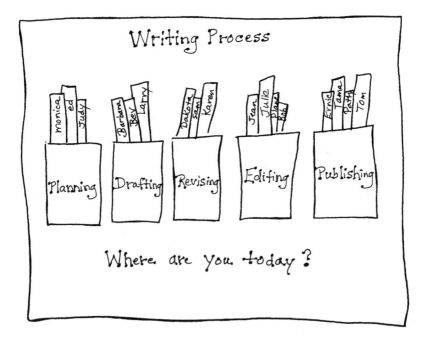

Figure 4.9.   This classroom poster helps Mr. Ducet and his students keep track of where each of them is in the writing process.

Mr. Ducet knows who is ready for a conference or who is prepared to share or present their work.

Each workshop usually begins with a 5- to 10-minute focus lesson on a skill that most of the class, or at least several students, need. Then, Mr. Ducet's students work independently or in small groups, depending on whether they are doing a special project or writing individual stories or reports. He either moves from student to student to offer help and support or works with one small group at a time.

The students in Mr. Ducet's class include 19 Caucasian students and 9 children from Africa, Russia, the Middle East, and Asia. Like other classrooms in this school, about two thirds of Mr. Ducet's class qualifies for free or reduced-price lunch and two students have learning disabilities. In order to optimize the learning experiences for these diverse groups, Mr. Ducet uses flexible groups that are based on student concerns, interests, and resources; group composition changes often depending on both Mr. Ducet's and the students' purposes. On one afternoon, for example, activity in the room looked like this:

- In preparation for writing a report, three students were analyzing a survey of sixth-graders' opinions for making the transition from elementary school to middle school easier.
- Four students were conferencing with Mr. Ducet at a table in the back of the room about inserting clues into the plots of the mystery stories they were writing.
- Six students were seated at a bank of computers located on one side of the classroom. Some students were drafting first reports on the early Native Americans of the region. Students were using graphic organizers they had created as planning tools. Other students were revising reports from hard copy that they had printed off previously and on which they and a peer reviewer had made corrections. Two were working together to add clip art to a nearly finished report.
- Ten students were writing various stories, reports, and letters at their seats.
- Two students were reading a book together and talking with each other.

On a wall in his classroom, Mr. Ducet has a poster with the steps in the writing process, as seen in Figure 4.10. He teaches the recursive steps in this process by sharing models of good writing, directly teaching specific skills, and demonstrating how to write for his students. But, much of what they write about originates from their own questions. For example, "What will it be like in sixth grade?" asked in a language arts class, and "Who lived here before us?" asked during a social stud-

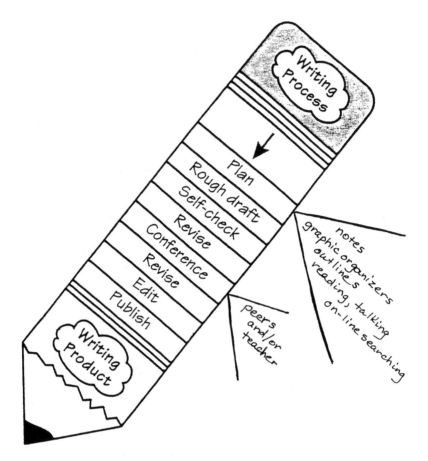

Figure 4.10. Examples added to the "Plan" and "Conference" steps on this poster remind Mr. Ducet's students of what to do.

ies unit. So, among other skills, Mr. Ducet teaches students how to survey and interview people and how to gather, analyze, and present data to answer questions. He uses both systematic teaching and constructivism to teach all aspects of the writing process: planning, revising, rewriting, editing, and publishing. He says,

> My job is to teach my students the skills, tools, and strategies they need to be good writers. My job is also to challenge and nudge them to use what they know to learn and create their own patterns for lifelong learning.

Several professional books help Miss Davis, Mr. Ferraro, Miss Murray, Mr. Ducet, and their colleagues, combine systematic and constructivist instruction as they teach writing. *Writing Workshop: The Essential Guide* (Fletcher & Portaluppi, 2001) explores the principles and components of writing workshop and includes a discussion of teaching writing skills. Two other excellent and practical resources are *Craft Lessons: Teaching Writing K–8* (Fletcher & Portaluppi, 1998) and *Nonfiction Craft Lessons: Teaching Information Writing K–8* (Portaluppi & Fletcher, 2001). These books contain lessons that teach specific writing skills within a writing process classroom. Lessons such as Crafting a Title, Unpacking a Heavy Sentence, and Using Surprising Imagery (from the first *Craft Lessons* book) show teachers how to demonstrate and model specific skills. Many lessons include examples of children's literature that teachers can read to, or with, students, in which the authors use the technique that is the focus of the lesson. For grades four to eight, *Descriptive Writing, Expository Writing, Narrative Writing,* and *Persuasive Writing,* by Tara McCarthy (1998), are loaded with mini-lessons and activities to help teach the four basic types of writing.

SUMMARY

The classroom practices described in this chapter represent only a brief glimpse into one school in which many teachers understand that "There is no one best way to teach children to read and write" (Allington & Cunningham, 2002). The mindful teachers you have read about blend systematic instruction and constructivism in ways that support the literacy and learning of all children. Mrs. Silbur, their principal says

> Our school's test scores improve every year. Even though we have a diverse population, we're one of the best-performing schools in the district. And, the district's performance is among the strongest in the state. We're doing lots of things right, and I believe one of them is that teachers use both teacher-guided and teacher-directed literacy instruction.

Mrs. Silbur and the teachers described in this chapter are seeking the common ground that enhances learning and boosts the achievement of all students. What can we learn from them? We can learn to be cautious about throwing out effective practices because of the current push to achieve higher standards and better scores on standardized achievement tests. We can realize that students become literate when we find the middle ground between constructivist and systematic approaches in literacy instruction. We can be assured that "best" literacy practices are explicit, systematic, mindful, and contextualized (Cambourne, 1999). These "best practices" blend reading, writing, listening, speaking, and viewing as students work and learn both alone and together to become literate.

REFERENCES

Allington, R.L., & Cunningham, P.M. (2002). *Schools that work: Where all children read and write.* Needham Heights, MA: Allyn & Bacon.

Anderson, R.C., Hiebert, E.F., Scott, J.A., & Wilkinson, I.A.G. (1985). *Becoming a nation of readers: The report of the Commission on Reading.* Washington, DC: The National Institute of Education.

Babbitt, N. (1986). *Tuck everlasting.* New York: Farrar, Straus & Giroux.

Bromley, K. (2002). *Stretching students' vocabulary: Best practices for building the rich vocabulary students need to achieve in reading, writing, and the content areas.* New York: Scholastic.

Cambourne, B. (1999). Conditions for literacy learning. *The Reading Teacher, 53,* 126–127.

Christie, J. (1990). Dramatic play: A context for meaningful engagements. *The Reading Teacher, April,* 542–545.

Coles, G. (2000). Direct, explicit, and systematic: Bad reading science. *Language Arts, 77*(6), 76–78.

Cunningham, P.M., & Allington, R.L. (1999). *Classrooms that work: Where they can all read and write* (2nd ed.). New York: Longman.

Cunningham, P.M., & Cunningham, J.W. (1992). Making words: Enhancing the invented spelling-decoding connection. *The Reading Teacher, 46,* 106–113.

Daniels, H., & Bizar, J. (1998). *Methods that matter: Six structures for best practice classrooms.* York, ME: Stenhouse.

dePaola, T. (1973). *Andy (that's my name).* Englewood Cliffs, NJ: Prentice Hall.

Duffy, G.G., & Hoffman, J.V. (1999). In pursuit of an illusion: The flawed search for a perfect method. *The Reading Teacher, 53,* 10–16.

Fitzgerald, J. (1999). What is this thing called "balance"? *The Reading Teacher, 53,* 100–107.

Fletcher, R., & Portaluppi, J. (1998). *Craft lessons: Teaching writing K–8.* Portsmouth, NH: Heinemann.

Fletcher, R., & Portaluppi, J. (2001). *Writing workshop: The essential guide.* Portsmouth, NH: Heinemann.

Fountas, I.C., & Pinnell, G.S. (1996). *Guided reading: Good first teaching for all children.* Portsmouth, NH: Heinemann.

Fountas, I.C., & Pinnell, G.S. (2001). *Guided readers and writers: Grades 3–6.* Portsmouth, NH: Heinemann.

Hesse, K. (1997). *Out of the dust.* New York: Scholastic.

Hopkins, G., & Bean, T.W. (1999). Vocabulary learning with the verbal-word association strategy in a Native American community. *Journal of Adolescent and Adult Literacy, 42*(4), 274–281.

Langer, E. (1997). *The power of mindful learning.* New York: Addison Wesley.

McCarthy, T. (1998a). *Descriptive writing: Grades 4–8.* New York: Scholastic.
McCarthy, T. (1998b). *Expository writing: Grades 4–8.* New York: Scholastic.
McCarthy, T. (1998c). *Narrative writing: Grades 4–8.* New York: Scholastic.
McCarthy, T. (1998d). *Persuasive writing: Grades 4–8.* New York: Scholastic.
Morrow, L.M. (1989). Designing the classroom to promote literacy development. In Strickland, D.S., & Morrow, L.M. (Eds.), *Emerging literacy: Young children learn to read and write* (pp. 121–134). Newark, DE: International Reading Association.
O'Dell, S., & Hall, E. (1992). *Thunder rolling in the mountains.* New York: Dell.
Portaluppi, J., & R. Fletcher (2001). *Nonfiction craft lessons: Teaching information writing K–8.* Portsmouth, NH: Heinemann.
Reutzel, R. (1999). On balanced reading. *The Reading Teacher, 52,* 322–323.
White, E.B. (1952). *Charlotte's web.* New York: Harper & Row.

CHAPTER FIVE

Beyond Constructivism and Back to Basics

A Cultural Historical Alternative to the Teaching of the Base Ten Positional System

JEAN SCHMITTAU

I n the debates raging between those calling for mathematics education to get back to basics and the advocates of constructivism, perhaps no instructional approaches have come under greater scrutiny or been subject to more sweeping changes than those directed at teaching the concept of our base ten positional system.

In the base ten system, the number seen does not necessarily indicate the number itself, but takes on different values (powers of 10) depending on where it appears in a multi-digit number. Therefore, in 3,124 the digit 2 represents 20, in 3,214 it represents 200, and in 2,134, it represents 2,000. Since the publication of the National Council of Teachers of Mathematics (NCTM) Standards (1989), the algorithmic drill approaches to this concept have been replaced by attempts to render the concept more meaningful for children. The former are favored by back to basics advocates and generally feature practice in adding and subtracting by applying rules; for example when 29 is added to 37, one must add 9 and 7 to get 16, then put down the 6 and carry the 1. One must then add the 1 to the 2 and 3 in the left-hand column to obtain 6, thereby giving a sum of 66.

Changes introduced to infuse meaning into operations such as addition and subtraction often feature the use of "base ten blocks." These blocks represent "ones" with centimeter cubes, "tens" with rods consisting of a row of ten such centimeter cubes, "flats," which are squares composed of 10 rows of 10 centimeter cubes each (or 100 centimeter cubes altogether), and large cubes comprised of ten flats and consisting of 1000 centimeter cubes. Trading activities using these cubes have now become common pedagogical practice. In adding 29 and 37 (the example just given), 29 is modeled with 2 rods and 9 centimeter cubes; 37 is modeled with 3 rods and 7 centimeter cubes. In the process of addition, the 9 + 7 or 16 cubes must undergo a trade of 10 cubes for one rod. This results in 6 rods and 6 cubes, representing the sum of 66.

Clearly this activity goes beyond drill, which has its purpose the rote memorization of rules. The child must perform the addition mindfully, with attention to the concept of positionality in the base ten system. Constructivists who believe that a child must "construct" his own mathematics concepts favor such a use of concrete manipulatives.

The trend toward the use of concrete materials to teach this concept was catalyzed by the research of Constance Kamii (1985). She found that none of the children in a first-grade class at a Chicago suburban school district had grasped the concept. Kamii determined this through an individually administered task, in which each child was asked to count and write the number of chips in a collection of 16 chips, then make a dot representing each chip on a piece of paper. Every child succeeded with this and the subsequent request to circle the number of dots represented by the 6 digit. When asked to circle the number of dots represented by the 1 digit, however, every child circled one dot. Oddly, they all circled 16 dots when required to indicate the number of dots represented by 16, but none gave evidence of any cognitive dissonance occasioned by the fact that 9 dots remained unrepresented by their circle designations. Kamii went on to administer the test in other grades in the school, finding that 49% of fourth graders, 40% of sixth graders, and approximately 22% of eighth graders failed at the task. These results were substantially corroborated at other sites.

Spurred by the widespread publication of these and similar research results (Ginsburg, 1982), the improvements noted previously featuring the use of manipulatives were developed and widely implemented. Children typically were introduced to the natural numbers ({1, 2, 3, 4, ...}) through counting quantities of discrete objects and, when the numbers became sufficiently large, the quantities were grouped by tens and the concepts of positionality and base ten were introduced and rendered meaningful through the use of base ten blocks and activities such as those requiring the trading of 10 ones for a single tension rod. Despite the fact that these instructional practices replaced the former rote drills and became commonplace after the 1980s, it is not unusual to hear teachers complain that students are still having trouble with this concept and its applications well into middle school. Clearly, the new approaches are more meaningful than the former algorithmic drill, but they are nevertheless inadequate.

In the next section, I provide a theoretical rationale for these inadequacies drawn from cognitive learning theory. I then offer an alternative model that has been researched for more than 40 years and used with thousands of students with wide ranges of abilities to improve the teaching of this concept. It is important to note that an understanding of bases and positional systems is absolutely central to the understanding of addition, subtraction, multiplication, and division of whole numbers. Because mastery of these operations comprises a substantial amount of the time allotted to mathematics in the early school years, the importance of an approach to the base ten positional system designed to enable a deep understanding of it for all elementary school students can scarcely be overstated.

THE INADEQUACY OF TEACHING BASE TEN FOR THE DEVELOPMENT OF THE CONCEPT OF BASE TEN

Both Skemp (1987) and Vygotsky (1962) suggested reasons for the continuance of difficulties with the concept of the base ten positional system despite the improvements of constructivist pedagogy. Skemp discussed the well-known fact from the field of psychology that concepts may be either basic level, superordinate, or subordinate. *Chair* and *sofa* appear to be basic level concepts, whereas *furniture* is a superordinate concept that subsumes these basic level concepts. *Rocking chair* and *recliner* are subordinate concepts because these are types of the basic level concept *chair*. Skemp pointed out that concepts are formed in the following order: basic level, then superordinate, followed by subordinate. Taxonomies such as those found in botany bear out this psychological fact. Skemp observed that a superordinate concept could not be formed from a single basic level concept. The concept of furniture, for example, cannot be developed from the single basic level concept *sofa*. Similarly, a superordinate concept (such as the concept of the base of a number system) cannot be developed from a single basic level concept (a single base of ten, for example). If one were to see only a single color—red, for instance—everywhere in the environment, it would not be possible to form a concept of *color*. One would have to experience several colors in order to attain the superordinate concept of color. Russian psychologist, Lev Vygotsky (1962), in the same vein, commented specifically on the concept of base ten.

As long as the child operates with the decimal system without having become conscious of it as such, he has not mastered the system but is, on the contrary, bound by it. When he becomes able to view it as a particular instance of the wider concept of a scale of notation, he can operate deliberately with this or any other numerical system. The ability to shift at will from one system to another... is the criterion of this new level of consciousness, because it indicates the existence of a general concept of a system of numeration. (p. 115)

It is interesting to recall that the concept of bases was explicitly taught during the time of the "new math" in the 1960s and 1970s. Children developed their own number systems in different bases, even inventing their own symbols for the digits and added and subtracted in base five, twelve, and so forth. I recall teaching all of the above as a student teacher to a class of ninth graders whose IQ scores ranged between 60 and 90. The students found it challenging but very motivating to create their own number systems in this way. They were successful in creating number systems from base two to base twelve. However, as the "back to basics" movement swept the country, displacing the "new math," it seemed superfluous within the back to basics paradigm to spend time teaching bases the students would never use. Because it appeared they would only need base ten, the others were peremptorily omitted.

The influence of these changes persists in the current curricula, despite the fact that, in the intervening years, much has come to light concerning the manner in which concepts are learned and mathematics is cognized. I refer in particular to the work of Ausubel, Novak, and Hanesian (1978); Vygotsky (1962, 1978); and Skemp (1987). The works of Ausubel et al. and Skemp had not yet been written and Vygotsky's *Thought and Language* had scarcely been translated into English when the "new math" was inaugurated. Nevertheless, the principles for the development of superordinate concepts enunciated by all three psychologists were incorporated into the earliest of the "new math" curricula for the teaching of the base ten system. The teaching of several bases other than the single base of ten was, however, subsequently abandoned. The reason for this is not difficult to ascertain: The field of mathematics education has, for the most part, not been driven by advances in cognitive learning theory.

Neither the algorithmic drill that characterized the back to basics movement nor the more recent constructivist approach featuring the use of manipulatives, such as base ten blocks, is adequate to develop the concept underlying our base ten positional system. It may also be important to mention the criticism leveled at the U.S. mathematics curriculum as a result of the Third International Mathematics and Science Study (TIMSS). The TIMSS study revealed that, in attempting to teach too many concepts, we have approached virtually all of them superficially rather than teaching the key concepts in depth, as many other countries do.

The concept of the base ten positional system deserves to be taught in far more depth than is typically afforded in our all-too-crowded curricula. There have, however, been bright spots. Kamii's (1985) games featuring exchanges apparently resulted in a much better understanding of the concept as is shown by her research. And the chip trading activities developed by Davidson, Galton, and Fair (1975) can be effectively used to develop a general concept of bases, because they can be used to teach several different bases. These, however, have largely been supplanted by trading activities primarily featuring base ten blocks. The most prominent approaches featured in textbooks of the early 21st century center on base ten virtually exclusively.

THE INADEQUACY OF COUNTING AS A BASIS FOR THE CONCEPT OF NUMBER

A second inadequacy is common to even these more effective approaches; they develop the concept of number out of the activity of counting. Only counting numbers (1, 2, 3, 4,...) can be generated in this way. Clearly, one must develop the concept of number on a basis other than counting given that later one must extend that concept beyond whole numbers to encompass fractions and irrational numbers (e.g., $\sqrt{2}$, $\sqrt{3}$, $\sqrt{5}$, π), neither of which are generated out of counting. The action of counting is inadequate for the generation of number in general. Therefore, as both Skemp (1987) and Davydov (1975) have shown, one is faced with the Herculean cognitive task of establishing a new foundation for number once fractions are introduced. This is rarely accomplished. Indeed, Skemp (1987) has reported that the counting number schema is so stable that most adults do not consider fractions to be numbers at all. Hinrichs, Yurko, and Hu (1981, cited in Fuson & Hall, 1983), and Schmittau (1991, 1994) also found that narrowly cardinal (whole number) concepts of number persisted even into adulthood. Clearly, developing an initial schema sufficiently general to subsume subsequent instances of a category is of primary importance. An initial schema inadequate to this task renders the future learning of mathematics very difficult.

The concept of number must be developed on a more general basis. Davydov (1975) and Minskaya (1975) asserted that even in the earliest years, schooling must develop in children the most general concept of number, based on real numbers (i.e., integers, fractions, and irrationals) and quantity, rather than allow their concept of number to remain at the level of positive integers (counting numbers). Davydov (1975) observed that the difficulty experienced by children in relating cardinal number to the more general concept of real number is due to the fact that children perceive them to originate in fundamentally separate contexts: counting and measurement. While cardinal numbers have their origin in counting, the general concept of real number arises from the context of the measurement of continuous quantity (e.g., length, area, volume, weight). Davydov (1975) noted that if their origins are perceived as different it is difficult to think of both as numbers.

It is interesting that a similar phenomenon occurred in the history of western mathematics. The Greeks admitted only counting numbers and a few fractions (representing pleasing harmonics) into the category of number, relegating the irrationals to the category of "magnitude." It took two millenia to unite these into a single category of real number. The current school experience of U.S. students, therefore, represents a kind of ontogenetic repetition of a general cultural phenomenon, and with similar challenges. Davydov (1975) advocated a very different approach to teaching the concept of number through measurement activities in which either a discrete or a continuous quantity is measured using some shorter length such as a paper strip, Cuisenaire rod, or wooden stick, as a unit.

THE CULTURAL HISTORICAL ALTERNATIVE

Davydov, Gorbov, Mikulina, and Saveleva (1999), working from the theoretical perspective of the Russian psychologist Lev Vygotsky have created a curriculum in which the concept of number is developed from the activity of measurement rather than counting. Children are asked to measure a length, for instance, with some smaller unit (paper strip, wooden rod, and so forth). The result may be a natural number, fraction, or irrational number. In Figure 5.1A, for example, the designated unit may be laid off three times on the line segment, which constitutes the quantity to be measured. Hence, the measure here is the counting number 3. In Figure 5.1B, the remainder may be laid off on the unit of measure twice, generating a measurement of $3\frac{1}{2}$, which is, of course, a fraction. Often, to obtain a measurement that is fractional, it is necessary to lay off successive remainders on the previous one several times in order to obtain the required measurement. In Figure

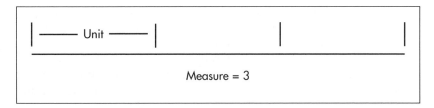

Figure 5.1A.   The designated unit may be laid off three times on the line segment, which constitutes the quantity to be measured.

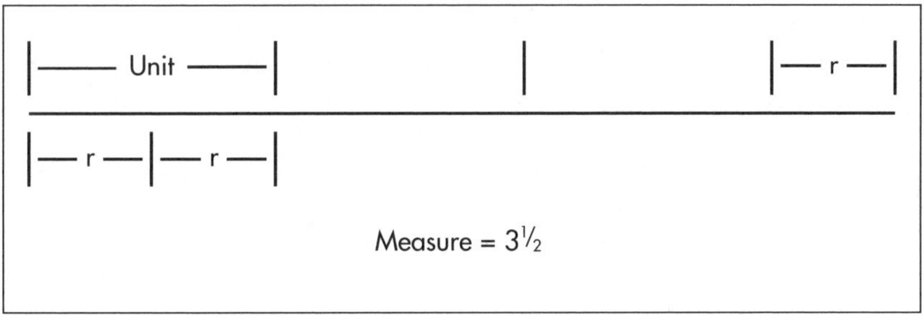

Figure 5.1B.   The remainder may be laid off on the unit of measure twice, generating a measurement of $3\frac{1}{2}$.

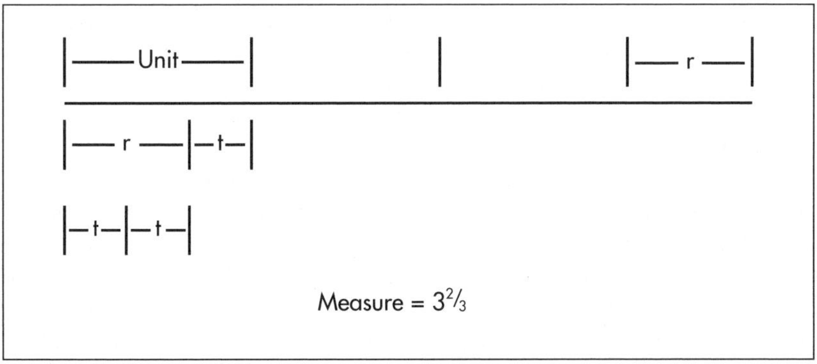

Figure 5.1C.   When the remainder of length r is laid off on the unit, it does not go into the unit evenly, and another remainder of length t, is left. When length t is laid off on the previous remainder (of length r) twice, the required measure is seen to be $3\frac{2}{3}$.

5.1C, when the remainder of length r is laid off on the unit, it does not go into the unit evenly, and another remainder of length t, is left. This second remainder, however, can be laid off on the previous remainder (of length r) twice. Hence the required measure is $3^{2}/_{3}$. When such an iterative process continues to infinity we say that the measure is an irrational number. Hence, whole numbers, fractions, and irrationals can all be generated out of the action of measuring.

No restructuring of a schema for number on a different basis need occur with the introduction of either fractions or irrationals. This facilitates the learning not only of these newly introduced numbers but also of their four fundamental operations (addition, subtraction, multiplication, and division) (Schmittau, 1993). Hence, measurement constitutes a more adequate conceptual basis for the generation and future development of the concept of number than counting. It is also important for developing the concept of bases. Fuson and Hall (1983) described our positional system as essentially a measure system, which utilizes units of different sizes that are only expressed implicitly. For example, the thousands, hundreds, and tens units are implicit in the designation 3,265. The relevant question then becomes, Might there be some way to develop the concept of our base ten positional system out of the measurement of continuous quantity, such as length, area, volume, or weight? Davydov and his colleagues (1999) have provided an affirmative answer to this question. The first-grade mathematics curriculum developed the concept of bases out of the notion of multiple measures of different sizes. This is precisely what Fuson and Hall (1983) suggested is lacking as a foundation for our base ten positional system. However, there are antecedent concepts that must be developed prior to multiple measures. If one envisions the concept of "measuring with multiple measures of different lengths," for example, as located at the top of a funnel, one must now go further down the conceptual funnel, so to speak, and ask what is prior to the development of multiple measures. Obviously, many things must go into the development of the concept of multiple measures.

United States curricula are inadequate in this regard because teachers emphasize primarily the finished, culturally accepted, and established systems of measurement ensconced in our society, which are the English and the metric systems. These are the endpoints, so to speak, of the cultural development of measure. There is much that must precede this on an informal level, both in individual development and also on a broader scale in the cultural development of measurement. So one must ask, then, in creating a curriculum, what must be done in the way of the development of the concept of measure. By going to the bottom point of the funnel (where the most basic concept is found), one can see that counting is far off and in fact does not come until two thirds of the way through the first grade in Davydov's curriculum (Davydov et al., 1999).

Instruction, in Davydov et al.'s (1999) curriculum begins with the comparison of quantities. These are quantities such as length or volume that differ in sufficiently gross ways so that they can be compared visually without being positioned next to each other. In the case of weights, children compare objects by simply hefting them in the hand. The teacher then poses problems in which finer discriminations among quantities have to be made. These are problems in which children cannot determine, for example, which of two weights is heavier by hefting both. A simple balance consisting of a fulcrum, an arm, and two pans is needed to find the answer. Similarly, in comparing lengths or areas, the child will have to align a pencil and a pen to determine which of the two is longer or actually attempt to cover one surface with another to see which of two areas is greater. In comparisons of volume, children may have to move two containers of similar shape close to each other in order to determine whether both hold the same amount of liquid.

Finally, students will be challenged to compare two lengths that are impossible to align (e.g., the length of a chalkboard and the height of the classroom door) or the volumes of liquids in two containers that have very different shapes. In these instances, children must discover that in order to accomplish the respective length and volume comparisons they will need to use an intermediary such as a length of string or a third container.

In these examples, just as the children become comfortable with gross methods of comparison of quantities, they are given quantities too close to compare through the use of the previous methods, and must come up with new ways (e.g., of aligning, covering) to make the determination. When comfortable with these, the child is then challenged to compare two quantities that cannot be brought into physical proximity and aligned, and so the children must create an intermediary (e.g., the use of a string, additional container) to affect the required comparison. Finally, the children will find that the only intermediary available is a stick, for instance, or a piece of string of insufficient length to encompass the length of the quantities to be compared. Here we have the beginnings of true measurement, and students must record the measure obtained by laying down counters (e.g., beans, chips) in one-to-one correspondence with the lengths of the stick or string laid off on the quantity in question. Eventually, it becomes convenient to replace counters with tally marks so as to create a record of the measurement. Evidence exists that early peoples used these methods. Once again, we have an instructional ontogenetic recasting of a sociocultural development, but one deliberately presented and framed in such a way that the child will find the problem intriguing enough to engage him or her. In this way, a curriculum is constructed based on the cultural historical psychology of Vygotsky.

CONNECTING MEASUREMENT TO THE CONCEPT OF BASES

At this point, I illustrate how the development of measurement concepts becomes linked to the development of the concept of base ten and share our experience implementing Davydov et al.'s (1999) curriculum in a school in the northeastern United States with a diverse group of children. The concept of base ten is introduced in such a curriculum only after laying a conceptual foundation that is far deeper than any found in U.S. textbooks. The concept of number is developed through measuring activities. Once a measuring activity is created, it holds the potential that a fraction or an irrational number may result, although the student is in no position to consider this possibility when just beginning. Later, however, such numbers can be considered and subsumed into the conceptual schema for number predicated on measure. Once students are comfortable with the concept of measuring with a unit, it is possible to introduce multiple units.

An appropriate task may be to find the most efficient way to measure a line segment 75 centimeters (cm) long, for example. Children may use three strips of paper labeled A, B, and C, of perhaps 20 cm, 10 cm, and 5 cm in length, respectively. They work in small groups. Each group is provided with a set of the strips of paper described previously. The members of each group can choose their own method of measure. They then report their results to the class in tabular form. Figure 5.1 illustrates three possibilities obtained by three different groups of children. (Other ways of measuring the line segment in question are possible, of course.) On discussion, they discover that the most efficient way to measure with multiple units is to lay off as many lengths as possible of the largest unit, then the next largest, and so on. This is reflected in the measure indicated by 3 1 1 in Table 5.1. They also quickly see that it is most inefficient to lay off multiple lengths of the smallest unit of measure first (as occurred in generating the third entry of 3 9 in Table 5.1). Such tasks lay the groundwork for the eventual introduction of the culturally accepted metric and English

Table 5.1. Measurements in tabular form of a line segment 75 cm long using lengths of 20 cm (A), 10 cm (B) and 5 cm (C), with the most efficient measurement indicated by 3 1 1

A	B	C
1	5	1
3	1	1
	3	9

systems of measurement wherein the length of an object may be measured using the multiple units of meters, centimeters, and millimeters or yards, feet, and inches. Later, children will measure a length of several yards with a yardstick first, followed by a one-foot ruler, and so forth. Eventually, feet and inches are incorporated into and marked on the yardstick, and similarly for centimeters and perhaps millimeters on the meter stick.

Such tasks can also lay the groundwork for the development of the concept of bases for number systems. As Fuson and Hall (1983) pointed out, a number such as 3,265 may be considered to be the result of a measurement with multiple units of thousands, hundreds, tens, and ones. The situation is similar for other bases. To develop these, children are told to pretend that they are in an ancient land in which people can only count to five, for example. If one can only count to five and one is confronted with a large number of buttons, one must form groups consisting of five buttons, and then groups consisting of five groups of five buttons each, and so on. A collection of 39 buttons would yield one group consisting of five groups of five buttons each (i.e., one group of 25 buttons), two groups of 5 buttons each, and four single buttons. This would lead to a representation of the number 39 in base five as $124_{(5)}$.

Similarly, if one could count only to three, one would have to count such a collection by forming groups of three, then three groups of three (nine), then three groups of three groups of three (27), and so forth. In base three, our collection would be written as one group of 27 buttons, one group of nine buttons, and one group of three buttons, with no single buttons left over, and be represented as $1110_{(3)}$. These results for the representation of discrete quantity correspond to the most efficient way to measure continuous quantity illustrated in the example of length measurement shown in Table 5.1, and are recorded by the children in a similar tabular form, seen in Table 5.2.

Table 5.2.   Base five and base three representations of the number 39, expressed in tabular form

IV	III	II	I	Place
U4	U3	U2	U1	
	1	2	4	(5)
1	1	1		(3)

In the United States, children typically begin the first grade learning the concept of number and progress more rapidly through computations with numbers than first graders do in Davydov et al.'s curriculum. We do not do the conceptual analysis that is prerequisite to establishing our curriculum on a sound conceptual basis of adequate depth. Obviously, it takes time to lay such a basis and we found that parents in the school in which we taught Davydov et al.'s program (so far as we could determine, the first such experiment in the United States) did not always grasp the necessity for it. Some became a little nervous as children in other first-grade classes were doing problems of a computational nature that our children had not yet started. We would not even introduce the concept of number until two thirds of the way through the first-grade curriculum. After the concept of number was introduced, subsequent to tallies and ordinality, children were asked to pretend that they were ancient peoples who could only count to three or five, and so forth. We worked a great deal with many different bases before concentrating on base ten.

During this extensive work with different bases, the children were typically required to solve problems such as the following:

- Mark on the number line the numbers that come before and after $10_{(8)}$, $20_{(8)}$, $30_{(8)}$.
- Place the following numbers on the number line in base ten: $41_{(5)}$, $10_{(6)}$, $12_{(3)}$, $11_{(4)}$, $3_{(2)}$, $12_{(7)}$, $11_{(5)}$. (Note to the reader: not all numbers are possible!)
- Write these numbers in order from smallest to largest: $12_{(7)}$, $11_{(3)}$, $11_{(7)}$, $12_{(5)}$, $2_{(3)}$.
- Write the next numbers (i.e., the number following each of these) in order from largest to smallest: $10_{(4)}$, $10_{(8)}$, $3_{(4)}$, $10_{(5)}$, $10_{(9)}$.
- Compare the following pairs of "fantasy" numbers: $\Phi\Gamma_{(\Psi)}$ and $\Phi\Gamma0_{(\Psi)}$. Compare $\Phi\Gamma_{(*)}$ and $\Phi0_{(*)}$.

Problems such as these are not easy. Yet, our results corroborated those of Davydov's research group in Russia, which found that "in the second semester, when they went over to using numbers, these children had no difficulty evaluating the numerical characteristics of an object from the standpoint of *any or a changing base* of counting" (Davydov, 1975, p. 159).

We ended the first grade without having done much work in base ten at all. Only single-digit computations in base ten were addressed. All the work with measurement allowed children to build their own number lines, however, and subsequently to use these to solve simple one-digit addition and subtraction problems (e.g., adding five plus four, subtracting three from eight) on a number line. But it was not until they entered the second-grade curriculum that computational problems in base ten, such as adding and subtracting with regrouping, were introduced.

Within 6 weeks of beginning the second-grade curriculum, I visited the children's class. The teacher was giving mental math problems such as $232 + 47 + 168$. The children were solving them easily by mentally grouping $232 + 168$ to obtain the partial sum and round number 400, then mentally adding 47 to obtain the sum of 447. The children begged me to give them some "hard" problems "like you give your students" (i.e., my students at the university). I continued to generate similar mental math problems for them, to their growing frustration and cries of "No! That's too easy!" Finally one little girl in exasperation jumped from her seat, went to the board, and wrote a problem consisting of a four-digit number minus another four-digit number, which required three regroupings for its solution. For some time the children refused to pick up their pencils despite my repeated exhortations to do so. One little boy actually solved the problem mentally, but all the others correctly solved it with paper and pencil and were able to give complete and correct explanations for the regroupings in terms of tens, hundreds, and thousands.

The children's teacher, a doctoral student and experienced elementary teacher from Korea, was incredulous. She stated that in Korea, children work with sums and differences of one digit numbers in the first grade, with sums and differences of two digit numbers in the second grade, and of three digit numbers in third grade, and four digit numbers in fourth grade. In only 6 weeks after the introduction of multidigit numbers in base ten, these children had mastered adding and subtracting of four-digit numbers at both the conceptual and procedural levels.

Our students did not seem to require a lot of practice. Clearly, children have to be expected to remember what they have learned and this is accomplished through usage. Often, the usage occurs in Davydov et al.'s (1999) curriculum through new problems with new levels of challenge. We did find that it was advantageous to use the *original* chip trading activities developed by Davidson, Galton, and Fair (1975). Their books *Chip Trading I, II, V,* and *VI* provided us with a concomitant and compatible framing of the concept of bases, and games and activities for the children. These gave the children practice that they found to be fun, and reinforced their understanding of bases, so we encouraged them to take the chips and tills home and to play the games in their free time.

DISCUSSION

Throughout Davydov et al.'s curriculum, the children are challenged to go beyond their present levels of competence to develop new understandings. The development of positional systems is perhaps the most challenging concept in the first-grade curriculum. Not only did the children solve difficult problems, however, they developed the ability to mount an argument (without becoming argumentative) to convince the other children of the correctness of their position. This often took time, but it developed in children the ability to reason and the power of logical thinking. It also developed clarity of linguistic expression, and promoted social development.

It is important to remember that this curriculum is developed for all students. For example, observe what happens when a child (Oscar) who is very articulate and grasps abstract concepts easily, but who has social, emotional, and behavior problems, finds the teacher calling on a different child (Mary) who happens to have a learning disability. Oscar, annoyed at being ignored despite his raised hand, promptly refuses to even pick up his pencil for the duration of the class period. The teacher has intentionally not called on him even though she suspects he has the correct answer. She wants to engage Mary and the others as they struggle through the process. To support Oscar and emphasize the importance of the solution process, she explains that she wants to hear how children arrived at the solution to the problems. In doing this, the teacher has made an intentional decision not to begin with a correct solution, which might end the possibility of discussion as to why solutions obtained by some children are incorrect. So, she calls on Mary, who is eager to answer but less likely to have the correct solution. This prompts others to join the discussion by sharing their own ideas, and finally coming to agreement on an answer. She knows that eventually Oscar will emerge from his self-imposed withdrawal from the class and explain the accurate process with the aplomb of a classroom teacher. And this is precisely what occurs. It is at this point that

Mary finally says that she understands. The teacher thanks Oscar for the explanation and the children for their good work.

It is also important to remember that from a Vygotskian perspective, it is not simply the obtaining of the right answer that is important. Rather it is the activity that produced this answer that is of even greater importance. The children do not simply internalize the result, but more importantly, the entire context of their goal-directed action in developing the solution. This includes all the processes of debating, producing counter arguments, reconciling the various viewpoints, resolving all the objections raised, and, finally, coming to a shared conclusion. When these processes are fully internalized as a result of the small group work and whole class discussions, then the child will be capable of performing them independently. That is, the child can then take a position with respect to a problem and simultaneously entertain a counter position or even a variety of different positions, and internally debate, analyze, and resolve them. This is one of the very important and powerful ways in which Davydov's program promotes the cognitive development of students. In the same way, it promotes the confidence of students and enhances their willingness to tackle ever more difficult problems.

In order to accomplish this, however, the teacher must open the discussion to student ideas. Frequently, teaching in a didactic manner closes the door to children's ideas and presents them with one correct way to do a problem, which they must then commit to memory. This not only controls the learning and limits what may be considered and discussed but it also results in children internalizing powerlessness in the face of difficult mathematics problems. Because the child must await the presentation of a method of solution by one more knowledgeable, the teacher, the child internalizes his or her own inadequacy.

Opening up the learning process in this manner may reveal to a teacher her or his own lack of confidence, however. When comparing volumes of liquid early in the first-grade program, a child asked whether the capacity of the container or the amount of liquid in it should be considered "the volume." A Russian researcher with whom I worked reported that a little boy had, on being asked to find something that illustrated volume, stretched out his empty trousers pocket and said, "This is an example of volume." Such sophisticated questions and illustrations from children may send teachers back to the textbooks they used in their own college mathematics courses in search of answers.

We could not help but notice that, unlike the situation that so often occurs in U.S. schools, in which children identified as high achievers early tend to continue as high achievers (and similarly for low achievers), this was not necessarily the case during the 3 years of Davydov's elementary mathematics program. It was not unusual for children to change places, struggling at one point and soaring at another. One child, identified with attention-deficit disorder (ADD), who had great difficulty early in the program not only concentrating, but paying virtually any attention at all to the class, emerged able to become engrossed in very difficult problems, and frequently came up with insights that would have been considered profound at the middle or beginning high school level.

It is also important to remember that Vygotsky began work in the 1920s with efforts to assist children displaced after the Russian revolution who were experiencing mental and physical disabilities. He believed that studying the manner in which cognitive functions were organized in those with disabilities illuminated the study of cognitive functioning in individuals who were not so challenged. His approach was to identify whether a disability was caused by an organic impairment or was the result of a cultural lag. If the former, everything possible was done to enable the individual to experience the full range of cultural mediation, so as to enable the development of the higher mental functions such as logical memory and voluntary attention. If the latter, efforts were made to bridge the cultural gap so that the individual could gain access to the full range of cultural means available to develop these higher mental functions (Vygotsky, 1993).

Vygotsky believed that developing higher mental functions could compensate for impairment. Thus, Vygotsky did not try to compensate for deafness by developing the other senses, which would have meant attempting to compensate on only the same sensate level. Rather, through cultural means, he worked to develop the higher mental functions and thus to compensate for the disability at a new higher level (Kozulin, 1990). It was interesting that, like the child with ADD who developed the ability to sustain high levels of concentration, children who were observed to be hyperactive often became more engaged with the problems, and those who caught on more slowly at first made credible advances later. This approach presents all children with high-level problems previously reserved for the gifted. Not telling children how to solve them creates the expectation that they can solve them on their own. Their experience of success, in turn, builds confidence, and in the process they experience a transformation in their own abilities.

The children we worked with advanced in their ability to persuade and communicate effectively. Several times, a child would be told a solution method by his or her parents and the next day come to class proclaiming it to be correct because "my father said so." I advised the teacher to ask the children if they understood the method, and, of course, they did not. The child who presented the method was then asked to explain it, and just as predictably, was unable to do so. Then the teacher and students concluded that they could not use the method, because they really did not understand it or how it worked. In this way, students learned to rely on their own thinking powers rather than on the authority of someone else (even an expert such as a parent or teacher), when it came to doing mathematics.

Growth in the ability to evaluate their performance is another benefit to children from this program. One typical way in which children evaluate themselves is to draw a vertical line segment in their notebooks and sometimes on the chalkboard and put an asterisk at the position they think they attained with respect to some quality on which they are rating themselves. If they believe they have done well on paying attention, contributing to the discussion, or some other dimension, they place their asterisk near the top of the line segment. If they think they could have done much better, they place it nearer the bottom. For example, one day the children had complained that the day before, one of their peers had been disagreeable when arguing a point. So at the end of the class, they decided to rate themselves on how considerate they had been in their discussion that day. This child, who had held to a particular point of view throughout the entire class period, rated herself a bit lower than the other children. The teacher, however, marked her higher and commended her for forcing the class to work through their own difficulty, because on the previous night's homework, they had all made the mistake she was now forcing them to reconsider!

Perhaps the most important thing we learned through our experience with the teaching of Davydov's curriculum is that if the conceptual foundation is adequate, then the payoff comes later, in the form of greatly increased facility in subsequent learning. First grade is the time for laying the requisite deep conceptual foundation. The cultural historical approach turns conventional pedagogy and school practice upside down. As Davydov has accurately observed, "The authors of textbooks and methods manuals try not to linger over the sources of concepts, but rather, to get pupils to work with the concepts themselves as soon as possible" (1975, p. 120). His curriculum takes a stand against this trend in school mathematics, and especially the rush to get to numbers quickly and then to confine mathematics instruction to manipulations of numbers. The cultural historical approach also does more; it reveals the inherent weaknesses in both the currently advocated constructivist approach and the default position of the back to basics advocates who criticize it. The algorithmic drill, on which the back to basics approach centers, ignores the fact that the algorithm is a cultural historical endpoint, and a concept cannot be grasped by starting at its developmental endpoint. Every algorithm was achieved after a long period of anthropological and historical development, and the child's mind must traverse in some form the significant moments of this development in order to arrive at a conceptual understanding of the algorithm. Absent this, the algorithm will not be easily comprehended, and so must be learned by rote and preserved in memory by frequent and continued drill. Constructivism also, although arguing for a teaching method that is oriented toward the problem-solving approach grounded in Vygotskian psychology, is unable to delineate what constitutes mathematical knowledge because, as Noddings (1990) has aptly pointed out, even misconceptions are "constructions." Therefore, it has nothing to contribute to the cultural historical development of a subject and the role of that development in curriculum construction. Furthermore, the child has little chance of adequately "constructing" his or her own concept of number and positional systems. These are theoretical concepts requiring considerable pedagogical mediation for their appropriation.

Cultural historical psychology removes us completely from the debate over systematic approaches versus constructivism by transcending both, while at the same time addressing the features advocated by both. It provides an intentionally designed curriculum consisting of a carefully sequenced collection of problems that actively engage students in their own learning, while at the same time requiring skill on the part of the teacher in tailoring the inquiry method to the concerns of all students. The curriculum content and instructional process are thoroughly grounded in conceptual analysis, with antecedent concepts such as quantitative relations and measure, for example, leading up to the concept of number. Not only are there observable and measurable objectives but also children themselves learn to evaluate their individual and collective growth toward meeting these objectives. Specific "helpers" such as the charts shown in Tables 5.1 and 5.2 function as tools that cue children to the initial information necessary to determine the most efficient way to measure with multiple units or to write numbers in different bases. Review problems and "mental math" are regular features of the curriculum, affording intentional opportunities for the reinforcement and maintenance of skills. In addition, the problems through which the curriculum advances build on one another, thereby not only challenging children to develop new insights but also providing a "built-in" reinforcement for previously developed understandings and skills. Finally, our use of chip trading as described previously was an intentional provision for additional reinforcement of the concept of bases, as well as practice on fact families for addition and subtraction in base ten. Because it is impossible to engage in chip trading games without reinforcing the concept that underlies the procedures, and because the games are fun, children were motivated to play them and practice was not a chore. It is important to point out that these are all features that teachers can incorporate in adapting this approach for use in their own classrooms.

Cultural historical theory encompasses all that constructivism and systemic instruction advocate, and more. It does not, however, promise a quick fix for our pedagogical problems, but instead brings to light their hidden complexity. The good news is that this approach, designed to accommodate the range of all children, has been subjected to 40 years of research and is taught in thousands of schools in the former Soviet Union. Our experience demonstrates that it can also be taught effectively in the U.S. The classroom teacher can use the activities presented previously, in the sequence indicated, to provide children with a more adequate grasp of concepts of measurement, number, and our base ten positional system. Furthermore, any teacher can profitably adopt a problem-centered approach to the teaching of mathematics, and engage all children in the process of solving challenging problems with the expectation that higher levels of mathematical understanding will result.

REFERENCES

Ausubel, D.P., Novak, J.D., & Hanesian, H. (1978). *Educational psychology: A cognitive view* (2nd ed.). New York: Holt, Rinehart & Winston.

Davidson, P.S., Galton, G.K., & Fair, A.W. (1975). *Chip trading activities. (Books I, II, V, & VI).* Fort Collins, CO: Scott Resources.

Davydov, V.V. (1975). The psychological characteristics of the "prenumerical" period of mathematics instruction. In L.P. Steffe (Ed.), *Soviet studies in the psychology of learning and teaching mathematics.* (Vol. 7, pp. 109–206). Chicago: The University of Chicago Press.

Davydov, V.V., Gorbov, S.F., Mikulina, H., & Saveleva, O.N. (1999). *Mathematics: Class 1.* Binghamton: State University of New York.

Fuson, K.C., & Hall, J.W. (1983). The acquisition of early number word meanings. In H. Ginsburg (Ed.), *The development of mathematical thinking* (pp. 49–107). San Diego: Academic Press.

Ginsburg, H. (1982). *Children's arithmetic.* Austin, TX: PRO-ED.

Kamii, C.K. (1985). *Young children reinvent arithmetic.* New York: Teachers College Press.

Kozulin, A. (1990). *Vygotsky's psychology: A biography of ideas.* Cambridge, MA: Harvard University Press.

Minskaya, G.D. (1975). Developing the concept of number by means of the relationship of quantities. In L.P. Steffe (Ed.), *Soviet studies in the psychology of learning and teaching mathematics* (Vol. 7) (pp. 207–261). The University of Chicago Press.

National Council of Teachers of Mathematics (1989). *Curriculum and evaluation standards for school mathematics.* Reston, VA: National Council of Teachers of Mathematics.

Noddings, N. (1990). Constructivism in mathematics education. In R.B. Davis, C.A. Maher, & N. Noddings (Eds.), *Journal for Research in Mathematics Education Monograph No. 4: Constructivist views on the teaching and learning of mathematics.*

Rieber, R.W., & Carton, A.S. (Eds.). (1993). *The collected works of L.S. Vygotsky: Vol. 2. The fundamentals of defectology.* New York: Plenum.

Schmittau, J. (1991). A theory-driven inquiry into the conceptual structure of multiplication. *Focus on Learning Problems in Mathematics, 13*(4), 50–64.

Schmittau, J. (1993). Connecting mathematical knowledge: A dialectical perspective. *Journal of Mathematical Behavior, 12,* 179–201.

Schmittau, J. (1994, April). *Scientific concepts and pedagogical mediation: A comparative analysis of category structure in U.S. and Russian students.* Paper presented at the Annual Meeting of the American Educational Research Association, New Orleans.

Skemp, R. (1987). *The psychology of learning mathematics.* Mahwah, NJ: Lawrence Erlbaum Associates.

Vygotsky, L.S. (1962). *Thought and language.* Cambridge, MA: MIT Press.

Vygotsky, L.S. (1978). *Mind in society.* Cambridge, MA: Harvard University Press.

CHAPTER SIX

Social History, Technology, and the Building of Inclusive Classroom Communities

LAURA LAMASH

I n this chapter, I explore a method of historiography called *social history* as a curricular framework that supports the meaningful inclusion of digital technology, the intersection of constructivist and systematic methodologies, and the foundation for establishing a deep and intrinsic classroom culture of inclusion. Social history uses primary sources and personal narratives to tell the stories of ordinàry people; social movements; and cultural, social, and political institutions. Social history is "history from the bottom up" (Metcalf & Downey, 1982, p. 182). Its purpose is to document and critique historical phenomena and to shift the focus of historical investigation from the "influential elite" to the ordinary citizen. For this reason, social histories often explore popular movements; issues of labor, race, class, and gender; and the impact of industrialization on the working class and poor.

In teaching social history, many different tools can be used to enhance the students' understanding. Instructional technologies are the

Portions of the Time Travel project were funded by a grant from School-to-Careers Partnership of Broome and Tioga Counties, New York. The author would like to thank Rebecca Hemzik for her patience, insight, humor, and editorial expertise. She thanks her principal, Douglas Green, for his support of her classroom work, the staff of the Roberson Museum and Science Center, Binghamton, New York, for their friendship, *Sensei* Hidy Ochiai, for his inspiration, and Adele Brown, who first gave her the camera.

"devices" available to teachers to extend the nature, format, interest, and effectiveness of instruction (Cuban, 1986, p. 4). Instructional technology has a long history that parallels the history of American schooling. In 1848, Henry Barnard, a progressive reformer and the first U.S. Commissioner of Education, described several innovations in the field of education. Among them was the Arithmeticon, "a most useful instrument" modeled on the abacus for the teaching of arithmetic and Allen's Education Table, "found very useful in teaching the Alphabet, Spelling, Reading, and Arithmetic, to little children" that was a large board with moveable type (McClintock & McClintoch, 1970, pp. 231–232). More recent devices that are now marginal to education such as the radio, film projector, and television were once considered innovations that could dramatically change the nature of education. The history of instructional technology reveals that such technology is only as powerful as the people who use it, the practices that embrace it, and the rationale that frames its inclusion (Cuban, 1986, 2001).

This chapter examines social history as a constructivist methodology that supports the conceptual and skill development of students with special needs in the context of the general classroom. I describe the planning, implementation, and culmination of a year-long social history project my fourth-grade class conducted called Time Travel. In this project, students examined the impact of the industrial revolution on the lives of working class children and adults. They established connections between the industrial revolution and the digital revolution. The design of the project supported a community of learners whose diverse concerns and abilities were validated by the cognitive paradigm advanced by digital technology. This cognitive paradigm establishes an open-ended model of inquiry and understanding that supports heterogeneous abilities, differential pacing, multiple representational forms, complex organizational structures, and the validation of various types of literacies (print, visual, oral). I also examine how the use of technology as a mere "tool" can actually interfere with the inclusion of constructivist and systematic approaches. What I demonstrate in this chapter is that social history is a curricular framework that sustains authentic achievement through the active construction of knowledge, the disciplined inquiry necessary to the development of academic skills, and the relevance of learning that has a value beyond school (Newman, 1996). As a project-based methodology, social history supports collaborative inquiry that can contextualize the building of a community of learners who value their work, recognize each other's unique contributions, and establish caring, supportive relationships with their classmates (Sergiovanni, 1994).

THE INTEGRATION OF THEORY AND PRACTICE IN INCLUSIVE CLASSROOMS

My theorizing about technology, social history, and inclusion is informed by my academic inquiry but oriented by my work with children during the past two decades and the dynamics of my school community. The inclusion of theory and practice, of action and reflection, is a critical element of my daily work as a classroom teacher and member of a diverse and exciting elementary school community. The demographics of my school describe a student population with high social, academic, and economic concerns. Eighty-five percent of our students are eligible for free or reduced lunches. Thirty-five percent of our students will have moved in or out of our school during a school year. One fifth of our students are acquiring English as a second language. These children come to our school through various refugee resettlement programs in the region. More than 10 languages are spoken at our school. One sixth of our students are eligible for special education services.

My fourth-grade class was comprised of more than 20 students during the year we engaged in the Time Travel social history project. This class was identified as an "inclusion class" and students with classification received part-time support from a special education teacher and the services of a full-time aide. Sixteen students were eligible for free or reduced lunches. Four students moved into or out of the class during the year. Ten students were below grade level in reading and writing. Six students were classified with special needs. Three students manifested varying degrees of learning disabilities that set them 2–3 years below grade level. Three students were characterized with multiple disabilities including cognitive, language, and speech delays, and emotional/behavioral challenges expressed through aggression, hostility, impulsivity, and defiance. Another four students received remedial support in reading. The level of hostility and anger manifested by this group could best be described as volatile. At any given moment a confrontation could erupt. Much of my day during the first three months of school was spent negotiating conflicts and working with parents. The academic and emotional concerns of the class were intensified by the dissonance between the model of total social and academic inclusion I promoted and the model of individualized remediation enacted by the inclusion support teacher.

Clearly, instructional technology alone could not unify my class into a thriving, kind community of active, motivated learners. This group of students needed to first learn how to co-exist. I knew that eventually this class could make it to higher ground, and, in fact, they did. No one element of curriculum, methodology, or instructional resources, however, enabled this journey. Rather, inclusion was required on multiple levels: social, academic, and emotional. Technology became one tool in this process of establishing a community with a "moral purpose"—a group of children with a commitment to the values of equity, compassion, civility, fairness, trust, and collaborative engagement (Fullan, 1999).

The type of students with whom I choose to work necessitate a reframing of the implications of technology to address how schools enable the emergence of different identities that support academic and social inclusion. A situation that occurred in my fourth-grade classroom several years ago underscores my concerns about technology's role in creating inclusive school communities. Along the far wall of my classroom, near the block corner, are computers. During the week, my students have opportunities to engage in free time when they use the room and its resources. Before the computers came into my classroom, two to 10 children would work in the block corner. One group would collaborate on building a farmstead spread out wide along the floor. They would discuss where the barn, stores, and houses would go. Someone would be in charge of the make-believe tractor. Another would organize the plastic figurines of livestock. Someone might have a horse out "galloping." Another group would be struggling with how to build a marble chute that could go from one end of the room to the other. For an hour, they would drop the marble down the chute, critiquing the chute's design, trying to figure out what made the marble "stick": "It needs to be steeper," "No the corner is too sharp," "Maybe we should make it higher," "Okay, let's try!"

Complicated processes were happening in this part of the room as children negotiated, argued, made up, shared, engineered, and problem solved their way through the rise and fall of many block buildings; and all the talking that went on! There was sincere, passionate, and engaged dialogue about their collective labor. I witnessed children that had been too often left out by their peers become active members of the block corner community. These children shyly entered the block corner and within 10 minutes were crawling around with the rest of their classmates. The block corner gave some children the simple permission to be children, something sadly missing from their lives.

All of this changed with the arrival of the computers. During free time, two to 10 children crowded around the computers. Their eyes were no longer directed at each other but focused on the screen. You could argue that they were working together, which is true—a lot of sharing certainly occurs when groups of children are at the computer. But as a teacher, I felt a qualitative difference in the nature of what they were doing. Their voices sounded different. When they spoke to each other, the focus of their enthusiasm was not about what they created, but the wizardry displayed on the screen: "Wow, look at that," "This is cool," "Hey, I can't see!" Loners worked alone quietly while others looked on. Girls had a more difficult time entering the crowds. As I listened to disputes over who could use the computer next, it occurred to me that computers foster a proprietary sensibility among children—they really want the computer all to themselves. Sharing is something they have to do but would rather not. In the block corner, sharing was an essential feature of the building process; social engagement was not imposed as a way to distribute a limited resource but emerged through the active engagement of children with each other and the blocks (Hirsch, 1974). Independent play at the computer lacked the kind of warmth, sincerity, and simple expressions of their playful imaginings and creative collaborations I had seen in other kinds of student-initiated activities. I became concerned that, as an unintended consequence of the introduction of computer technology, these subtle changes might be a foreshadowing of the slipping away of community building in my classroom.

This experience made me vigilant about the implications of technology and my commitment to sustaining a thriving community of heterogeneous learners. The block corner had been the perfect enactment of an inclusive environment that freed children from the discriminating gaze of the school curriculum. As educators, we need to address the demise of block corner "culture" and what it represents in schools. Although I am a strong advocate for the dissemination of educational technology and the advancement of technological literacy, my classroom experiences make me proceed cautiously. I have since limited the use of computers during free time. My approach to technology inclusion in elementary classrooms incorporates the "relational view of technology," advanced by Burbules and Callister (2000). They considered how changes in technology initiate changes in social patterns and processes that may, in actuality, "have the greatest overall impact in changing society, not the 'technologies' themselves." Their recognition that "transformation is not intrinsic to the technology itself" (p. 7) should redirect the focus of technology inclusion from a preoccupation with hardware and machines, to a reconceptualization of curriculum.

The analysis of technology inclusion presented in this chapter is a delicate one. Organizations that promote technological advancements in education do not address the material impact of that technology on students' lives. Technological literacy requires a child's comprehensive ability to use technology to support his or her creative, intellectual, social, and aesthetic development. For this to happen requires attention to the cultural, social, and cognitive impact of educational technology. The new discourse of educational technology assigns great significance to technology's capacity to transform outmoded educational practices without a deep or complex analysis of the systemic reforms necessary for such transformations to occur. International Society for Technology in Education (ISTE) prefaced its National Educational Technology Standards for Students (NETS) with the following:

> The challenge facing America's schools is the empowerment of all children to function effectively in their future, a future marked increasingly with change, information growth, and evolving technologies. Technology is a powerful tool with enormous potential for paving high-speed highways from outdated educational systems to systems capable of providing learning opportunities for all, to better serve the concerns of 21st century work, communications, learning, and life. (2000, p. xi)

ISTE asserted that the "concerns of the 21st century" can be met by technological advancements. Technology can eliminate "outdated educational systems" and empower children to "function effectively in their future." The actual needs for functioning successfully in the 21st century, however, are not acknowledged. What skills will children need to negotiate their lifetime of labor? What types of employment will be available to them? The hyperbole that characterizes the uncritical proponents of technology masks the role of the technology industry in promoting economic inequities. The language of technological advancement obscures the degree to which a technological society is dependent on the inequitable distribution of technological and financial resources. If everyone aspires to be a systems analyst, then who will run the cash registers, assemble the circuit boards, or care for our older adults?

It is important to place these new initiatives advanced by ISTE in a historical context in order to understand technology's actual impact on ordinary lives. Significant parallels exist between the industrial revolution and the current digital revolution. Both have radically transformed the way things are done and how lives are lived. Both are also marked by a great disparity between the wealthy and the poor. The labor force projections published by the U.S. Bureau of the Census (1998; see Table 6.1) reveal that the two occupations that have the

Table 6.1. Ten occupations with largest projected job growth: 1996 and 2006

Occupation	Employment		Change		Education and training category
	1996	2006	Number	Percent	
Cashiers	3,146	3,677	530	17	Short-term on-the-job training
Systems analysts	506	1,025	520	103	Bachelor's degree
General managers and top executives	3,210	3,677	467	15	Work experience plus bachelor's or higher degree
Registered nurses	1,971	2,382	411	21	Associate's degree
Salespeople, retail	4,072	4,481	408	10	Short-term on-the-job training
Truck drivers light and heavy	2,719	3,123	404	15	Short-term on-the job training
Home health aide	495	873	378	76	Short-term on-the-job training
Teacher aides and educational assistants	981	1,352	370	38	Short-term on-the-job training
Nursing aides, orderlies, and attendants	1,312	1,645	333	25	Short-term on-the-job training
Receptionists and information clerks	1,074	1,392	318	30	Short-term on-the-job training

Reprinted from U.S. Bureau of the Census. (1998). *Statistical abstract of the United States: 1998* (118th ed.). Washington, DC: Author.

highest projected growth in job openings are cashiers and systems analysts. The 1996 employment rates for these two fields showed that there are more than six times as many cashiers (3,146,000) as systems analysts (506,000). Furthermore, the employment projections for 2006 estimate that employment in both fields will grow by 500,000. Seven of the next eight-largest growing occupations are in service occupations that require workers to interact directly and in some cases intimately with the public: registered nurses, salespeople, truck drivers, home health aides, teacher aides, nursing aides, orderlies and attendants, and receptionists. All told, of the top 10 occupations showing the largest projected growth in job openings, 7 of them require only on-the-job training, minimal compensation, and limited benefits or long-term gain.

Proponents of the development of a technologically literate work force ignore these employment trends. Given the economic outlook of the early 21st century, many of my students and others across the

United States will be employed in low-wage service sector jobs as adults. Those who are not successful academic achievers will most likely become the new working poor of the service economy. Technology alone cannot ameliorate the social inequities that many of our students confront and that frame their educational experiences. Those who claim that the introduction of computers will rectify inefficiency in learning and/or transform classroom practices risk simplifying and masking the complexity of the situation. One feature of this complexity is the degree to which technology is tied to corporate and economic structures and the demands of a capitalist system to maintain profitability and expand markets. As in education, although the mainstream model of advancement may benefit some, it neglects many. Children with special needs require a more complex restructuring of the educational context that relates their academic success to their social realities and development. This restructuring necessitates the development of curricula that blend systematic and constructivist approaches in order to support academic advancement and critical literacy. Children must be allowed to understand that their inability to thrive in certain educational contexts is not the result of their inadequacy, but a weakness of the system to address their needs. If these children become adults who are marginal to the economic mainstream, they risk similar self-blame and may engage in counterproductive attitudes that undermine their effectiveness as workers, parents, partners, and citizens. An integrated approach within an inclusive community can mitigate the psychologically damaging forces of marginalization and help children who are not part of the academic mainstream develop the self-esteem and inner strength to grow into adults who can effectively comprehend and navigate the economic structures that impact their lives. The digital revolution has created a climate responsible for the restructuring of the economy in ways that benefit some and hurt many (Ehrenreich, 2001). At the same time, digital technology has the capacity to enlighten and empower us so that we can use it for the good of all. The educational use of technology must occur in this context.

The next section offers an overview of the evolution of classroom applications of technology. This overview underscores the primary argument of this chapter—that people, and not technology, build thriving communities of learners. The section following the overview explains my rationale for adopting social history as a framework for curriculum and technology inclusion. This section describes aspects of one social history project called Time Travel, created in collaboration with my fourth-grade students. My examination of the Time Travel project explores some of the underlying theoretical and pedagogical concepts of the social history approach that are necessary for framing authentically inclusive communities. The Time Travel project's focus on the industrial revolution demonstrates how technology inclusion requires attention to the history and social impact of technology.

TECHNOLOGY AND CLASSROOM COMMUNITIES

Instructional technology has a history that predates computers. Cuban (1986) defined instructional technology as "any device available to teachers for use in instructing students in a more efficient and stimulating manner" (p. 4). In his research, Cuban traced the historical evolution of instructional technology. There has been a consistent belief that instructional technology can make education more efficient and support educational reforms. Cuban's research lead him to conclude that the reality of technology inclusion is quite different. He said, "The search for improving classroom productivity through technological innovations has yielded very modest changes in teacher practice without any clear demonstration that instruction is any more effective or productive after the introduction of radio, films, instructional television, or computers" (p. 109). Nonetheless, contemporary rationales for technology inclusion continue to pursue this reasoning and assert that technology can radically transform the nature of learning.

The ISTE, in conjunction with private industry and the U.S. Department of Education have pioneered a national framework for technology inclusion. The National Educational Technology Standards for Students (NETS) were developed by ISTE (2000) to provide teachers with models for teaching with technology that can transform classroom practices. ISTE illustrates this transformation by creating a dichotomy between "traditional learning environments" and "new learning environments" (ISTE, 2000, p. 5). The authors of these standards use disparaging language to demonstrate how new learning environments are exciting and dynamic alternatives to traditional learning environments. Traditional learning environments, as defined by ISTE, are "teacher-centered," "single-sense stimulation," "isolated," "passive," "factual," "single media," and "artificial." They define new learning environments as those that can liberate children from this dreary and lonely condition because they integrate technology to create "student-centered instruction," multisensory stimulation," "collaborative work," "active/exploratory/inquiry-based learning," "critical thinking," "multimedia," and "authentic, real-world context." This contrast between traditional and new learning environments distinguishes between systematic and constructivist models of instruction. This hard distinction fails to critique the underlying structure of schooling or recognize that instructional models require a blending of approaches within a framework that supports authentic achievement.

This dichotomy dismisses the complex interaction of instructional styles necessary to support diverse instructional needs. On the surface, the constructivist model promoted by ISTE appears hopeful, and I agree with its recommendations. The authors of the National Educational Technology Standards, however, created a faulty and deceptive comparison that masks the lived consequences of classroom technology use. This model does not critique the basic structures in place for the organization of the school day, models of curriculum, the role of the teacher and administration, models of supervision, assessment, and professional development; or the nature, purpose, and scope of standardized assessments.

Teachers are receiving mixed messages about the use and inclusion of technology. ISTE disparaged models of systematic instruction. The standards movement, however, is supporting the resurgence of traditional learning environments that focus on content mastery and skill acquisition (U.S. Department of Education, 2003). These contradictory messages indicate the degree to which private industry and governmental agencies influence educational programs. The establishment of dichotomies such as ISTE's distinction between the "traditional" and the "new," incite debate in the educational community and compel practitioners to take sides. It is a reductionist mentality that distracts educators from attempts at deep systemic school reform.

Put another way, the constructivist model advanced by ISTE is valid and necessary. To be effective, however, it requires a more complex restructuring of the educational agenda that is beyond the scope or purpose of technology. ISTE's agenda neither addresses nor articulates the broader political and cultural implications of their position. Many of the issues educators face result from social, political, economic, and cultural inequities. The development of inclusive schools and classrooms is one response to these inequities. Inclusion can either remain superficial, like the simple description of "New Learning Environment," or it can provide teachers and students with a language and context for personal and political empowerment through the structural transformation of classroom practices.

Another rationale commonly given for the inclusion of recent technological innovations is the need to prepare students for citizenship in the global community. What I wish to consider, however, is the significance and complexity of the local community—the material and geographic present—that can support the framing of a viable and humanizing relationship to the global community. Local and global awareness must co-exist in a dynamic, dialogic relationship. The building of community should become the locus for the interaction of technology, curriculum, and inclusive environments. In the next section, I explain my rationale for inclusion of digital instructional technology (digital still photography, Internet, digital video production and editing, word processing and imaging software, scanners) within the context of social history, and the relevance of this inclusion to building authentically inclusive communities that recognize that the disciplined acquisition of skills is one component of a holistic educational program.

SOCIAL HISTORY AS A FRAMEWORK FOR INCLUSIVE PRACTICES AND TECHNOLOGY INCLUSION

Social history is the inclusive study of the past and present through the stories of ordinary people and the artifacts that trace their lives. Social history emphasizes the processes that result in the creation of historical narratives. In my classroom work, I thematize these processes of historiography (the writing of history) to support the inclusion of skill development and content areas. For example, to draw attention to the historicity of names and the act of naming, I begin the school year by having children ask their parents and family members to record the story of how they got their names. This is effective because the act of naming is both personally relevant and historically significant to every child. We also read literature that emphasizes the process of naming. One book we read together, Ada's (1993) *My Name is Maria Isabel,* gives children the opportunity to talk about names, name calling, and a people's right to name themselves. Tehanetorens' *Migration of the Iroquois* begins

> This is a story about the Hotinonsonni, as we say in our language, or the People of the Longhouse as it is translated into English, or the Iroquois as the French called us, or the Six Nations as the British called us. (1976, p. 3)

History shows us how naming is an assertion of power and control. Understanding the past and present through the process of naming is an example of how social history has the capacity to provide a seamless curriculum because subjects, disciplines, and perspectives can be conceptually unified and contextualized by the formation of the individual child's emerging self-concept. This holistic conception of curriculum parallels the holistic conception of the child.

The study of social history requires a commitment of time and energy. A comprehensive social history project in an elementary school can be a year-long program that culminates in the creation of various products or artifacts that demonstrate poignant elements of the students' research, academic endeavors, and social engagements. These culminating experiences incorporate a range of media and technology—books, songbooks, videos, web sites, photography, dance, recitation, digital presentations, simulations, and animations. They also require a range of talents that simultaneously build on and support the cognitive and social diversity inherent in inclusive education.

My commitment to social history programs is the direct result of my work in inclusive settings. Through years of teaching, I came to see how inclusive classroom communities celebrate the idiosyncrasies, talents, gifts, and limitations of all members. An intellectually diverse classroom compels us to build learning environments that foster creativity and do not stigmatize children. A project-based approach allows for open-ended activities that support children's varied levels of pacing, complexity, and skill development. Inclusion, then, through the process of social history, becomes the engagement of an intellectually and socially diverse group of students in a collective undertaking.

A social history curriculum dissolves the dichotomy often established among skill-based or systematic approaches and thematic or conceptually organized approaches through the requirement of embedded learning. Children learn through connections—among themselves, their lives, their communities, and their understanding of the world. Thematic curricula display these connections and relationships through organizing concepts or a general organizing idea. Concepts incorporate a level of abstraction that evolves through immersion in the processes of analysis and inquiry rather than through direct instruction. Vygotsky asserted that "a concept is more than the sum of certain associative bonds formed by memory. It is a complex and genuine act of thought that cannot be taught by drilling" (1986, p. 149). Social history, as a prolonged engagement with social and historical themes, supports the type of immersion that leads to complex and deep understanding and gives children the time and space to internalize new knowledge and articulate new insights. A conceptual approach of this kind stimulates ways of thinking and manners of inquiry that are expansive, open ended, and generalizable.

Delpit (1995) captured the complex dynamic and interplay between constructivist and systematic models. I am drawn to one observation she made because it describes situations that I have witnessed in the context of well-intentioned academic support programs: "Children who may be gifted in real-life settings are often at a loss when asked to exhibit knowledge solely through decontextualized paper-and-pencil exercises" (p. 173). This decontextualization of skills may actually increase rather than decrease the need for remediation when it weakens a child's self-concept and diminishes his or her identity as a learner. When left to stand alone, methods that focus only on the surface expressions of knowledge, or require the acquisition of skills as a prerequisite to making meaning, can impede social and academic success.

At the same time, Delpit (1995) argued that we must provide children with the necessary skills to negotiate the educational system. As a classroom teacher, I struggle constantly with the lived implications of what Delpit described as "teaching less":

> Those who utilize "skills-based" approaches can teach less by focusing solely on isolated, decontextualized bits. Such instruction becomes boring and meaningless when not placed in any meaningful context. When instruction allows no opportunity for children to use their minds to create and interpret texts, then children will only focus on low-level thinking and their school-based intellect will atrophy.... Teaching less can also occur with those who favor "holistic" or "child-centered" approaches. Although I believe that there is much of value in whole language and process writing approaches, some teachers seem almost to be using these methodologies as excuses for not teaching. (p. 175)

As an educator, I have a responsibility to teach my students the skills and content necessary for their academic success. Direct instruction validates my role as a facilitator of my students' education by attending to the foundations for their intellectual development. Teachers must be articulate, knowledgeable about, and conscious of everything they do in order to avoid the contentiousness of the dichotomy between "skill-based" or systematic and "child-centered" or constructivist approaches. Dichotomies are dangerous, and we become manipulated by them when an informed pedagogical framework and a complex view of child development is reduced to a simplistic struggle between "right" and "wrong" methods. What is necessary is a thoughtful and dynamic interplay among systematic and conceptual approaches. I rely on methods of social history to provide a conceptual framework for the creative inclusion of these two pedagogical approaches: the rigorous development of basic literacy skills and the empowerment of children to take responsibility for their learning.

Delpit's recognition that children need to "use their minds to create and interpret text" resonated with my own belief that skill instruction must occur in a meaningful context. Social history's emphasis on the making of meaning through active inquiry and artifact-based research provides this context. With a social history approach, what becomes important and "historically" relevant to the child begins with the child's basic process of remembering and forgetting. Artifacts and records are introduced as methods of remembering. Then, children begin to assess the role of culture and community in the creation of their individual artifacts and how these artifacts contribute, as a group, to the building of collective memories. Underlying this process of remembering (and forgetting) is storytelling. Social history is the telling of stories and learning how artifacts and people all have stories to tell. Typically, history instruction uses chronological sequencing to organize historical events in an objective and balanced fashion. The reliance on ostensibly objective data promotes an objectified worldview that, by its nature, cannot express the impact of history—how history is lived, tolerated, understood, and interpreted in the course of its happening. Objective approaches also require a kind of conceptual framework for the understanding of history that young children are lacking. The absence of a context in which to locate "facts" undermines young children's ability to integrate and make sense of objective historical data.

The elementary program should, therefore, begin the process of establishing a conceptual framework for historical information. I often find that when I ask children to recall a historical event, their accounts are somewhat disjointed and illogical. For example, every September I ask children to explain what they know about history. During one such discussion the most salient historical event my students recounted was that George Washington had wooden teeth. Now, at first, this seemed like a strange recollection to me until I realized that this is exactly what children would respond to—artifacts, twists of fate, and the bodily realities of "great men" that humanize the past and connect it to the present. The impact of decontextualized learning expresses itself most succinctly in history. When I asked my student Lizbeth to tell me one moment in history that made an impression on her, her response revealed conflicting tendencies of insight and confusion. She had responded, "How people did something and stuff and how they made the world good or bad. Martin Luther King he wanted everything not races and stuff and to make the world bad—I don't know who made the world bad." Often I find that when elementary children recall their knowledge of the past, it does not quite make sense. Children try to make sense of disconnected information by putting it into a narrative form. But when you really listen to children, the superficial imposition of a story schema cannot mask the deep confusion arising from the absence of a conceptual understanding.

Levstik and Pappas (1987) examined how children make sense of historical narratives. They noted that sixth-graders understood a historical event as something that brought about change, whereas younger children focused more on the relationships between people. Levstik and Barton's (1996) study of children's interpretation and sequencing of historical photographs revealed the framework children employed to organize historical knowledge. Their research findings revealed the following:

> The most accessible historical knowledge for early and middle grade children apparently relates to changes in material culture and the patterns of everyday life.... Family stories and activities often relate to material culture—visits to historic sites, conversations related to artifacts and the like. (p. 570)

The references children use to make sense of history—popular media, artifacts, family narratives, and material culture—do not fall within the parameters of traditional textual sources. Instead, these references are situated in the present and imply that children rely on what they already know to organize what they don't know. Seixas' (1993) research into the historical understanding of adolescents paralleled these observations. His findings showed that family stories and family history affect how students understand history.

The findings of these researchers show the importance of experiential learning in the development of historical knowledge. Experiential learning must lead to and have a basis in a conceptual framework if it is to support intellectual development and historical fluency. Personal experiences, however, require the conscious application of analysis, critique, and synthesis to support abstract levels of understanding and interpretation. The students who succeed in school are able to generate a broader conceptual framework by themselves. These students can make connections, draw parallels, and establish relationships within and across content areas. And because of this, learning is interesting and meaningful. Children with learning disabilities and cognitive delays are often steered away from activities that require conceptual orientations because these are assumed to be "too hard" or beyond their cognitive abilities. To a certain degree, this represents a self-fulfilling prophecy that evolves despite well-intentioned teachers. Students who are academically marginal need to internalize conceptual and thematic orientations to learning in order to inspire their investment in the learning process and their ability to articulate the personal relevance of newly acquired knowledge.

Social history promotes the child's active engagement with the process of historical research and documentation and results in representations or artifacts that resonate with personal and cultural meaning. Social history relies on three concurrent strands of activity for the accumulation and organization of understandings: research, representation, and dissemination. In the next section, I will describe the year-long project called Time Travel and demonstrate how technology advanced the ability of students to engage in the rigorous processes of research, representation, and dissemination. I will also explore how technological innovations such as the Internet and digital video require a different way of organizing knowledge that challenges mainstream approaches and advances the building of inclusive communities.

TIME TRAVEL: A SOCIAL HISTORY

When I design a social history curriculum for the children, it validates my own fascination with the process of creating histories. As time passes, everything we do becomes a type of "history" if we are able to connect events to our life story. I have come to this understanding because I have been teaching long enough to see the transformations in myself, the culture of American education, my community, the national and global community, and, most important, children. Recognizing these forces of change and transformation was the context for my interest in building a curriculum around the idea of my fourth-grade students as "time travelers." Underlying the design of a Time Travel project was my desire to inspire this awareness in children. I wanted children to assume a different perspective on their lives that would foster their appreciation of the passing of time and make them conscious of themselves as historical beings. Once the children began to articulate and internalize a relationship between their past and present lives, they could begin to understand how the future is shaped.

The Time Travel project served several purposes. Conceptually, it provided my elementary students with a preliminary framework for understanding history as a process of remembering. This process relied on the simultaneous listening to and telling of stories. These stories emerged by way of personal and family accounts, the reading and analysis of historical narratives and documents, and the interpretation of past and present artifacts. As a framework for technology inclusion, the Time Travel project also created a context for the practical uses of digital resources that provided a critical understanding of the history of technology and its impact on human life and the environment. The development of print literacy (reading and writing) was embedded in this process of history-making and defined by the broader demands it placed on students to engage in research, formulate representations of their subjective and objective knowledge, and disseminate these representations in public contexts.

The concept of traveling through time and its rich associations challenged my students' imagination. I began the first week of school by very simply stating to the class, "This year we will travel in time to many different places and meet many different people." At first, of course, the children thought that would be impossible. They said, "You can only do that in the movies" or "Time travel isn't real; it's just made up" or "That's silly." The resistance was very interesting; it demonstrated the children's thinking at a concrete level. Themes allow for conceptual teaching that creates spaces for metaphors and symbols that shift children's perceptions away from the obvious meanings of phenomena to a consideration of implied and embedded meanings. I intended the theme of Time Travel to instill in children a basic conception of history as the process of traveling through time. It is significant, however, that this conceptual model also requires a basis in concrete information and experiences. The year-long study would integrate concrete experiences such as field trips and interviews with a broader historical awareness derived from local and regional history. Most important, the theme of Time Travel would be reiterated in the literature read to and by the children and the other activities we did throughout the year. This immersion made it possible for the children to become invested in history. By year's end, the children did see themselves as time travelers and they began to identify all the different ways you can travel through time and space (i.e., symbolically, metaphorically, aesthetically, and emotionally). "Time machine" became a metaphor for anything that could transport our thoughts and feelings (e.g., books, movies, songs, objects, stories, pictures, photographs, museums, artifacts). Time Travel also became the theme of the children's own projects and defined the class's culminating experience, a videotape titled *A Blast to the Past.*

Social history as "history from the bottom up" provides an alternative perspective on the movements and developments that shape cultural, social, and economic institutions. Time Travel, as a social history, was a study of the industrial revolution from the perspective of child laborers. Inherent in this approach is a critique on industrialization and the inequitable distribution of wealth. Understanding the forces of industrialization—the mechanization of production, the concentration of workers, the division of labor, the colonization of natural resources, and the expansion of markets—precedes an understanding of the digital revolution that began in the late 20th century. Both represent technological revolutions that dramatically altered the structure of society. This historical awareness is also a type of technological literacy.

Technological literacy, like any type of literacy, should eventually foster the capacity for critique, evaluation, and deliberate action. It is not enough for children to learn how to use computers. Children and adults alike need to be able to explain the intended and unintended effects of the digital revolution. If we can understand technology's past, then we are in a much better position to control its future rather than have it control us. The historian Kirkpatrick Sale's analysis of the cultural and environmental impact of the industrial revolution framed his assertion that "technologies are never neutral, and some are hurtful" (1996, p. 261) He tells the story of the 18th century Luddites in England and their rebellion against the mechanization of their looms, the subsequent demise of their vocation as skilled textile workers, and the dehumanizing practices of mass production. The Luddites were rebels who challenged the radical upheaval of their lives by the politics, economics, and material practices of industrialization:

> The real challenge of the Luddites was not so much the physical one, against machines and manufacturers, but a moral one, calling into question on grounds of justice and fairness the underlying assumptions of this political economy and the legitimacy of unrestrained profit and innovation at its heart. (Sale, 1996, p. 5)

The notion of "unrestrained profit and innovation" struck a chord with me. For the economically disenfranchised—the poor, the unemployed, the workers replaced through "downsizing," or the movement of manufacturing to Third World sites, the new manufacturing poor of the Third World, and the many underpaid service workers in health, education, and retail—the digital revolution represents social and economic upheaval. Technology is power (Apple, 1986), and part of what gives it power and profitability is its inequitable distribution. How do we prepare children to make sense of this technology and its relationship to their lives? There is a lack of critique pertaining to technology's impact on culture, society, and the environment in school curricula. I wanted to bring this critique into our classroom through the methods of social history that draw on the records, voices, artifacts, and recollections of the laboring classes.

The Time Travel project, therefore, enacted multiple levels of technology inclusion. The academic and creative demands of the project required my students to develop a facility with the practical and creative uses of the technology and digital resources available to us: video production, web page design, word processing, multimedia presentations, electronic mail, and Internet resources. Concurrently, Time Travel examined the historical, cultural, and felt significance of technology through a focused study of child labor in the United States during industrialization and into the present (Bartoletti, 1999; Colman, 1994; Deitch, 1998; Freedman, 1994; Mofford, 1997; Reynolds, 1992; Saller, 1998; Seguin, 1996). A historical analysis of child labor seemed a potentially compelling entrée for my students and me. Children have a deep capacity to empathize with other children. Learning about the lives of children during industrialization could provide a concrete framework for examining their own lives and the meaning of technology or "machines."

The next three sections examine how each of the simultaneous processes of research, representation, and dissemination was enacted in the Time Travel project to allow for the inclusion of students with diverse cognitive and creative abilities. Through the interaction between my classroom experiences and academic inquiry, I began to consider how digital technology has transformed the way we think and organize our thoughts. The organization of knowledge has been altered in complex and exciting ways by the digital environment. This transformation has significant implications for the establishment of authentically inclusive environments that celebrate cognitive pluralism. In the following sections I write about the different processes of research, representation, and dissemination in order to emphasize particular elements of the reconceptualization of knowledge and learning brought about by the digital environment. These processes, however, should overlap; research requires varying degrees of representation and dissemination. Students' efforts to represent knowledge are validated by the dissemination or distribution of that knowledge among an audience of peers, family, and community members. Representation is, inherently, dissemination. It is a complex interplay that typifies the orientation to intellectual development fostered by a new paradigm for the organization of knowledge brought about by the digital revolution.

Research and the Implications of Hypertext

Methods of research have been significantly expanded by access to the Internet and digital libraries. During the planning stages of the Time Travel project, I needed to expand my own knowledge of industrialization and child labor and locate resources for my students that they would find engaging and accessible. As I navigated the Internet and helped my students to do the same, I reflected on the nature of the "information superhighway" and how it contrasted to print-based research. The Internet challenges accepted models of meaning-making. Hypertext is a technological innovation that raises significant issues about the nature and purpose of traditional instruction. Hypertext is media linked to other media. It is a divergent media of expanding and seemingly infinite pathways that carry users far from their initial point of origin. It is easy to "get lost" on this "highway" because the associated links are as compelling as the originating one. Often, I would begin my own search looking for information on one topic and arrive at some equally compelling yet unintended site. Burbules and Callister argued that these associative links of the hypertext environment complicate the making of meaning by decontextualizing and fragmenting meaning:

> If hypertexts do make possible the manifold linkage of nodes to different points of association, they also have the effect of fragmenting and decontextualizing each node, freed up from its position in some original narrative or line of argument. "Lateral" associations may turn out to be more useful in certain contexts than the original "linear" ones; but the leveling of all associations without privileging any particular one may make every association appear arbitrary. (2000, pp. 49–50)

I have found that it is the associative and divergent qualities of the Internet that most fascinate children. Books and printed text are convergent, and the nature of literacy instruction in schools emphasizes a linear progression of ideas and events. Schools continue to support linear narrative structures that move from an introduction through a complicating event to a resolution and conclusion. In many ways, hypertext is a more accurate representation of how children think. Every elementary school teacher has had the experience of associative storytelling. One child's account of a scar or bicycle accident or a pet's death triggers multiple stories of similar occurrences that eventually lead to yet other stories of seemingly unrelated events. As teachers, we feel compelled to get the topic back on track, yet often, children do not have this investment and would, if they could, go on all day.

The hypertextual environment of the Internet made me more attentive to the support of divergent styles of discourse in my classroom. The language of teaching and learning is typically convergent. Lesson plans model this type of thinking in which objectives establish the direction of a given lesson and the intent of instruction. To approach the Internet with a narrow objective would impede its fundamental design and utility. I realized that it is imperative for children to model and internalize conceptual strategies that enable them to weave meaning from multiple associative threads; children need to learn how to build contexts.

Without an organizing theme, research on the Internet would be a series of stops and links that held superficial interest—perhaps some interesting graphics or pictures or a compelling web page design. Time Travel provided a context that included and unified ostensibly unrelated subjects. For example, while researching on the Internet songs about life in the coal mines, I came across the popular railroad song, "Casey Jones." I liked it and I wanted to sing it with my students so I followed various links to get the lyrics and to learn about Casey Jones. I realized it is not just a song about a specific train accident. Rather, it is a mild critique of the impact of machines on people presented by certain folk songs and popular stories during this period. Further research led me to an alternative version of this song written by Joe Hill (1879–1915), an activist and union organizer, who presented Casey Jones as a scab crossing a picket line.

Following the links, the Internet brought me to the "Casey Jones Accident Report, May 10, 1900," which states, "Reports received to date indicate that Engineer Jones of the passenger train, who lost his life in the accident, was alone responsible for the accident..." The web publisher of this primary source demonstrates their credibility by prefacing this account with a comment that there are other conflicting reports. Pursuing these led me to the account of Casey's fireman, Sim Webbs, an African American (Farmer, 1999); and on it went. What I initially thought was a song about a train accident initiated a chain of associations that eventually incorporated issues of race and class. It was not part of my plan, but because of the concept of time travel and the conceptual framing of industrialization, Casey Jones was able to "join" the program and his complex story intrigued the children and deepened their understanding of the lived, complex realities of industrialization.

Research represents an area in which technology and social history overlap to sustain an intellectually diverse community. The diversification of concepts and multiple strands of inquiry support the abilities and interests of a heterogeneous community of learners. The power of digital resources lies in their capacity to support the inclusion and use of divergent forms of media. The hypertextual environment of the Internet parallels the type of diversity that occurs in inclusive settings. The teacher's role is to help children learn how to synthesize concepts and build contexts that support the convergence of this information. What results should be a range of artifacts produced by students that simultaneously represent and preserve their expanding knowledge of the world. This underscores the second element of social history made possible by digital technology: the students' use of diverse representational forms.

Representation and the Creation of Artifacts

The phrase "social history" is often preceded by the words "to do." This is because it involves an individual, group, or community actively documenting and representing a conception of the past and present that cannot be expressed by broader historical categories and periods. Often, it is the documentation of the reactions to larger events that becomes the work of social historians. I have had students interview elder members of the community to ascertain their reaction to events such as the death of Dr. Martin Luther King, Jr., or World War II. These social interactions humanize the past for children so that eventually they understand that all objective historical data has somebody, somewhere, who could tell about it subjectively, with feeling and insights. These interactions place responsibilities on the social historian to preserve what was learned in a manner that respects authenticity. This act of preservation is conveyed to my students as the material process of making and interpreting artifacts.

Artifacts are material representations of a culture's present and past. The Time Travel project directed most of the students' work in research toward the creation of individual and group artifacts. To consider the process of representation as the production of artifacts introduces another dimension to the nature of literacy education in elementary schools. What makes an object an artifact is the process of interpretation and contextualization that we apply to it. Aidarova (1982), a curriculum theorist influenced by Vygotsky's program of social constructivism, documented the ways in which children's imaginative play transforms the meaning of objects. For example, she observed how, in their play, children would turn a stick into a sword or a rock into a gem. Aidarova's program of language instruction validated this tendency as an opportunity to develop the child's *polyse-mantic* capacity. In other words, the symbol and sign substitution that occurs during a child's imaginative play prepares students for the understanding of literary texts that have multiple levels of meaning. She argued that "to tear the idea (the meaning of a word) away from the objects is of paramount importance for the development of thinking in symbols" (1982, p. 62). Transforming an object into a culturally and historically significant artifact activates polysemantic fluency. Aidarova suggested ways to build instruction that support cognitive development through the social processes of play, talk, imagination, and storytelling. Contexts and concepts emerge from the accumulation of interpretations and experiences. Students move back and forth among the literal and abstract, the specific and the general. A polysemantic environment that frames the creation and interpretation of artifacts helps students to meaningfully navigate the hypertext world of the Internet. Both situations require educators to build contexts and embed knowledge within broader organizing concepts. The making of meaning becomes a type of conversation between the self and the artifacts that is expansive and ongoing.

Social history creates an environment for the conceptual development of literacy by applying the process of semantic decoding to artifacts. The idea of "listening" also takes on different implications. To develop a capacity to tell stories or create narrative structures requires immersion in a culture of storytelling. With children, the telling of stories can be stimulated by the concrete, tangible reality of an object. An object externalizes thought processes so that children can structure their stories initially as descriptions of the objects, and from this, broaden the scope of their analysis to include its personal, cultural, and chronological significance. As the description of the artifact moves from a story about it to the meaning behind it, the teacher can facilitate more abstract levels of comprehension. The following examples of students' interpretations of personally important objects reveal various levels of analysis and narrative development. Tanya wrote the following herself:

MY BABY ARTIFACT IS A HAT
By Tanya

My baby artifact is a hat. I had the hat when I was a baby.
It is special to me because, I got the hat from my mom
and dad. The hat was made from goat's hair. Too bad
the hat doesn't fit my big head.

> Like I told you that the hat doesn't fit me any more because, my head is too big. But it can fit my baby doll or when I have a baby and if the baby will not fit in the hat. Guess who will? The baby's baby doll and it will keep on going on and on. If you would like to know more about my hat or other things just ask me and I will tell you more.
>
> If you also like to see my hat go ahead. Be my guest.

Tanya was able to project her story into the future. Her baby hat channeled her insights on the passing of time. The baby hat takes on multiple levels of meaning. It is her hat, but it will become another's hat. The hat becomes a symbol for her passing from childhood ("my baby doll") to different stages of adulthood. At first she is the parent ("I have a baby") and then the grandparent ("the baby's baby doll").

The following story by William of something that is precious to him shows a more concrete level of analysis. He is not able to say why his "toolbox" is important. Rather, for William, simply being able to identify something precious in his life marks a transformation in his self-awareness.

SOMETHING PRECIOUS
By William

> Something that is precious to me is my toolbox. I love taking stuff apart. Once I took a Hess truck apart. I have a hammer, a screwdriver, a pair of pliers, and a wrench in my toolbox. I have more screwdrivers in my toolbox than anybody else. I have a remote control car in my room.

William was identified as having multiple disabilities, including cognitive delays, a speech disorder, and emotional and behavioral immaturity, which led to hostility and instigating situations in which he would become the victim of the hostility of others. His speech was marginally intelligible to most unfamiliar listeners. He often needed to repeat himself and was reluctant to talk in front of the class. William's differences in speech and demeanor made him a target for ridicule, a dynamic he had come to internalize and, sadly, recreate in his social interactions. He came to my class from a self-contained classroom in another district; he was angry and distrustful. All he wanted to do was sit at the computer and withdraw from his classmates. This was safe for him. My year with William was spent helping him "speak" literally and symbolically. He would tell me stories that I would transcribe. He rewrote them and then typed and formatted them on the computer. William's description of his precious toolbox gave me important insight into what engaged his mind and feelings. He worked with his hands and this became how he distinguished himself among his classmates. This story also marked a turning point in William's feelings about writing. He realized that writing could be about him and the things he liked, and that he didn't need to do it alone. Eventually, William did strike out on his own. The following piece he wrote himself several months later:

MY MOM
By William

My mom takes care of me. She gives me a bath. I like my mom. She gives me popcorn. My mom likes to watch movies. My mom likes to make macaroni and cheese for me. She gives me potato chips. My mom says goodnight too. I say goodnight to my mom.

William cannot yet name in the abstract the feelings and thoughts his mother evokes. What he can do is identify the concrete representations of these abstractions. Reading this passage, I know William's mother loves him, he feels this love, and he loves her. For a boy with William's challenges, these simple expressions were major achievements. Talking about, and then writing about, people and objects provided concrete starting points for the development of Tanya and William's thoughts about themselves and their relationship to others. The use of artifacts drawn from a child's life—bicycles, games, memorabilia, souvenirs, sports equipment, clothing, and photos—supports the modeling of narrative and interpretive techniques.

The use of artifacts is critical in inclusive environments because it is often the inability to decode written text that excludes students from general education programs. Digital photography has made the process of recording and preserving artifacts through images more expedient and accessible. In addition to recording three-dimensional artifacts, digital photography allows children to integrate images of their immediate world as a type of artifact and a basis for critical examination. When children read and examine images they have made of their surroundings, they begin to understand and articulate the stories behind them (Ewall, 2001). For children who struggle with reading, the act of decoding text may interfere with their participation in the abstract and analytical models of interpretation that they need, but in which they often cannot engage. Artifact-based activities allow students with differing abilities to participate together in these intellectual processes. Tanya and William are engaged in the same things as students but are doing them differently in accordance with their cognitive development and narrative skill. As their teacher, I recognize and interact with these differences. What is most important, however, is that in the eyes of their classmates, both William and Tanya are joining them in writing about their lives.

The use of artifacts as representational forms helps students experience history as a creative process they can participate in. I sought out historical resources that modeled the use of artifacts to preserve and record the past and establish traditions. In particular, I was interested in graphic forms of representation that used images or stylized symbols to record the past. The historical use of wampum belts by the Native Americans of the northeast region of the United States demonstrates the complexity of graphical forms of representation (Graymont, 1988; Tehanetorens, 1976, 1999; Wallace, 1994). For this reason, and in the spirit of time travel, my students were required to "write" about themselves using symbols to create wampum belts of personal significance. Out of respect to the Native tradition from which this activity was derived, the children also had to create and narrate wampum of historical importance to the Haudenosaunee people. We built simple wooden looms and used yarn and beads to create the patterns of the Hiawatha and Kahswentha belts and other belts of significance to the Iroquois Confederation. Once each child completed a belt he or she had to learn the story of the belt.

The "examination" or assessment that coincided with this activity consisted of a recitation. They would tell me when they were ready to be "tested." Together, the student and I would stand in front of the class. I would hold the wampum while the child told its story. I would then ask questions about the belt such as, "Who was Deganawidah?" "What is the Great Peace?" "How do a bundle of arrows symbolize the meaning of unity?" For the child to receive the belt, he or she had to demonstrate the ability to be responsible bearers of it—they had to accurately tell its story. The repetition necessary to learn the story was embedded in the recurrence of the testing process, as each child participated in the examination. Children who were weak at decoding printed text thrived in this environment when their expertise as "griots," or storytellers, became evident and their developing literacy was based in orality rather than textuality.

Ultimately, everything the children created during the course of the year became an artifact. Each student had a Time Travel portfolio. This was a large file that served as a conceptual "container" for organizing the year-long accumulation of writing and documentation that became, in the process, an artifact of the child's life and learning in fourth grade. The Time Travel portfolios were a way for children to realize the historicity of their lives. "Writing Workshop" was an extended period of time 2 or 3 days a week when children developed these portfolios. They had writing folders with a chart that they could add topics to and which helped them organize and monitor their own progress. Children worked at their own pace according to their different abilities. The work that each child included in his or her portfolio was varied. Writing was a critical element of the portfolio process. What liberated students to write freely (or in some cases dictate their writing), was their awareness that everything they produced became, through this process of documentation, historically important. Direct instruction in writing was embedded in this portfolio process and individualized to each student's level of need and development.

To emphasize the preciousness of these documents, the portfolios—large manila envelopes organized alphabetically—were stored in a portable file that the children could have access to only once their hands were clean and their desks clear. The students would ask, "Ms. Lamash, can I look at my Time Travel portfolio? My hands are clean." I would say yes only after making a fuss about them not wrinkling or misplacing anything. My fussing was intended to make them feel special and to have them internalize the extreme importance of their work. The scanner and digital camera significantly extended the scope of what could be included in the child's portfolio and validated as historically significant. Important documents such as birth records, report cards, family photographs, and immigration papers were scanned and preserved. Artifacts such as baby toys, memorabilia, and objects of personal significance were digitally photographed and inserted into word documents.

The students' portfolios modeled the type of *polysemantic organization* (Aidarova, 1982) that is defining the new discourse of information technology and postmodern practices. Polysemantic approaches recognize that contexts and concepts emerge from the accumulation of experiences. The student portfolios became a "container" for the accumulation and organization of each child's written and graphic representations of their social historiography. Each child's final collection of documents was bound into a book called *Time Travel.* This shared title unified the material conceptually, but there was no attempt to organize the content of the books according to any general model. The organization of the books evolved through each child's interaction with the activities and experiences of the year-long social history project. These portfolios came to symbolize the dynamics of an inclusive environment. No one book was more outstanding than any other. Each book was uniquely beautiful in its own style and way; each book followed its own logic and aesthetic agenda. At the same time, each book shared with all the others a conceptual relationship. What unified the books and, ultimately, the class community, was not the standardization of the curriculum, but its conceptualization. Working with the concept of traveling through time allowed for the simultaneous diversification and unification of the classroom community.

The importance of the children's work was emphasized by its preservation and dissemination throughout the portfolio process. The portfolio was an assessment tool and a historical artifact. The portfolio process also took on social significance when it presented a child's work for others to see and respond to. This process of dissemination fostered students' awareness that what they were doing would be for others to see. It motivated the children to take their work seriously. Also, digital technology expanded the portfolio process by allowing for student-created multimedia.

The next section describes the group project that served as the class's collective portfolio. Students used digital video to create a documentary about child labor during industrialization. What became evident in this activity was that a digital environment not only restructures the way things get done in a classroom, but also the conditions that support creativity.

Dissemination and the Creative Process

Social history is an open-ended process; it does not stop once certain information or data is acquired or internalized. On the contrary, the pathways of inquiry actually multiply as stories, research, information, discoveries, and experiences initiate new directions of exploration and curiosity. Social history evokes a hypertextual environment that extends beyond Internet research. Structures of organization are not inherent in the material or its presentation. These structures emerge and are shaped by the interaction between what we bring to the context— our initial curiosity—and the new curiosity stimulated by the associations brought about through inquiry.

A word that captured the spirit and intent of the type of inquiry that is emergent and unfolding in my classroom is *bricolage*. The sociologist Sherry Turkle adopted the concept of bricolage from the work of the French anthropologist Claude Lévi-Strauss. Bricolage is the process of "theoretical tinkering...by which individuals and cultures use the objects around them to develop and assimilate ideas" (Turkle, 1995, p. 48). The bricoleur "does not proceed by abstraction, but by thinking through problems using the materials at hand" (1995, p. 51). Turkle considered bricolage a necessary alternative to the accepted and validated analytical methods of computer programming. She referred to the psychologist Carol Gilligan's feminist critique of analytical methods. Gilligan's (1982) research demonstrated that dominant analytical models repress and devalue embedded or contextualized processes of thinking, doing, and feeling. This kind of embedded reasoning is viewed in our culture as the "soft" or feminine stages that lie at the base of a hierarchical model of moral and intellectual development. Gilligan disagreed with this analysis and demonstrated that contextual, situated reasoning is not a stage, but a style (p. 58). Turkle concurred, describing problem solvers "who do not proceed from top-down design but by arranging and rearranging a set of well-known materials" (1995, p. 51) as "bricoleurs." "For planners, mistakes are steps in the wrong direction; bricoleurs navigate through midcourse corrections. Bricoleurs approach problem-solving by entering into a relationship with their work materials that has more to do with the flavor of a conversation than a monologue" (p. 51).

The concept of bricolage reflects my way of thinking about the type of activity occurring in my classroom. Many teachers lack methods and contexts that recognize the process of bricolage as a framework for integrating activities that support students' acquisition of skills and information. The classroom application of bricolage requires that curricula be simultaneously divergent and convergent. The culminating experience for Time Travel included both and represents a shift from a top-down model of planning and enactment to an emergent, context-derived model.

Blast to the Past was a video documentary that recreated salient elements of what my students had learned about the lives of children during industrialization. It was initially conceived as a culminating activity in a very conventional manner, based on my years of working in an analog or VHS format. What first led me to the instructional use of video was how it allowed my nontraditional students to "write" with images. The conventional model of video production proceeds in stages, beginning with various outlining structures: a script or narrative, a storyboard or visual outline, and a production plan. Students select a video treatment from among various types: educational, dramatic, humorous, or documentary (Black, 1989). Different production crews are created and assigned tasks. Although the taping of the footage can occur out of sequence, the editing must progress in a linear fashion. This is where digital technology changes everything. Digital editing is referred to as *nonlinear editing,* which means that editing can be done out of sequence. With digital editing, inserting new footage does not require a reconfiguration of the whole videotape. You can drop in or take out portions or whole segments of footage while retaining the general structure and format of the overall piece. Digital editing allows for constant conception and reconception of a production's narrative and visual sequencing.

The conventional approach to video production follows a "top down" model in which a written script or outline precedes and determines the visual treatments of the scenes and events. This is how we initially approached the video project. I directed the class in generating a written outline for the script. Once this outline was established, the "writers" would develop it and then we would pass it along to the "producers" for story boarding. First, we would describe what industrialization is and then talk about the coming of steam power and the meaning of mass production. We would explain factories and reasons for immigration. Then we would talk about the lives of children in the textile mills and garment factories and the lives of boys in the coal mines. All of this initial planning was done in writing. The visuals were to come later, with the exception of some drawings inspired by a boy, who was found to be an exceptional artist. During the process of planning our script, we discovered that the boy, Justin, could do beautiful drawings of photographs by the documentary photographer Lewis Hine (1874–1940). I discovered this when, one day, Justin, a quiet boy who struggles with reading and writing, was looking through a book of Hine's photographs (Freedman, 1994). Justin liked to sketch and on his own he sketched Hine's photograph entitled "doffer boys" showing a young child, barefoot, climbing a spinning machine to replace bobbins as seen in Figure 6.1. His classmates became inspired to do their own drawings of Hine's photographs of children in the coalmines, textile mills, and fields. Although I was preoccupied with the script, the children were busy sketching Hine's photographs on their own.

It was then that I realized that the whole structure of the video project had to change. Clearly, the children were establishing their own agendas and priorities based on what engaged their imaginations. They were ripe with ideas. We had been immersed in this project for almost a year. We had visited a coalmine and toured several museums that displayed artifacts of the Industrial Age. We had read historical fiction, viewed slides of the work of documentary photographers from this period, watched video documentaries, studied the evolution of

Figure 6.1.   Justin's drawing of Hine's photograph of doffer boys.

technology and machines, and read primary sources. We sang songs such as "Miner's Strawberries," "My Sweetheart's a Mule in the Mine," and "Cotton Mill Girls." We had toured our own neighborhood and seen the traces of the Industrial Age in the abandoned factories, overgrown train tracks, and preserved mansions of local manufacturers.

Reorganizing (and reconceptualizing) the production of *Blast to the Past* was also necessitated by the children's enthusiasm for the medium of video. Everyone wanted to do everything. My initial attempts to develop production crews gave way to a more open-ended creative process. I found that once I trained several students in the use of the editing software, they trained each other. Different groups of students became responsible for different segments. As portions of the video were assembled, the whole class would screen and critique the project and individual students would take on the task of integrating the changes. Revision of the project was ongoing. The script was altered many times to allow for new scenes, improve transitions, and establish continuity between existing scenes. As students developed greater technical facility with the camera and software, they wanted to retape different scenes.

One technique in particular that the children wanted to experiment with was stop action animation. This technique uses a series of still images or frames to create a sense of movement. For example, to show the hands of a clock moving, we would record for 1 second, pause, move the hands of the clock slightly and then record for 1 second again. (Doing this repeatedly results in the creation of a series of still frames that simulate movement when played continuously.) One group wanted to create a moving time machine. Once they started, others also wanted to animate scenes. This led to animations of a boy on a mule cart, cotton being picked, a trapper boy opening and closing the ventilation doors in a mine, and, what became the beginning and end of our video—students in the class being transported from the present to the past in a time warp.

The children's interest in songs also shifted the emphasis of the production. One morning, a student named Thu came in and handed me a pile of drawings. "Ms. Lamash," she said proudly, "I decided to illustrate 'Cotton Mill Girls.'" "Cotton Mill Girls" is a song written by Hedy West in 1964. It describes the futile experience of women mill workers trying to survive on inadequate wages.

Thu created still drawings that were refined and used as slides in the video to accompany the class singing the song. Her initiative created a whole other area of interest. The class felt that if we were going to have a song about the textile mills, we also needed one about the coalmines. They picked one of their favorites, "My Sweetheart's a Mule in the Mine" (Donegal Weavers, 1994). These two songs were not part of the initial outline of activities. By the time we were finishing the video, however, they became central organizing elements, integrating the coal mine and textile mill segments. The children's reaction to the music and their desire to incorporate it into the video demonstrated their deepening investment in this historical period. To completely rearrange the video to fit in the musical segments was never a question. It simply had to be done, and it had to be done well. The nature of the video was no longer in my hands.

The children asserted a different narrative format than what I had originally intended. As a documentary treatment, it was my assumption that the narrative would be in the third person. As the children appropriated the planning and script writing by way of their associative model, they rewrote much of the script in the first person. Billy's animated character, derived from Lewis Hine's photograph of a trapper boy, spoke in the first person:

> Billy: My name is Billy and I am a trapper boy. Air is forced into the mine from the outside. The trapper doors should be kept closed so that clean air stays where the men are working. My job is to open and close these doors so that the coal

cars can go from one chamber of the mine to another. It's a real lonely job. Sometimes I don't get out of the mine until after dark. I work in total darkness too. When I get bored I draw pictures and write on the door things such as "Don't scare the birds." I like to draw birds on the door because I never get to see any.... Look, here comes Justin the mule driver.

Justin: I am the mule driver. I drive the mule to the front of the coal mine. My mule's name is Justy. My mule spits on me when it's mad. If I stand in back of my mule, its gonna kick me. My mule can pull five tons of coal in a coal car. That's how much each coal car holds. A miner has to fill three coal cars a day. If my mule gets sick or dies, I'll get fired.

William's comment, "Look, here comes Justin the mule driver," was added after the class reviewed the script and realized that it was not clear how scenes fit together. When I revisited the script for the writing of this chapter, I noticed that those parts of the script written in the third person were the result of my influence and input. As I think about this now, I am reminded that when working with children's representations of reality, whether it is graphic or textual, it is important to allow their own perspectives and strategies to emerge through the process of creation and re-creation. Digital technology not only facilitates this but also compels it.

The making of *Blast to the Past* demonstrates an approach to the creation of artifacts by students that incorporates the type of contextual or situated reasoning that Turkle (1995) referred to as bricolage. *Blast to the Past* became a much more complicated process as the students' creative vision expanded and circumscribed mine. It also became more intellectually rigorous. The initial convergent style of the script's focus narrowed the scope and depth of the video's content. This preliminary framework for the video showed me what I thought the children should know. Once the children became empowered as bricoleurs, the video began to reflect what they had internalized, both intellectually and emotionally. I came to understand their relationship to this period of industrialization and the ways it had altered their worldview. The students began to empathize with their historical counterparts and sympathize with the difficulty of their lives. Because this process was divergent in scope and form, we actually had to revisit and redress a great deal of information and ultimately, we did more reading, rereading, writing, and rewriting than I had originally intended.

Finally, perhaps what was most critical in my own understanding of this process was that, as bricoleurs, my class came to understand and value the diverse strengths of their classmates. Justin, once perceived by others to be a quiet boy who struggled with reading and writing, became the driving force behind whole segments of the video. It was not simply a surface inclusion of his talents or his being able to collaborate with more academically proficient classmates, but a complete shifting of the very paradigm of achievement.

Children began to make more connections between what they were doing and the types of techniques they saw on television or at the movies. One student asked if what we did with voice-overs and sound effects was the same thing done when voices were put in cartoons. Many students were amazed by the amount of work animation takes. One day when we watched an animated video, the children wanted to know how many different frames were needed to make a character move. When I told them that film uses about 20 frames for each second, they were shocked. One boy thought about this and replied, "Well maybe they use something like an assembly line to make a cartoon, in which a whole bunch of people do different scenes and then they put them together." Comments such as these suggested that the children were moving beyond an awareness of the surface attributes of historical events and technological innovations and were beginning to inquire into the material and human processes that brought them about. They were starting to see the "big picture." How often does learning actually change a child's perceptions of the world in such a way that they see new things differently and familiar things in a new light?

In the Time Travel project, students were not simply proud of what they had done, but of what the whole class was capable of doing. All of this came to a climax the night of our open house, during the final week of school. It was a celebration we had spent 10 months working toward. The children led their parents, siblings, and grandparents in the singing of songs. They read from their books, interpreted their wampum, and showed off the assortment of artifacts we had accumulated. And of course, we watched *Blast to the Past*. Only then, on the last Friday of the school year, when the open house was over, could we actually say our work was done and successful. The project was divergent, expansive, and, at times, almost unwieldy. There was a moment by mid-May when we did not think we would get our books and video done by June. At this point, children voluntarily worked on their portfolios or the video script at home. The activities typical of most classrooms at the end of the school year generally do not provide elementary-age children with the kinds of tangible symbols of their academic efforts and achievements that were the outcome of our project. The hustle and bustle of our classroom came from children's desire to get a meaningful project done on time. What if we were to think of the end of the school year as meeting this kind of deadline?

RETHINKING CURRICULUM
AND TECHNOLOGY INCLUSION

The Time Travel project demonstrates the potential of conceptually organized, process-focused methodologies to restructure curriculum and develop a model of embedded instruction. Embedded instruction modifies systematic and constructivist approaches by the conceptualizations it brings to the curriculum. Lasting or productive changes do not occur when only teaching practices or material resources are altered. Change occurs when the conceptualization of the educational encounter is altered to the extent that paradigms shift (Cuban, 2001). This happened for me through the course of the Time Travel project.

My understanding of social history methodology achieved a greater degree of cognitive pluralism and social relevance because of the freedom offered by digital technology. This new technology significantly redefined my pre-existing models of thinking and creativity. The connections I made between hypertext, polysemanticism, and bricolage represent the structural inclusion of technology to transform my existing practices to more adequately support a heterogeneous group of students. The interaction between social history methodology, the conceptual framework of Time Travel, the availability of digital resources (e.g., the Internet, word processing, digital imaging), and a rationale informed by a social vision of an equitable world, sustained a culture of inclusion for my students that ultimately turned them into a community of happy, proud, and unified learners. No one feature, standing alone, would have been enough to make this experience effective. If I attempted a social history project that did not provide resources for multiple representational forms or thematic inclusion, then I would not have been able to invite all of my students to participate fully. Likewise, if I focused solely on computer applications without any curricular or conceptual inclusion, then students' relationship to this technology would have been shallow and divorced from their intellectual and social development. Similarly, to pursue a social critique of technology without any connection to the curriculum or the instructional needs of students would have neglected students' academic and intellectual development.

Issues of technology inclusion and the building of inclusive class-room communities are connected on a very deep level in that they both require a humanizing presence and a compassionate framework. The blending of constructivist and systematic approaches must be more broadly contextualized within a framework of community. Technical proficiency, whether it be manifested in a child's capacity to write, solve a math problem, or design a web page, is contingent on, and made relevant by, our deep understanding of the social, ethical, and political implications of the technology we employ. Apple (1986) asserted the need for this type of "social literacy" to contextualize "technical literacy" and redirect our attention to the lived conse-quences of new technology, "To the degree that new technology trans-forms the classroom in its own image, the more technical logic will re-place political and ethical understanding. The discourse of the classroom will center on technique, and less on substance" (p. 171). The discourse of technique may also risk displacing considerations of the child, the felt consequences of curriculum, the lack of meaning in education, and the reasons why so many children are marginalized from inclusive educational programs. In other words, the technical dis-course precipitated by technology use parallels the instrumentalist ap-proaches to the treatment of students with special needs or children who simply do not fit in.

The "social literacy" of which Apple speaks is the capacity of indi-viduals to critique the underlying structures that sustain those of us who benefit from a system of inequitable distribution of wealth and re-sources and those who do not. "Unless students are able to deal hon-estly and critically with these complex ethical and social issues, only those now with the power to control technology's uses will have the capacity to act" (1986, p. 173). Technology does not change people; people change technology. Technology inclusion that does not incor-porate critique is simple indoctrination and sustains economic in-equity. Addressing these issues compels educators to build environ-ments in which our students—especially those who do not benefit from the material and educational resources of our society—work with us to name our world, our relationship to it, and our responsibility to improve it. Social history can establish the relationship between the transformation of the self and the transformation of the world by mak-ing possible what Paulo Freire spoke of as an investigation into a peo-ple's "thematic universe" and the "thought-language" that scripts it (2000, p. 96). It is a dialogic process framed by love for oneself and the world, and the passionate desire to elevate both. Children with special needs challenge us to articulate and refine our beliefs and actions as educators. They challenge us to develop core values that support not just their inclusion but the celebration of all diversity and the recognition that heterogeneity is a resource and not an impairment.

The conceptualization of learning as time travel will continue to shape my relationship to the curriculum, my students, and my own development. The complexity of it allows me to be human. It allows me to feel the curriculum as part of my lived reality. And because it is part of my lived reality, it continually expands and enriches my worldview. I believe that my students have had, in varying degrees, similar feelings of connection. I recall one student, Malcolm, who came into my class many years ago as a child who showed little emotion. He did not respond to conventional methods of instruction. Consequently, teachers did not know what to do with him. He was characterized as unmotivated, unresponsive, and as not doing "anything." That year, we made a video documentary about the history of our school and neighborhood. Once Malcolm took hold of the video camera, something shifted. He knew what to do. What struck me at year's end was his physical transformation. He stood up straight and was able to look at people. He began to smile, laugh, and engage in conversation. He found a connection to school and an avenue for communication.

Years went by. One afternoon, after I had spent the week photographing the demolition of the Endicott-Johnson shoe factory, a local factory of significance to the history and economic development of our community, there at the door was Malcolm with a paper bag in his hand. "Ms. Lamash," he said with a shy smile, "I have something here that I think you would really like." I took the crumbled bag and opened it up. It was a brick! He said, "I got it from the Endicott-Johnson factory. I knew you would want it." And he was right! Malcolm and I both had an investment in this event because of the work we did years earlier. We could both look at the brick and see a whole other world. Our perception of the world transformed our experiences in the world. If we cannot see it, then we cannot know it. Malcolm would have never seen that brick if he had not learned how it came to be. It is this process of unfolding enlightenment that a culture of inclusion, tied to a curriculum that celebrates the making of meaning, can inspire. That was the lesson Malcolm taught me. It is the lesson inherent in my account of a year of traveling through time with my students.

REFERENCES

Ada, A.F. (1993). *My name is Maria Isabel.* Glenview, IL: Scott Foresman.
Aidarova, L. (1982). *Child development and education.* Moscow: Progress Publishers.

Apple, M. (1986). *Teachers and texts.* New York: Routledge.

Bartoletti, S. (1999). *Kids on strike!* New York: Houghton Mifflin Company.

Black, K. (1989). *Kid vid: Fundamentals of video production.* Tucson, AZ: Zephyr Press.

Bromely, H., & Apple, M. (1998). *Education /technology/power: Educational computing as a social practice.* New York: State University of New York Press.

Burbules, N.C., & Callister, T.A. (2000). *Watch IT: The risks and promises of information technologies for education.* Boulder, CO: Westview Press.

Colman, P. (1994). *Mother Jones and the march of the mill children.* Brookfield, CT: The Millbrook Press.

Cuban, L. (1986). *Teachers and machines: The classroom use of technology since 1920.* New York: Teachers College Press.

Cuban, L. (2001). *Oversold and underused: Computers in the classroom.* Cambridge, MA: Harvard University Press.

Deitch, J. (1998). *The Lowell mill girls: Life in the factory.* Carlisle, MS: Discovery Enterprises.

Delpit, L. (1995). *Other people's children: Cultural conflict in the classroom.* New York: The New Press.

Ehrenreich, B. (2001). *Nickel and dimed: On (not) getting by in America.* New York: Henry Holt.

Ewall, W. (2001). *I wanna take me a picture: Teaching photography and writing to children.* Boston, MA: Beacon Press.

Farmer, N. (1999). *Casey Jone's fireman: The story of Sim Webb.* New York: Phyllis Fogelman Books.

Freedman, R. (1994). *Kids at work: Lewis Hine and the crusade against child labor.* New York: Clarion Books.

Freire, P. (2000). *Pedagogy of the oppressed.* New York: Continuum International Publishing Group.

Fullan, M. (1999). *Change forces: The sequel.* Philadelphia, PA: Falmer Press.

Gilligan, C. (1982). *In a different voice: Psychological theory and women's development.* Cambridge, MA: Harvard University Press.

Goodman, K. (1996). *On reading.* Portsmouth, NH: Heineman.

Graymont, B. (1988). *The Iroquois.* New York: Chelsea House Publishers.

Hirsch, E.S. (Ed.). (1974). *The block book.* Washington, DC: National Association for the Education of Young Children.

International Society for Technology in Education. (2000). *National educational technology standards for students: Connecting curriculum and technology.* Eugene, OR: Author.

Levstik, L.S., & Barton, K.C. (1996). They still use some of their past: Historical salience in elementary children's chronological thinking. *Journal of Curriculum Studies, 28*(5), 531–576.

Levstik, L.S., & Pappas, C.C. (1987). Exploring the development of historical understanding. *Journal of Research and Development in Education, 21*(1), 1–15.

McClintock, J. & McClintock, R. (Eds.). (1970). *Henry Barnard's school architecture.* New York: Teachers College Press.

Metcalf, F.D., & Downey, M.T. (1982). *Using local history in the classroom.* Nashville: The American Association for State and Local History.

Mofford, J. (1997). *Child labor in America.* Carlisle, MS: Discovery Enterprises.

Newman, F.M. (Ed.). (1996). *Authentic achievement: Restructuring schools for intellectual quality.* San Francisco: Jossey-Bass.

Reynolds, R. (Ed.). (1992). The history of labor. *Cobblestone, 13*(8).

Sale, K. (1996). *Rebels against the future: The Luddites and their war on the industrial revolution: Lessons for the computer age.* Reading, MA: Addison-Wesley Publishing Company.

Saller, C. (1998). *Working children.* Minneapolis, MN: Carolrhoda Books.

Seguin, M. (1996). *Silver ribbon Skinny: The towpath adventures of Skinny Nye, a muleskinner on the Ohio & Erie Canal, 1884.* Boston: Branden Publishing.

Seixas, P. (1993). Historical understanding among adolescents in a multicultural setting. *Curriculum Inquiry, 23*(3), 301–327.

Sergiovanni, T.J. (1994). *Building community in schools.* San Francisco, CA: Jossey-Bass.

Tehanetorens. (1976). *Migration of the Iroquois.* Rooseveltown, NY: Akwesasne Notes.

Tehanetorens. (1999). *Wampum belts of the Iroquois.* Summertown, TN: Book Publishing Company.

Turkle, S. (1995). *Life on the screen.* New York: Touchstone.

U.S. Bureau of the Census. (1998). *Statistical abstract of the United States: 1998* (118th ed.). Washington, DC: Author.

U.S. Department of Education. (2003). *No child left behind act of 2001.* Retrieved March 2, 2003, from http://www.ed.gov/legislation/ESEA02

Vygotsky, L. (1986). *Thought and language.* Cambridge, MA: MIT Press.

Wallace, P. (1994). *White roots of peace.* Sante Fe, NM: Clear Light Publishers.

Weavers, D. (1994). *Last day of the northern field: Memories of Pennsylvania's coalmines.* Wilkes Barre, PA: Author.

CHAPTER SEVEN

Inclusive Education Through the Arts in a Collaborative Community-Responsive Elementary Team

A Day in the Life

BARBARA L. REGENSPAN

This chapter takes the reader on a journey into the life of two adjoining multi-age classrooms, one primary (first through third grade) and the other upper elementary (fourth through sixth-grade) in a socially diverse, urban public elementary school. The classrooms are unusual in their vision of a coherent first through sixth grade curriculum that inspires appropriately challenging work for all of the children, including the oldest and youngest. The teamed teachers enjoy a continual and collaborative relationship around a shared commitment to inclusive, arts-based first- to sixth-grade curriculum and teaching in which the children's questions, responses, and products from one day's pursuits find their way into future lesson plans. This process of a spiraling curriculum, which takes its inspiration from John Dewey (1902/1990), determines the organic quality of these classrooms in which growth is experienced on multiple levels.

Vignettes and descriptive summaries focused on specific lessons and activities in both classrooms during one day of this teaching team's ongoing urban–rural unit will reflect an expansive interpretation of "inclusive" classrooms. The children's long-term study and comparison of urban and rural environments exemplifies the broad and content-rich themes that ensure coherence, flexibility, and challenge in classroom life. Also, the reader will be presented with evidence that the commitment to the arts as the motor of the curriculum is both inspired by and makes possible the enactment of such an expansive conception of inclusion.

The adjoining multiage primary and upper elementary classrooms, whose collaborative urban–rural unit is explored anecdotally in this chapter, represent a "best practices" composite. That is, the school, teachers, curriculum, and these specific adjoining classrooms, including the children and their families and the multiple communities to which they belong, are based on my teaching, research, and observations of "best practices" in a wide range of classrooms and community arts projects over many years.

Five broad principles organize and/or characterize the life of both classrooms:

1. The featured teaching team relies on the families of the children in the classroom and members of the communities that circumscribe the school, both for teaching artists who can collaborate with them as curriculum-makers and for creative, humanistic, and artistic inspiration for the curriculum in general. Furthermore, the team is assertive about finding and using the arts resources available in the community.

2. Morning meeting is a business meeting in which all parties concerned help to organize the day and clarify expectations. Issues of appropriate behavior are negotiated in a manner that resets the tone each morning; the point is for children to be attentive enough to enjoy the fruits of this exciting curriculum and to not "miss out" because they have allowed themselves to become distracted from the important and gratifying business at hand.

3. Specific artistic techniques and challenging historical information are taught to the children, giving them the tools to enrich their independent work and create high quality—and therefore, gratifying—written, graphic, and plastic (three-dimensional) products.

4. Consistent blocks of time are provided for play and independent exploration of the rich resources available. Products of play and independent exploration periods are prominently displayed in the classroom and efforts are consistently made to spiral the curriculum from interesting pursuits of the children initiated during these blocks of time.

5. Often, unpredictable classroom incidents and accidents are used to spiral curriculum. In other words, the need to respond appropriately to real and interesting occurrences, certainly part of what gives life meaning, becomes the context for further learning. Even events of systematic instruction in these classrooms acquire a "response to...." context that makes them compelling.

The bulk of this chapter is correlated with each of the five broad principles identified. In turn, each of these principles is used to place specific aspects of the rich curriculum of the two classrooms in a highly pragmatic context. At least one vignette or description centered on curriculum or the negotiation of behavioral norms is offered to concretize each principle's implications for classroom practice. Yet, the broad principles provide an accessible link between the curriculum itself and the theory that motivates that curriculum. Therefore, theoretical discussion and/or interpretation that speaks to both the vignettes and the highlighted principle of each section is typically labeled and set apart from the vignette for the reader's ease. Occasionally, such discussion is more seamlessly woven into the content of the vignette, reminding the reader that thoughtful teaching represents the continual enactment of the teachers' best response (informed by theory) to what happens in the classrooms and the communities in which they are situated. In turn, such thoughtful response can generate new theory.

It is clear that some of the vignettes correlate equally well with more than one principle; in some cases, my matching may feel arbitrary. Yet the ease with which the curriculum can be correlated to multiple principles might be seen as an argument for the cohesiveness and thoughtfulness of all aspects of classroom life.

An introduction to the featured teaching team and its general guiding perspectives or philosophy follows and immediately precedes the five sections. After the five sections, a brief conclusion summarizes the chapter's content with an emphasis on the transferability of its "lessons."

SOCIAL RECONSTRUCTION AS GUIDING PHILOSOPHY

The perspective of the teaching team featured in this chapter is that the arts are about creating or making things happen in response to interpreted experiences of life in community. The community cited in the definition, however, both practically and theoretically, represents many communities. It includes the actual families of the children in these classrooms and the multiple communities to which they belong ethnically, geographically, historically, and geo-politically. Whenever possible, these communities are invited to be active players in the curriculum.

The teaching team's practices confirm its members' belief in "social reconstructionist" teaching. Although social reconstructionism is the philosophy that grounds the educative project of reconstructing society to make it socially equitable (Kliebard, 1987; Sleeter, 1999).

The curriculum of social reconstructionist classrooms, then, is characterized by intentionality with regard to selecting what knowledge
should be passed on to learners: knowledge that is considered useful
and important by communities interested in challenging social inequities and promoting democracy. Such knowledge, then, becomes
the basis for experiential learning in the classroom and local community as part of a process of reconstructing the cultural worlds of the
school community and the communities that circumscribe it; this re-
constructive process is deemed the goal of education. Some of the vignettes in the chapter should illustrate for readers how the relationship of mutual responsibility among the classrooms and these
overlapping communities helps this teaching team determine what to
teach, how to teach it, and to whom. In the two featured classrooms it
is assumed that the children, often in collaboration with one another
and their teachers, parents, and community members, will generate
new understandings in response to knowledge made available both
through text and experience. Both the knowledge presented and the
new understandings take the form of some combination of language,
graphic, music, culinary, plastic, or building arts.

Again, speaking specifically to the theme of this book, classrooms
with a strong, arts-focused curriculum can provide the unique data
with regard to a continual balance between constructivist practices and
systematic instruction, that social reconstructionism requires. This is
precisely because the curriculum keeps demanding creation, and therefore illuminates those underlying skills and knowledge bases required
to make very different creative acts possible. Although some children
learn this knowledge and these skills through the interpretive and creative activities themselves, the overwhelming majority of children
need systematic instruction in some areas, some of the time.

Therefore, the classrooms featured in the vignettes are guided by
the belief that certain skills and some previous knowledge are always
required in order to understand and produce interpretation; this belief
is both observable and explicitly stated. Members of the teaching team
articulate with and for the children the (loose) division of much of the
work they pursue together into the categories "practice for..." and "the
real thing." "The real thing" includes the work of understanding, interpreting, and creating, whereas "practice for..." generally applies to
phonetic decoding skills, math facts, and formulas including skills with
measurement, research and study skills, procedural knowledge with
regard to use of art and science materials, and information deemed
useful to memorize or "know." Sometimes, this last category includes
the historical background to appreciate a particular art form or innovation or to understand how some idea became thinkable.

Often, but not always, systematic instruction supports the sequential building of a set of skills and, therefore, correlates with the "practice for" category. This means that these skills, sometimes acquired sequentially, are required in order to pursue analytic, interpretive, and creative work, but in and of themselves, do not constitute analytic, interpretive, or creative work. Yet, in these classrooms, aspects of the process by which children are given access to artistic texts of all types—graphic, literate, visual, and plastic—can be both systematic and constructivist. The fluidity sometimes found in these categories will be explored further in the discussions that examine the practice implications of each of the five principles more deeply.

Principle 1

The featured teaching team relies on the families of the children in the classroom and members of the communities that circumscribe the school.

VIGNETTE 1: TUESDAY MORNING BEFORE SCHOOL

It is 7:45 A.M., and 8-year-old Luis has returned from the main office to his multiage primary classroom carrying 40 copies of the following unpublished poem:

COTTON PICKIN' TIME
By Henry J. Ausby

Early, early on Saturday morning
ever so slowly I climb out of bed
find myself a string to hold up my britches
make a newspaper hat to put on my head
make my way into the kitchen
help myself to the syrup and bread.

Throw my daddy's old shirt on my back
pull my raggedy sneakers upon my feet
getting myself ready to go to the cotton patch
gotta help my mother make ends meet.

The big green truck pulls up to the door
like sheep to the slaughter we all pile in
the family and me, everybody on the back!
To be driven to the fields where the pickin' will begin.

From sun up to sun down we'll labor
row after row we'll pick
headache, finger ache, back ache, never mind
I ain't got time to be sick.

The grass still all wet with dew
although it's morning, there is yet no sun
and my legs get wet from my knees on down
not exactly my idea of fun.

But the two bucks a day
which will be my pay
gotta go a long way.

So I get used to it. It's no big deal
that's the way it is. I don't complain
it's not blood!
Besides before this day is over. It'll be so hot
I'll be wishing for that dew. And praying for rain
or a flood.

'Cause when them cotton bows get open
and I ain't got a dime
it don't matter about the weather.
For me, it's Cotton Pickin' Time!

Two of Luis' teachers, Mrs. D. and Ms. R., greet both Luis and the poem with enthusiasm. Local African American minister, Reverend Ausby, wrote the poem when he was 16 years old about growing up as son of a Mississippi sharecropper. Now a clergyman/activist in this medium-sized city in central New York state, Reverend Ausby is the minister of Luis' family's small Haitian congregation and an advocate for new immigrant families in this historic refugee resettlement area. Many of the children in these families, such as Luis, attend this high-poverty public urban elementary school.

The consulting special education teacher in Luis' classroom, Ms. R., had recently attended the "opening" for the Saratoga Cultural Histories Mural featuring Reverend Ausby's poem. The mural was painted at a municipal housing authority residence where Luis' family lives, less than a mile from school. It was a project of the elementary teacher education program from which Ms. R. graduated and whose student teachers she and her team regularly sponsor.

Last week, a regularly scheduled parent conference was held for Luis, which included Ms. R., his general education classroom teacher Mrs. D., Luis, both of his parents, and his grandmother. Knowing that Luis' family attended the small Haitian congregation to which Reverend Ausby ministered, and that Luis' entire extended family had attended the mural opening, Ms. R. had arranged during the conference that Luis would request permission from Reverend Ausby to copy the poem for use in their team's current urban–rural unit. It was also agreed at that conference that Luis would have the poem duplicated in the office as part of his before-school-helper assignment, a job held at least once during each school term by every child on this team.

After Ms. R., Mrs. D., and Luis reached agreement to wait until the morning meeting to distribute Reverend Ausby's poem, the two teachers sent Luis next door to the multi-age upper elementary classroom, where he would continue his before-school-helper job. Here, in the classroom, Luis works with Mr. G., the teaching assistant who divides his assignment between Luis' classroom and this one. Mr. G. is a comfortable and well-loved adult in Luis' school life. Mr. G. and Luis begin unpacking and remounting, on large collapsible foamboards, the Lewis Hine photography exhibit on loan from the Southern Tier Institute for the Arts in Education, which Mr. G. picked up from the institute's downtown office on his way home from work the previous afternoon. (Lewis Hine was the early 20th century photographer whose work exposed child labor practices while capturing aspects of the humanity of his subjects beyond their victimization. See Chapter 6.) Luis has experienced traveling exhibits before and is able to follow Mr. G.'s instructions for sorting the 8- by 10-inch photographs according to their vertical or horizontal orientation in preparation for mounting them in the photo brackets already glued to the foam board. The two continue working to ready the exhibit for the children who will be stepping off their busses shortly.

The collaboration between Mr. G. and Luis is continual; just yesterday, Mr. G. had written the word "emergency" in Luis' personal wordbook while helping Luis and his friend Michael write a sign to identify the hospital in the city being built in the primary classroom block area. That drama related to the same urban–rural unit for which both Reverend Ausby's poem and the photography exhibit are important resources. Luis' sign will appear in a later vignette.

"MATERNAL THINKING" AND RECONSTRUCTION OF THE "CODES OF CULTURAL POWER"

The artfulness of the arts-based curriculum is as visible in the relationships orchestrated by the teachers as in the actual curriculum created by collaboration among these players: children, teachers, poets, artists, and community activists. It is a classroom community in which teachers continually tell and model for the children the idea that intellectual and social connection-making is the point. The teaching team, male and female members alike, recognize that the prototype for their own elementary teaching is the commitment that women have historically made as mothers. Such a paradigm invokes philosopher Sara Ruddick's conception of "maternal storytelling" to characterize the teachers' role in the teacher–student relationship.

> Ideally, a mother's stories are as beneficial to her children as they are to her. As she pieces her children's days together, a mother creates for herself and her children the confidence that the children have a life very much their own and inextricably connected with others. (1989, p. 98)

Thus, this team helps the children contextualize their own life experience in a hugely encompassing classroom community, one which pulls in the historical community of the area, the children's communities of family and friends, and ultimately, even the human community of knowers and artists. Ms. R. and Mr. G. literally tell Luis a story of his "inextricable connectedness" in the first vignette. Reverend Ausby's poem introduces Luis and his classmates to a potentially inclusive identity as poets, and the Lewis Hine photography exhibit reminds him as well as them that this country was built by immigrants like him. Reverend Ausby is an African-American poet and Luis can become a Haitian-American poet and one of the poets in his classroom or school. Here is the enactment of an expanded notion of the "codes of the culture of power," the tools that this team agrees must be systematically taught to children of color and other marginalized children in order for them to succeed in a culture whose "codes" are determined by a white and middle class dominant culture (Delpit, 1995). This teaching team includes the canon of poetry written primarily by white men as one such code, while recognizing that poetry can be used to include, even celebrate, all immigrant cultures and all people. In this social reconstructionist classroom, the code of poetry will be passed on to the children; indeed, selections from Walt Whitman,

Langston Hughes, and Emily Dickinson grace the prominent bulletin board to which Reverend Ausby's poem, and poems produced by Luis and his classmates, will be added. The code, "poetry," is transformed by the new contributions of this community. It is expanded, literally reconstructed by the additions to the bulletin board of "Cotton Pickin' Time" and then by poems produced by the children in the poetry workshop convened this morning by Mr. G. and, in turn, by the children, themselves (captured in the next vignette). No longer primarily the province of the canon's dead white men, "poetry" is available for the children in this classroom to nourish, express, and share their own stories, thereby reconstructing both the canon and the membership of "the culture of power."

VIGNETTE 2: POETRY WORKSHOP AFTER MORNING MEETING

Mr. G. works with eight children immediately after morning meeting, six from the primary classroom and two from upper elementary. Charles, an 11-year-old, volunteers to read aloud "Cotton Pickin" Time" for this self-selected group of poets, whose primary level members have already heard it read by Luis earlier in group meeting. Mr. G. then reiterates the purpose behind gathering the group: writing poetry about rural work. In the brief introductory discussion he facilitates, the children are reminded, and remind one another, of some of their most recent sources of information about rural work. Last Friday, Mr. Estavez, a former migrant apple picker from Wayne County, New York, had visited both classrooms and shared oral histories from his crew (compiled through a grant from the Cornell Migrant Program, whose director is a friend of Mrs. D.'s). Yesterday, Mrs. D. read to the primary group the picture book, *A Green Horn Blowing* (Birchman, 1997), an imaginative Depression-era tale narrated in the first person by an unnamed young boy living on his aunt's farm. The story featured an itinerant farm worker, John Potts, who temporarily came to do odd farm jobs and live in Aunt Frita's barn with the cats. But John Potts was also a skilled trumpet player and he discovered for the little boy narrating the story a fantastic playable green squash called the trombolia. Although a joyful fantasy, the book reminded the children of Mr. Estavez' presentation in which he had pointed out the low pay of farm workers and their special vulnerability in times of economic crisis. With Mr. G.'s recursive questioning, Charles recalled that Mr. Estavez was particularly passionate about one point: Those who helped to ensure that all of us could eat deserved to feel secure about their ability to provide good food and shelter for their families. Luis pointed out that although John Potts made beautiful music and worked hard on Aunt Frita's farm, he was unsure where his own meals or shelter would come from, let alone providing for a family.

Two younger children mentioned Mr. G.'s stories about bailing hay on his grandparents' farm in Iowa. And two other children were reminded that their families bought corn from a farm stand only 10 minutes outside the city; one of the children knew a boy from this school who worked at the stand selling corn in the summer. Ten-year-old Aveen spoke of her grandfather's farm in New Jersey, which she loved to visit; her grandfather grew corn but earned most of his income training horses.

This discussion segues into Mr. G.'s explanation of the specific lesson plan, which will involve the children in actual teaching. He asks the children to listen for characteristics of the language or ideas as he rereads Reverend Ausby's poem. He identifies specific choices the poet made in the writing of "Cotton Pickin' Time" as "variables." Again, through recursive questioning he has the children identify some of these variables. The children name the presence of rhyming words; the use of informal, family, and community-based language (sometimes called *street language* without derogatory connotations in these classrooms); images related to the realities of "making ends meet"; and the use of details of ordinary life, such as the specifics of getting dressed and eating bread with syrup. When it is her turn as leader, Aveen selects rhyme and a description of someone eating as the two variables to which the children's poems must conform.

CATEGORIES OF TEACHING PRACTICES BLUR

This anecdote provides an example of the blurring of categories, systematic instruction and constructivist practices, as well as the teachers' informal categories for use with the children: "practice for…" and "the real thing." For instance, generating a list of words that rhyme with "corn" could be part of a lesson representing systematic instruction in mechanical decoding and encoding skills. In that case, it would represent the category "practice for…." Yet, the generating of such a list might also be part of a poetry writing lesson in which students are being encouraged to play with and produce rhymed verse in the context of an exploration of rural work, as is the case in this poetry workshop.

The organization and facilitation of the poetry workshop itself, though, also invokes questions of what is "real" and what is "practice." Through Mr. G.'s facilitation, children are reminded of Ruddick's very "real" proposition that they have a "a life very much their own and inextricably connected with others" (1989, p. 98)—others such as Reverend Ausby, their teachers, and even John Potts with his fantastic trombolia. Aveen wants to experiment with rhyme, for example, and has an idea for a poem of her own that features the hot water without tea that her grandma drank as a new young mother in a village in Kurdistan. For Aveen, the writing of this poem will be very real as is her experience facilitating the workshop as a practice teacher. For the other children in the group who are writing poems following Aveen's specifications, will the experience represent "the real thing" or "practice for..." ? The answer is unclear. But is it not quite systematic to identify the different ways "how a poem means" (Ciardi, 1959) as variables and to have children selecting and assigning them for use by the community of poets in their classroom?

Principle 2

Morning meeting is a business meeting in which all parties concerned help to organize the day and clarify expectations.

VIGNETTE 3: EXPECTATIONS EXPLAINED IN MORNING MEETING

Two morning meetings proceed simultaneously in the younger and older elementary classrooms. Much of what will unfold during the day, including, for instance, Mr. G.'s poetry workshop described previously and the use of the Lewis Hine photography exhibit, are introduced in these parallel morning meetings. The younger children will receive a copy of and hear Luis introduce and read Reverend Ausby's poem. The older children will receive their first pictures taken on a recent downtown field trip, developed by Dunja's dad, Bosnian immigrant photographer Sead Hadziabdic. Mrs. H. reminds the older children that most of them will have the opportunity to study the Lewis Hine exhibit and to plan their individual and small-group multi-media research projects related to the urban–rural unit. Some of them will participate in groups that directly support an aspect of their research. In both classrooms, children are reminded that because Mr. Hadziabdic will return this afternoon for a workshop on lighting with the upper elementary children, math instruction groups will convene this morning after snack. Mrs. H. has arranged to meet with children working with Unifix cubes (interlocking plastic cubes) on multiplication towers in the downstairs resource room again because that room is equipped with many more Unifix cubes than the classrooms.

In the primary classroom, the participants of this morning's watercolor group with primary teacher Mrs. D. identify themselves, as do the cooks working with parent volunteer Debra to produce the applesauce and the flier for tonight's PTA meeting. Members of the cross-team writing support group are reminded of their regularly scheduled meeting with consulting special education teacher Ms. R. in the upper elementary classroom directly following this one. A number of children in these classrooms participate in Odyssey of the Mind, a state-sponsored, challenging, problem-based math curriculum involving periodic regional competition. The primary and upper elementary students involved, including 11-year-old Thomas, who has severe cerebral palsy, will meet in the hall with 9-year-old student captain Dinesha and Ms. S., classroom aide assigned to Thomas. They will continue plotting the scale and provisional plan for the model city construction project to begin tomorrow in the upper elementary art area. Thomas will hold the cardboard in place and hand out markers to the other children. Ms. S. will also brainstorm with the students about how they plan to individualize the model city project into their own urban–rural research project. And in both meetings, teachers will restate the authentic recording requirement, whereby every student must "leave a trace" in the form of a written or graphic chronicling of some activity they performed during the day.

In the primary classroom, examples are offered this morning, as they are every morning to clarify what will be considered acceptable chronicling. Will the leaflet count for the children in Debra's group? Will poems produced in Mr. G.'s group count? If you are working on the Unifix tower problems, can you write up your process solving one of the problems with words? Can you illustrate a problem with a diagram? Can Michael do a block story or diagram with Luis about the emergency room of the hospital? The answer to all of these questions is, "Yes!"(Luis feels obligated to point out that he will be working with Mr. G.'s poetry group first thing.) Mr. T. offers that he will be with Michael in blocks. Might he help Michael write such a story, possibly including the other children who are starting the morning there? Michael is clearly delighted that Mr. T.'s shared attention connects him to the two other children who plan to work in blocks. In the elementary classroom, in which children are already well-versed in authentic recording, children suggest ways that Thomas also can record his work.

GROUP MEETING, ORGANIZATION OF THE DAY, AND ISSUES OF BEHAVIOR

All teachers can appreciate how the best intentions with regard to curriculum making can be sabotaged by lack of cooperation on the part of the children, or even the "acting out" of a few children. Arts-focused social reconstructionist teaching requires the full engagement of the children as a community. Yet, the process of achieving such engagement is an art form in itself. Although the long-term goal is to have a curriculum that continually spirals from the preceding inquiry, creative project, or other work of individual and small groups of children, in reality, constant compromises are required by state-mandated curriculum and contradictory school and community. Then, there is the issue of differences in skill level and background information on the part of individual children, requiring different amounts of, and/or different timing in the provision for, systematic instruction.

These realities help explain why the teachers call the first block after morning meeting "assigned morning activity time" even though more than half of the children are typically working in a teacher-facilitated group whose initiation or content the children themselves helped negotiate. Afternoon independent work time allows similar flexibility for teacher direction, and both writing workshops and whole- and small-group math instruction are typically teacher-directed. All of these blocks are regularly scheduled, some daily and some bi- or tri-weekly. The children know that only blocks specifically labeled "play and independent exploration" are consistently free choice.

Clearly, assigning activities and confirming ongoing commitments and choices in morning meeting proceed conversationally and involve a great deal of negotiation. They require a kind of maturity and patience that some of the children find too challenging without assistance. Yet, assistance comes in many forms, not typically requiring one-to-one aides. For instance, Mrs. D. has a gift for successfully reinforcing behavioral expectations in light and humorous interactions that are consistent with the social reconstructionist philosophy. Two such interactions are featured in the following vignettes.

VIGNETTE 4: CEDRIC IN PRIMARY GROUP MEETING

Cedric is a 7-year-old who generally functions well in the primary classroom. He arrived from another school in the fall with a 5-inch-thick folder, mostly documenting what others had labeled his "behavioral challenges" and "emotional problems."

Before the assignment and selection of activities, Mrs. D. announces lunch count. "I need every child's attention to complete this process without wasting too much of the morning's assigned activity time. If everybody hears all the lunch choices the first time, then they can be prepared to make their selections in one round," Mrs. D. explains, as she often does in morning meeting. Instead of listening, Cedric is fooling around with a rubber band at Mrs. D.'s feet, trying to keep a fast-moving spider encircled. "I appreciate your gentleness with that spider, Cedric. Do you think we could catch it in a cup and release it out the window?" Although many children volunteer, Mrs. D. encourages Cedric to complete the job by himself as she hands him an empty coffee cup from the desk just behind her. She knows Cedric well enough to know his skill in such matters; this interruption will not take long, and it will bear long-term fruit. The children get reinforcement for an important rule in this community: We respect all living things. And Cedric—at times annoying to the other children—is seen at his most gentle, kind, and thoughtful in this brief sequence of events. The situation, under Mrs. D.'s skillful guidance, "constructs" Cedric as gentle, kind, and thoughtful.

Before long, the lovely, quiet moment occurs during which everyone watches Cedric coax the spider off the rim of the cup held just outside the cracked-open window. Mrs. D. waits respectfully, modeling the awed silence she intentionally chooses to cultivate as a resource for this classroom in which beautiful things are regularly observed and made. Cedric completes the job and seats himself in his original place. But the children immediately surrounding him feel gifted now to have him in their midst. There is some shifting around of bottoms and legs to make room for him, yet somehow everyone is seated even closer to him than before. The child immediately behind him places his hand on Cedric's back. With a rejecting movement, he shrugs off the hand. The spell is broken. Cedric is a child who cannot tolerate too much attention for a sweetness he cannot maintain.

Mrs. D. returns to the first agenda of the meeting, lunch count. But she will bring a kind of closure to the incident with Cedric and the spider, recognizing the need to welcome him back as the Cedric who is not always so gentle, not always so appropriate. She accomplishes this with an almost offhand wry remark, made with her head turned to the board and chalk in hand, ready to write the egg noodle casserole tally. The comment she makes is directed to the more cynical side of Cedric, the side of him that has seen a bit too much in his fairly chaotic life outside of school.

"There must be an oversupply of those noodles this week, Cedric, because they're certainly appearing regularly on this week's lunch menus," she comments.

"There was a special at the warehouse, huh, Mrs. D.?" asks Cedric, now grinning.

He is a child who already knows that education and human services agencies too often put administrative convenience and cost containment ahead of benefits to the children and families supposedly being served. The hand of the boy behind him replaces itself on Cedric's back, and this time it is not shrugged off.

Her comment represents Mrs. D.'s very personal approach to keeping Cedric sufficiently connected to her, to the other children, and to the complex agenda of this exciting classroom. He cannot be a gentle "good boy" much of the time; it is too great a contradiction with his life outside of school in which he is being raised by a single, often well-intentioned but "macho," father living in poverty. Just 2 days ago Mrs. D. had to interrupt Cedric's gleeful narration of how he witnessed his father throw a brick through his girlfriend's car window. (I add this detail not in the spirit of negative gossip about children and families, but to offer readers insight into both this child's difficult negotiation of home–school boundaries and the delicate balancing act of teachers working to maintain positive relationships with families.) But this classroom will offer Cedric many opportunities to do and be both gentle and good. Mrs. D.'s comment about the oversupply of noodles lets him and the other children know that there is space here for Cedric in all his complexity.

THEORIZING A RELATIONSHIP AMONG SOCIAL RECONSTRUCTION AND BEHAVIORAL NORMS

The point of the preceding vignette is that social reconstructionist teaching includes the reconstruction of all of the players, including the children. Cedric's goodness gets stretched further in the sequence of events described, just as his harder edge gets softened a bit because Mrs. D.'s noodle comment is not rude or inappropriate, just aware in the way Cedric is. One could argue, relative to the focus of this chapter, that there is an artful approach to inclusion modeled here. Children are reshaped and reshape themselves in order to fit into this humane, humorous, and expansive community.

The author would be remiss in not articulating what most teachers certainly appreciate: the reality that economic, social, and cultural factors combined with individual psychological issues can lead to difficult behaviors in a classroom. In addition, children's conflicts, regardless of their causes, can cause significant disruption in any environment. It is important to note that children can reject physical contact for many reasons. Cedric does not have an autism spectrum disorder, nor does he suffer from other neurological problems, but some children who behave similarly do have disabilities of these types. Most teachers are familiar with "tactile defensiveness" more serious than Cedric exhibits that sometimes appears in children who have been abused or have certain sensory disabilities. Increasingly, children with tactile defensiveness are offered desensitization treatments in school; for many of them, the consistent support of an aide with training is essential to their success.

In addition, a teacher in Mrs. D.'s position could have just as realistically reminded the class about the need to ask permission before touching. Many teachers in active classrooms hold all meetings while children are seated at their desks or tables to minimize such complications. And sometimes it is important to give children appropriate information about the special concerns of their peers. The point here is that there is always a balance between allowing the raw data of life to play out for all of its educative potential and maintaining the levels of order, confidentiality, and peace required by both the "players" and the complex, sometimes systematic curriculum.

VIGNETTE 5: WANDA IN PRIMARY GROUP MEETING

Wanda is a 6-year-old whose family refused to have her "held back" in kindergarten, despite the strong recommendation of the school psychologist and kindergarten teacher, both of whom perceived her to be too immature for first grade. Although not necessarily opposed to young children repeating kindergarten, this teaching team thinks Wanda's family made a good decision.

After Mrs. D. has completed the lunch count, Ms. R. reviews the morning's group assignments and choices. She publicly welcomes Debra, a community volunteer who visits weekly to cook with a rotating group of children from both classrooms. Ms. R. reminds the children that Debra is here to help this week's cooks with the applesauce they are making for today's snack and for tonight's PTA meeting. The cooking group will also be responsible for completing the leaflet to be distributed at the PTA meeting. That leaflet will include, as has already been agreed, the recipe, the diagram of the bisected apple that Wanda produced last Friday, and whatever else this week's group decides to include.

Wanda is stimulated by the mention of her name and raises her hand. "Couldn't Reverend Ausby's poem be included in the leaflet for the PTA too?" In the conversation that ensues, a number of children restate the opinion that Reverend Ausby's poem "Cotton Pickin' Time" would not match the theme of the leaflet. Mrs. D. suggests that there may be time to produce a poem about applesauce making. A child sitting next to Wanda counters, "No, we'll make the recipe rhyme." Debra is as visibly delighted by a couple of the "cooks" who now gaze at Wanda with new admiration.

Again, there is a kind of subtle shaping of a child into a gradually more responsible community member. Wanda's immaturity sometimes takes the form of needing to talk even when she does not really have something compelling to say. In classrooms that invite student input, this common pattern can become a problem. But Wanda is a natural connection-maker; she proposes a connection that is not quite direct enough to make sense to this community but evidences her awareness that the point is this continual effort to make connections. Subsequently, she is immediately rewarded by Mrs. D.'s modeling of the effort to work with her thinking, and of another child's quick grasp of an exciting possible compromise. The process of negotiating the curriculum itself, in this case, the creation of a rhyming applesauce recipe, is decidedly constructivist.

Principle 3

Specific artistic techniques are taught to the children, giving them the tools to enrich their independent work and create high-quality—and, therefore gratifying—products.

VIGNETTE 6: WATERCOLORING THE SKY

Students who experiment with the combination of blue watercolor, water, white paper, and masking gum are learning through "practice" how to represent the sky. Indeed, this is the immediate goal of the group that works with Mrs. D., who does watercolor painting in her life outside of school. They are systematically instructed in a technique that represents knowledge worthy of being preserved and passed on, one that will make it possible for them to create convincing and very different kinds of skies. Yet the children's experimentation with the technique is part of an artistic, creative, and literate response in this lesson in which the youngest children, mostly 6-year-olds, work with Mrs. D. to create the sky in pictures for their book comparing urban and rural environments.

Following the writing workshop, during independent work time, they will use a combination of drawing and collage materials to continue crafting their pictures. The pictures are inspired by research in books, films shown to the class, two field trips, another community artist, and the Lewis Hine exhibit. Finally, their completed pictures will require the children's own captions, produced in a series of writing workshops in which the same children will use a combination of methods to re-represent, in words, the meaning they make of their graphic representations. Such methods include dictating to an adult or older child who does the actual writing, requesting words to be written in their wordbooks and transcribing them onto the book page, and "sounding out" the whole caption.

This lesson, then, represents a constructivist response to a number of different encounters with professional art even during this one day. The children have briefly viewed the Lewis Hine exhibit next door at the beginning of this lesson, and have been asked to focus only on the way the sky appears in the photos during this first encounter. Also, a number of books that feature skies, including the beautifully illustrated children's picture book read yesterday morning in group meeting, *A Green Horn Blowing*, the rural depression-era fantasy, are available for their perusal on a display shelf adjoining their current painting workshop space in the primary classroom.

Mrs. D. reminds them of Luis' reading of "Cotton Pickin' Time" in group meeting. "Can you imagine the sky not described in the poem?" A child points out that the day is very hot, and adds, "We know the sun must be a ball of fire."

This afternoon the children will briefly visit next door to examine the foreboding sky in a famous photograph taken by Dunja's dad, Sead

Hadziabdic. Do the children's opportunities to research skies represent events of systematic instruction because they lead to the children's ability to make their own sky pictures? Are these research opportunities a "practice for..." or "the real thing"? Or is no separation of categories possible in some of the complex constructivist events that constitute the core of this arts-based curriculum?

INTRODUCTION TO THE PHOTOGRAPHY WORKSHOP

Certainly, the same questions arise in the case of the activities related to the upper elementary classroom featuring the Lewis Hine photography exhibit that is central to the current urban–rural unit. The Lewis Hine photographs capture the lives of poor and working class new immigrants to New York City at the beginning of the 20th century. As part of the urban–rural unit, pursued at different levels of academic and intellectual challenge for different children in the two classrooms, all of the children have been given reuseable black and white cameras provided by a grant through the local Roberson Museum's partnership with a number of classrooms in the local school district. Some of the older children are doing their research in the form of photo essays about urban work. Some will correlate research with their work on the model city project. Others will use poetry, including their own, to explore their choice of themes. Some photography will be a part of every project.

This afternoon, the older children prepare to take their own photographs in workshops in which they learn from a visiting parent photographer not only how to operate the camera but also how Lewis Hine captured different qualities of the urban immigrant experience in his photographs.

VIGNETTE 7: A PARENT'S PHOTOGRAPHY WORKSHOP AND A TEACHER'S LECTURES

Mrs. H. welcomes Dunja's dad, Sead Hadziabdic, well known to the upper-elementary children, to the class. She delivers the good news that in the future, they will be developing their own pictures in the temporary darkroom Mr. Hadziabdic will be setting up in the storage closet. Dunja is proud to announce that her dad has been awarded a small grant from the New York State Council on the Arts that will fund his work with the children in the darkroom. Mrs. H. had written the grant with the input of Mr. Hadziabdic and the editing help of three of the older children in two special after-school meetings.

This afternoon, Mr. Hadziabdic focuses on how the use of lighting contributed to the mood of heaviness and oppression conveyed in many of Lewis Hine's photographs. He shows the children his own award-winning photograph of the bridge at Mostar, which he took just days before it was destroyed in a bombing during the war in Bosnia, and explains the choices he himself made about lighting. He emphasizes with the children the variables over which they have control with their own black-and-white cameras before they proceed outside to experiment with these variables.

In the course of his work with the students, Mr. Hadziabdic articulates another "maternal story": that understanding the use of light is part of the knowledge base of the community of "inextricably connected" artists who call themselves photographers. It is a community that includes himself—with his desire to capture for the human community a gorgeous and important piece of architecture from his own and Dunja's own former homeland—and Lewis Hine, who likewise wanted the world to know about the exploitation of immigrant workers, including children. It could also include the children in this classroom who might choose to master the required skills to produce pictures that reflect aspects of life they want to capture and share.

THE UNFOLDING OF UPPER ELEMENTARY RESEARCH PROJECTS

In addition to the background information about the Lewis Hine photographs offered by Mr. Hadziabdic, Mrs. H. has been giving brief mini-lectures to the whole class about the turn-of-the-century urban immigrant experience, including how Lewis Hine took his pictures and for what political and humanitarian motivations. Mrs. H.'s lectures are also inspiration and support for the upper elementary research projects. She would argue that her mini-lectures represent systematic instruction in that she is providing a gradually deepening background for examining different aspects of that historical era.

For instance, a number of children have chosen to do their research in the form of a collective photo-essay about the history of work in the local area since the beginning of the 20th century. Mrs. H. has introduced the concept of exploitation of the labor of new immigrants including children. Ten-year-old Catherine has decided to focus her research on the famous New York City newsboys' strike. Does Catherine's experience of Mrs. H.'s mini-lecture represents "practice-for…" or "the real thing" in terms of a learning experience? What could be more real than the challenging historical-materialist information being passed on by Mrs. H.?

VIGNETTE 8: WRITING SUPPORT GROUP

Following group meeting, five children (three from primary and two from the upper elementary classroom) convene for writing support group with Ms. R. Half of the members of this group have remained constant this school year and half have moved in and out of the group. Membership is negotiated among teachers, families, and children, but the idea of a writing support group came out of the ongoing school-wide faculty research seminar of which Mrs. H., Mrs. D., Ms. R., and Mr. G. are members. For a few months the previous year, the seminar considered the concerns of children who, for various reasons and at different times, resisted the group editing processes that were a standard component of the writing workshop in a number of the classrooms in this school, including the two classrooms featured in this chapter.

THEORIZING WRITING SUPPORT GROUP

Last year the faculty research seminar read both Ann Haas Dyson's (1993) *Social Worlds of Children Learning to Write in an Urban Primary School* and Elizabeth Ellsworth's (1989) *Why Doesn't This Feel Empowering?* Working Through the Repressive Myths of Clinical Pedagogy. Faculty members designed teacher action research projects related to inquiries potentially illuminated by either or both texts. These projects affirmed that the questions raised by Dyson about a specific homeless child featured in her research resonated with the experience of a number of teachers in this school, including those on this teaching team. At various times, a few children seemed too fragile to tolerate questions about their intentions and meaning relative to a written or performance piece. Ellsworth's article introduced to the teachers African American writer Barbara Christian's (1987) conception that she was "writing to save her own life." Mrs. D. realized how well that characterization periodically applied to some of the children in the classroom. Like Christian, they voiced experience that had not figured in to the dominant culture's conceptions of worthy human realities. They wrote to save their own lives by making them real. Others who had no understanding of their experience could not validate their views. Parallel to Christian's argument about her writing on the realities of the lives of African American women writers, some of the written and performance pieces that these children created needed to be appreciated as a unique source of information. Such an interpretation did not invalidate the need for these children to learn the "codes of the culture of power" (Delpit, 1995), including conventional English grammar and syntax. However, the more public editing process through which skills were taught and reinforced with the students' own writing used as object (a process that, therefore, objectifies that writing to some extent) did not always feel safe.

The writing support group, then, could serve two functions. It could provide a more selective audience for certain more sensitive written, graphic, and performance pieces. It could also provide a place to systematically teach conventional English syntax, grammar, and spelling skills ("codework") using a combination of materials other than the students' own writing. These materials included older linguistic readers, Glass analysis (1973) techniques similar to methods of Reading Recovery (Clay, 1985) and selected work of published poets and writers.

The preceding faculty research seminar findings continued to influence the practices of the teachers on this team outside of the writing support group. For instance, the teachers in both classrooms tended to use what they articulated as "discoveries" made in the writing support group for whole group and small group lessons that isolated a particular "decoding trick" or "encoding trick." All of the children on this team continually wore a personal wordbook, attached to a belt or necklace (e.g., the one in which Mr. G. copied the word "emergency" for Luis). The idea was that everyone was at all times an authentic chronicler and poet, needing access to the words that could be "given" by anybody in the school (or in the wider community) who could spell them. People collect words much like they collect life experience; some of the experiences remain private or are only shared with a carefully selected group. Words, however, are always available to everyone for the giving and taking as both "practice for..." and "the real thing."

Principle 4

Constant blocks of time are provided for play and independent exploration of the rich resources available to the children.

VIGNETTE 9: THE BLOCK AREA

With regard to the social reconstructionist philosophy that guides the curriculum, the children's independent exploration time can yield both play, and the creation of formal curriculum for the classroom, equally useful outcomes. "Practice for..." and "the real thing" can each take on somewhat different meanings, now reflecting the interpretation of "play" as "practice for" real life. In the context of building their city as part of the urban–rural unit, three of the younger children who spent part of the morning with Mr. T. in the block area also discovered how a pulley works. In their efforts to rig up an appropriately dramatic door for Luis' and Michael's hospital emergency room, they were able to direct Mr. T. to attach a pulley arrangement to a hook already imbedded in the ceiling above the block area and to attach its string to the cardboard handle on that door.

Mrs. D.'s group is now at the library checking out astronomy books for more inspiration about the sky. She walks over to the block area to help during the transitional time just before Mr. T. will be offering Michael one-to-one attention. Mr. T. suggests that the children read to Mrs. D. the story they have written, which focuses on how they helped Mr. T. by taping and retaping the handle on the door to their hospital emergency room and finally discovered a way to get the cardboard attached to the pulley. She admires the detail and precise language they have used, and suggests that they share their story with the whole group before lunch.

As Michael leaves with Mr. T., Mrs. D. notices the elaborate and extremely tall clock tower at the center of their city. Would the two remaining children be interested in measuring their clock tower that Mrs. D. believes is the tallest structure built this year? The inquiry that ensues inspires in Mrs. D. her idea for a demonstration lesson in transition to standard measurement that Mrs. D. will reconstruct with the two block-builders for the entire class during the next formal math instruction block. How many color cubes high is the tower? How many dog biscuits high? (Dog biscuits were introduced in math groups just yesterday and so far they have measured only distances on the floor.) This requires more taping and engenders much excitement. Not now, but in the formal group, Mrs. D. will proceed to "How many inches? How many centimeters?" The process of conversion to standard measurement is "systematic" in its movement from dog biscuits to color cubes to inches to centimeters. The children are engaged in "practice for later" work with standard measurement. The skills of measurement will offer these children a background in appreciating the more elaborate and scale-modeled city construction that the older children next door will begin tomorrow.

Yet, the contextualization of the measurement lesson in their own work of city building, connects measurement to one of its very "real" locations in the world: a part of the knowledge base (even code, such as poetry) called "architecture." The same is the case with the story about the specific design of the pulley that controls the emergency room door. Indeed, the sharing of that story will spiral into an extensive study of pulleys and levers, integrating beautifully with the focus on inventions and technology that will naturally emerge during this urban–rural unit.

VIGNETTE 10: HATTIE AND SARAH "INTERNET SURFING"

The controversies about use of the Internet in classrooms such as these are particularly charged. The teachers on this team continually discuss, argue, and compromise based on their different perspectives about the potential positive and negative effects of Internet use, even general computer use in school by the children, particularly in the context of the commitment to arts-based curriculum. Compromises have evolved on this team: both computers with Internet access are located in the upper elementary classroom and there is a clearly articulated rule that children may only access bookmarked sites. Bookmarked sites are many, varied, and fully available during play and independent exploration blocks, however. Partly because of his fascination with the intersections between computers and the arts, Mr. G. monitors computer use and continually bookmarks appropriate new web sites.

Yesterday afternoon during a free choice time, 12-year-olds Hattie and Sarah discovered one of Mr. G.'s newest finds from a university archive: a film clip about the minstrel show tradition from Marlon Riggs' "Ethnic Notions" (1987) in which Riggs himself portrays a famous African American singer of the early 1950s removing the blackface makeup required of him in order to perform. Moved by this image, the girls proposed to Mrs. H. that their research project for the urban–rural unit take the form of an in-class museum installation they would call "Artifacts of Slavery." This morning, the girls brainstorm with Mrs. H. other ideas for their museum, eventually leading them to an Internet site featuring the manumission papers of slaves.

THEORIZING THE IN-CLASS MUSEUM

Hattie and Sarah's project includes their own acquisition (a "passing on" to them) of a number of different kinds of knowledge including Internet access skills, the rich content and context of actual historical documents, and reinforcement that a concept of continual social change can help people organize and understand their worlds. In the context of these classrooms, the reality that artifacts represented separately in graphics and language can be unified for representation to others in museum installations is a specifically practical lesson in interpretation that Hattie and Sarah have learned well, and now reinforce for the other children. Again, modeled for all of the children is reinforcement for their own invention of the curriculum of their classroom.

Principle 5

Not necessarily predictable classroom incidents are used to spiral curriculum.

MATERNAL THINKING AND THE
MAKING OF MEANING IN DIVERSE CLASSROOMS

The practice of writing process has added much to the curriculum of elementary classrooms in the early 21st century, including a renewed appreciation for using stories—both telling and writing them—to make sense of life experience in school. Especially significant for these classrooms is Sarah Ruddick's (1989) contention that a mother's stories can help her children locate the meaning of their lives, not just in their individual developing competence and independence, but also their connections to others. Represented here is a subtle shift in perspective from the conventional view that mothers instill confidence so that children can successfully separate in order to achieve and fulfill themselves. Ruddick appreciates that mothers also instill confidence geared at helping children appreciate the importance of their connectedness to others. It is this shift that makes her thinking so valuable to this social reconstructionist teaching team. Much of the social reconstructionist project is the revaluing of connection and community in the context of the increasingly global dominant culture that overvalues independence and autonomy.

In addition, Ruddick's thinking is particularly intriguing in the context of teachers committed to critically facilitating meaning-making in public school classrooms with children from different social classes and cultural backgrounds who have therefore suffered different kinds of social hurts. A convergence of theory from diverse fields including post-structuralist literary criticism and autobiographical or narrative inquiry seems to confirm what many resourceful mothers have long understood: that self does not generate autobiographical memories. Rather, the reverse is the case. In the words of coresearchers Craig Barclay and Rosemary Hodges (1990), "the self is composed anew" in each presentation of autobiographical information.

Those who study the effects of internalized oppression in themselves, in their students, and in an academic context, understand that all internalized oppression causes feelings of social isolation. The potential to contradict feelings of social isolation in the classroom is certainly a strong motivation for teachers who believe that public schools can foster democracy.

Yet, there is a problem with an uncritical understanding of "welcoming the child's home communities into the classroom" as a paradigm for curriculum making. In this chapter, we have appreciated the appropriateness and richness of the connections Ms. R. helped forge among Luis, his Haitian community, Reverend Ausby, and poetry, and the comparably inspired curriculum-making involving the Bosnian refugee photographer Sead Hadziabdic, his own moving photograph, his daughter Dunja, and the urban-rural unit. Yet, the reality is that for some children and their families, it is or feels unsafe for a child to reveal aspects of home life and family history in the classroom. Although the most obvious situation is the potential revelation of illegal alien status, it is also the case that children of gay or lesbian families, children who have survived wars, children living in poverty, and children of nondominant cultures can learn very quickly how unsafe the experience of revealing life stories sometimes is or feels. Children who do not have the privilege of publicly connecting home and school experiences can become untrusting or will shut down emotionally in classrooms that require a kind of boundary-lessness between the two communities.

Still, the inability to articulate the meaning of events in a community with a shared history can deprive children of what this teaching team defines as *education*. It is not just the joy of identification that is at stake, it is also the reality that group identification makes possible all acts of interpretation.

All of these ideas offer the rationale for Principle 5, which recognizes the classroom itself as a real community in which things happen, many of them unpredictably. Spontaneous or unpredictable classroom events have a safe community-with-a-history context in which to explore their meaning. The classroom gives its members a shared history; events in its life can be safely chronicled and interpreted publicly by all, including children who have no other publicly safe communities. Also, children who have learned not to call attention to themselves, or who have learned to seek attention for negative behaviors for reasons including internalized oppression, can find a less-threatening form of attention through their association among others with a funny or unexpected or otherwise meaningful classroom event.

Mrs. D., in particular, has long understood the potential to help shape stronger "selves" through sensitive orchestration of autobiographical history generated in the classroom. She often seizes spontaneous classroom events as subject for the whole-group mini-lesson that typically precedes writing workshop. These mini-lessons usually represent events of systematic instruction, in which a particular language arts skill is emphasized in each lesson. In the final two vignettes, such "instruction" is focused on both the skills of "being good reporters" and "viewing events from multiple perspectives." These vignettes, however, are selected for placement at the end of this chapter because of their demonstration of the natural blurring of the categories of "systematic instruction," constructivism, "practice for…" and "the real thing" in effective arts-based social reconstructionist teaching. Also, in situating the reader with Cedric when he had his accident, vignette 10 introduces to the reader an example of a historical-materialist social studies lesson suitable for all ages of children and adults, a useful resource in arts-based social reconstructionist teaching.

VIGNETTE 11: CEDRIC'S ACCIDENT

The subject of this afternoon's writing mini-lesson (which precedes writing workshop) requires some introduction. Today's lesson, "Seeing events from different perspectives" was a powerful social reconstructionist response to yesterday's "Being good reporters." And "Being good reporters" was, in turn, a collaboratively planned response to a classroom accident that happened the previous Friday, when Mr. G. was convening a group of clay pot makers at the art table responding to the following assignment:

Directions: You are a member of an early human community living by a clay-bottom river. You have realized for the first time the possibility of inventing "a container." Take your time creating this pot out of clay. When everyone in your group has a pot, come together for the following brainstorming activity: How is this discovery of the pot going to change the life of your community in both positive and negative ways?

The gist of the story, dictated by the children one sentence each to Mrs. D. (writing furiously on her chart paper) yesterday, was that Cedric decided to use slab construction to build his pot and reasoned that he needed a heavy object with which to flatten his clay into a pancake. Although Mr. G. was present, Cedric made his move to claim a large plastic jar of white paint from the supply crates behind him before Mr. G. looked up from his conversation with Bonita, another child in the group. Cedric immediately positioned the gallon container of white poster paint above his head and, using all of his (notorious) physical force, slammed it down smack in the middle of a presently very flat clay pancake. Unfortunately, the paint jar's previous user had been careless regarding tightening the jar's lid. Cedric, Mr. G., Bonita, Sandi, Nathan, the art table, and much of the surface area of nearby walls and floors were suddenly plastered with thick, dripping white paint.

Yesterday, Mrs. D. had probed for correct sequencing, details, and exact quotes. As the story was orally reconstructed for her transcription into the classroom chronicle, it became clear that the children had absorbed Mrs. D.'s perspective on classroom accidents; in its retelling, "Cedric's accident" was about connection-making, specifically about how the members of this classroom community were linked through shared experience, caring, and the broader school-wide community. Recreated was a portrait of the principal, Mrs. N., who, hearing the commotion while passing down the hall, rolled up her sleeves and pitched right in with paper towels. Next, the irascible head custodian was called in, and, having quickly sized up the required clean-up operation, supplied Cedric with a person-sized garbage bag, cut a head-size hole in the center of the bottom, and slipped it over Cedric's head so he could get out of his paint-soaked clothing "in privacy." The art teacher, Mrs. Mott, being the only teacher with access to a large sink, was consulted by telephone in her room. She agreed to wash Cedric's clothes herself. Later, the class observed her hanging them on a tree out on the school's front lawn to dry.

This story for the classroom chronicle was completed during yesterday's writing workshop by Cedric and Mrs. D. working with a small group of volunteers while the other children pursued their ongoing writing. But this particularly productive session could not begin until the "lessons" of the whole-group narration had been summarized by Mrs. D. for application to the children's individual work: "Use the speaker's exact words. Show us the envidence!"

VIGNETTE 12: SEEING THINGS FROM DIFFERENT PERSPECTIVES

Today, Mrs. D. begins the mini-lesson by invoking a character out of her own life story that is familiar to the children. Mrs. D.'s very old Aunt Vy, a woman quite dependent on Mrs. D. despite her bluster to the contrary, frequently navigates into this classroom by way of humorous stories. The stories typically focus on some aspect of the conversation during their regular Sunday afternoon outings. The children know that Aunt Vy is hugely entertained by the stories from their own classroom that Mrs. D. brings her.

The entire class is intently focused on the whiteboard at the front of the classroom as Mrs. D. writes the following:

Sunday, Aunt Violet didn't think the story about Cedric and the paint jar accident was funny. She was angry with me!

"Why [are you angry with me]?" I asked her.

"Well, Judith, you shouldn't have put the paint can near the children."

The children are predictably delighted. That Aunt Vy! Always giving Mrs. D. trouble!

MATERNAL STORYTELLING AND THE NURTURANCE OF TEACHERS

The story of Aunt Vy just recounted provides a fine example of the modeling of the tension between "hav[ing] a life very much [one's] own" and being "inextricably connected with others" accomplished by good maternal story-telling, contended Sarah Ruddick (1989, p. 87). But now, in front of the children, the lesson is applied to an important adult authority figure in their lives. The children know from the stories she regularly tells them that Mrs. D. loves and cares for Aunt Vy, even though Aunt Vy clearly drives Mrs. D. crazy. Mrs. D. also values many things about Aunt Vy, including their relationship. Mrs. D.'s commitment to Aunt Vy is an important, moral one; but Mrs. D. is a moral person who requires moral commitments.

Today, Mrs. D. has drawn Aunt Vy into the classroom community as a potential ally for Cedric, which helps Mrs. D. teach him about other possible perspectives on himself and on adult authority. There is somebody looking out for him even outside the safe haven of this classroom. From Aunt Vy's perspective, Mrs. D. is the culprit, the irresponsible adult who gets a little kid in trouble. There is certainly no "bad boy" in Aunt Vy's version of the story.

Aunt Vy, however, is also an important resource for Mrs. D. as a subjective being, outside of her complex maternal story-telling role in this community. In Mrs. D.'s "life very much [her] own," Aunt Vy is a valuable ally to her storyteller self and her writer self. She is funny, and the telling of her stories makes Mrs. D. funny. These realities intimate the potential for nurturance of the teacher herself in a classroom such as this one. Such nurturance is a particularly important consideration when teachers like the ones on this team are taking on, as the point of their work, the difficult challenge of fostering in the children in their care an appreciation of their positive connections with others.

CONCLUSION

By requiring teachers to develop a community of artists in the classroom, the arts-based social reconstructionist curriculum provides an opportunity to attend to the educative place of community and/or communal connections in life. It also provides a model for creating a community in which the world is re-shaped in microcosm. Teachers are part of this re-shaping, having the opportunity to grow in their capacity to artfully shape the life in the classroom by offering a careful balance of (often overlapping) systematic instruction and constructivist practices while simultaneously challenging themselves to expand the boundaries of their own lives. Finally, a more global kind of boundary-expansion is accomplished, in which "the codes of the culture of power" are appropriated for use by everyone in the community engaged in the constructivist project of growing (educational) life itself.

ACKNOWLEDGMENTS

The author wishes to acknowledge the very real individuals who inspired the curriculum featured in this chapter. Reverend Henry Ausby is the poet and social activist minister who contributed his poem "Cotton Pickin' Time" to the "Saratoga Cultural Histories Mural." The mural was a collaborative project between the Binghamton Housing Authority, for which Reverend Ausby was at that time Resident Activities Coordinator, and the students in the Social Action as Curriculum course, a core course in the social justice-focused Master's programs in elementary education at Binghamton University (SUNY). Sead Hadziabdic, the father of Dunja and the Bosnian refugee photographer whose award-winning photo, "The Bridge at Mostar" is also featured in the mural, served as consulting artist to this New York State Council for the Arts Decentralization Grant-funded project. The primary classroom teacher, Mrs. D., is based on the now-retired multi-age primary teacher Judith Davis, the case study of whose classroom literacy curriculum in Sodus, New York, was the subject of the author's dissertation. Judith Davis is the niece of the very real late Aunt Vy. The fourth-grade teacher, Laura Lamash at Woodrow Wilson Elementary School in Binghamton, New York, inspired the upper elementary teacher, Ms. H., including the museum collaboration and photography component of the urban–rural unit. Ms. Lamash has been a powerful force behind the long-term collaboration between Binghamton's Roberson Museum and the Binghamton City School District. The Southern Tier Institute for the Arts in Education does generously loan collections including the Lewis Hine exhibit to educators such as myself, in addition to the school districts who participate in its excellent arts inclusion programs.

REFERENCES

Barclay, C.R., & Hodges, R.M. (1990). La composition de soi dans les souvenirs autobiographiques [The composition of one's self in autobiographical memories]. *Psychologie Française, 35*(1), 59–65.

Birchman, D. (1997). *A green horn blowing.* New York: William Morrow & Co., Morrow Junior Books.

Christian, B. (1987, Spring). The race for theory. *Cultural Critique, 6,* 51–63.

Ciardi, J. (1959). *How does a poem mean?* Boston: Houghton Mifflin.

Clay, M. (1985). *The early detection of reading difficulties* (3rd ed.). Portsmouth, NH: Heinemann.

Delpit, L. (1995). *Other people's children.* New York: The New Press.

Dewey, J. (1990). *The school and society, the child and the curriculum: An expanded edition with a new introduction by Philip Jackson.* Chicago: University of Chicago Press. (Original work published 1902)

Dyson, A.H. (1993). *Social worlds of children learning to write.* New York: Teachers College Press.

Ellsworth, E. (1989). Why doesn't this feel empowering? Working through the repressive myths of critical pedagogy. *Harvard Educational Review, 59*(3), 297–324.

Glass, G.G. (1973). *Teaching decoding as separate from reading: Freeing reading from non-reading to the advantage of both.* Garden City, NJ: Adelphi University Press.

Kliebard, H. (1987). *The struggle for the American curriculum: 1893–1958.* New York: Routledge.

Riggs, M. (1987). *Ethnic notions* [videorecording]. (Available from California Newsreel, 149 Ninth Street, San Francisco, CA, 94103).

Ruddick, S. (1989). *Maternal thinking: Toward a politics of peace.* New York: Ballantine Books.

Sleeter, C.E. (1999). *Making choices for multicultural education: Five approaches to race, class, and gender* (3rd ed.). New York: John Wiley & Sons.

"All" Children
Really Means All Children

When discussing "schools for all children," thinking often focuses on children with cultural or linguistic diversity and children with mild disabilities. Educational policy and research have given increasing attention to how these children can and should be included in general education and educational reform efforts. Too often, however, these discussions exclude children with challenging behavior and children with severe cognitive disabilities, who are often considered "too disruptive" or "unable to benefit." The chapters in this section illustrate how *all* students, even those with more severe disabilities, can be successful members of inclusive schools.

Chapter 8 addresses the needs of students with challenging behavior. An underlying assumption in this chapter is that challenging behavior communicates student concerns. These may be personal needs, such as safety and acceptance, for example, or educational needs, including those related to the curriculum content and instructional strategies. Understanding and responding to these student concerns is our best hope for teaching students with challenging behavior to become responsible citizens in a democratic society. Traditionally, however, the typical response has been to punish and exclude challenging students until they conform to school dictates, with little reflection on the success of this approach. This chapter examines psychoeducational and behavioral perspectives and how related strategies can be combined to support inclusive education for students with challenging behavior.

Chapter 9 addresses the concerns of students with severe cognitive disabilities, who may also have physical and/or sensory disabilities, and who, traditionally, have not been considered candidates to participate in even modified academic programs. The belief underlying this chapter is that classrooms with rich curricula, such as those described throughout Section Two, offer the ideal environment for educating students with severe disabilities. In these classrooms, the learning activities and interactions among children provide a motivating context for students with severe disabilities to learn essential cognitive, language, and social skills.

Providing meaningful, effective, and inclusive education for students with challenging behavior and students with severe cognitive disabilities requires collaboration with teachers, psychologists, and therapists who bring additional skills and perspectives. Some teachers may back away from these students—seeing them as too different or too hard. Teachers who have taken the step forward, however, have discovered that their efforts to accommodate, support, and educate these students has made them better teachers of *all* students. We invite all teachers to take that step forward.

CHAPTER EIGHT

Meeting the Needs of Students with Challenging Behaviors

ROBERT L. CARPENTER & MELISSA A. PRICE

E ducators have struggled with workable approaches to educating students with challenging behaviors since the Education for All Handicapped Children Act of 1975 (PL 94-142). Prior to this federal mandate, children with emotional and behavior disorders were seen as the purview of psychologists and mental health professionals and sometimes the police, but not school teachers. Skinner, Bandura, and many others provided a clearly objective perspective for understanding and dealing with challenging behavior (Bandura & Walters, 1963; Homme, 1969; Meichenbaum, 1977; Skinner, 1953). This perspective emphasizes carefully observing and defining a behavior in question, and viewing that behavior as a function of the environment that surrounds it. Behavior is learned and maintained through external events.

Erickson, Redl, Rogers, and others provided the contrasting theoretical basis for a psychoeducational perspective (Erickson, 1968; Redl, 1966; Rogers, 1969). A psychoeducational perspective focuses first on children as possessing internal processes—feelings, needs, and wishes that they seek to satisfy through their behavior. Interventions involve helping children to reconcile these motivations in their everyday school and community functioning through self-awareness, self-control, human relationships, and realistic problem solving. As we describe and illustrate, neither perspective has been entirely satisfactory for helping children with challenging behavior in the context of a public school.

More than twenty-five years of including students with disabilities in public schools, however, has mellowed theoreticians and has sharpened the skills of teachers and related service providers working with such children. Although a truly unified theory synthesizing various lines of thinking and research still eludes the field of emotional and behavior disorders, day-to-day work with children goes on, practice and pragmatics have informed theory, and some principles for improving the futures of children with challenging behaviors are emerging. This chapter elucidates current practice in terms of both limitations and promises in a context of an inclusive educational environment.

Other chapters in this book describe approaches that can be characterized as systematic, constructivist, or an integration of the two. In general, behaviorism tends to align with systematic approaches, whereas psychoeducational approaches tend to be more constructivist. These are not, however, clean matches, and in this chapter it is more useful to focus initially on the behavioral and psychoeducational approaches. The fundamental problem in writing on this topic was finding a way to discuss approaches to teaching and learning that does not describe the behavioral perspective as the problem and psychoeducational approaches as "the answer, the one right way to intervene," or vice versa. Children and schools are far too diverse and complicated to bifurcate such a discussion, and discussing interventions as either behavioral or psychoeducational may reify something of a false dichotomy. Contrasting and comparing is such a useful and powerful organizational approach, however, that we employ it in explicating the subject of interventions on challenging student behavior. We do not wish to imply any sort of linear continuum between these two perspectives. Our interest is in respecting both the behavioral and the psychoeducational perspective and in providing a framework for making good choices in how to intervene.

Behavior management cannot be considered apart from the established conditions for learning in classrooms and schools. Learning conditions and student behavior are inherently entwined. Other chapters of this book discuss those conditions for learning that constitute the essential ecology within which the classroom operates. At first glance, however, employ a more constructivist philosophy of learning contradicts more established approaches to behavior management. Likewise, much of the current, systematic approach to behavior management seems quite contradictory to a student-centered approach to learning. In this chapter, we explore the apparent dichotomy between constructivist learning and behavioral approaches to management and suggest that the possibility exists for creating a middle ground in which a teacher can create a constructivist environment for learning. In doing so, a teacher will reduce, somewhat, the necessity of intervening frequently in behavior-related problems while still having the option of employing more systematic, intrusive approaches for students who have a greater need for external controls.

FUNDAMENTAL CONSIDERATIONS IN CHOOSING INTERVENTIONS

Conceptualizing a plan for intervening on challenging behavior in a constructivist environment is complex. Some of the principles for guiding thinking, however, emerge from examining three important areas of contention: relationship building, ways of knowing what is happening, and issues of control.

Relationship Building

Central to the child-centered perspective is an emphasis on the teacher's developing a positive relationship with each child. The importance of this relationship follows all we know about child development. For many, this may even be the central reason they became teachers—they enjoy relating with children and youth. Therefore, it should come as no surprise that burnout is so frequent under conditions in which relationship building is difficult, as it sometimes is when working in programs for students with emotional and behavior disorders. Given that children with challenging behaviors are often so rejecting, or seemingly incapable of relationships with adults, it is easy to understand why efforts to include students with emotional or behavior disorders are so problematic.

Paradoxically, relationship building is rarely emphasized in most texts on behavior and classroom management that approach the topic from a behavioral perspective. Behavioral psychology and its emphasis in nationally popular textbooks on behavior disorders (e.g., Kauffman, 2001), coupled with its strong empirical rationale (e.g., Alberto & Troutman, 2002; Miltenberger, 2001), appear to have won the minds of many teacher educators and school administrators. Thus, in too many classrooms, harried teachers have replaced relationship building with rules of behavior.

In contrast, other bodies of literature (e.g., Brendtro & Ness, 1983; Kunc, 2000; Long & Morse, 1996) and many first-person accounts of teachers (e.g., MacCraken, 1977; Marek, 1988; Paley, 1989; Pelzer, 1995) asserted that it is in the hands of the teacher to forge relationships with children because many children do not make relationship building easy at all! They believed that nearly anything is possible in the context of a relationship with a particular child. A child may have had few positive experiences with adults or may have had experiences that would engender serious mistrust of adults. The child's innate need for nurturing relationships may have been so frustrated that he or she may appear to simply have given up on the possibility altogether. Although not all children are "reachable" by every adult (and teachers who continue working with students with challenging behaviors must reconcile themselves to that fact), a positive child–adult connection based on trust, respect, and caring is the fundamental ingredient for the eventual development of children's self-management skills. Children who are able to forge bonds of this type come to construct their behavior with optimism, enthusiasm, and hope. In a strictly systematic environment, however, the same children will likely come to despair in a world of frequent, tangible, but fundamentally irrelevant rewards.

Even rigorous behavioral psychologists working with children who seem unable to respond to a caring relationship would probably acknowledge this fundamental developmental need of nurturing relationships. Traditional behavioral approaches, however, emphasize reinforcement of desired behaviors and suggest a more detached relationship between student and teacher. Some feel that to become emotionally involved is not only unscientific, it risks putting oneself in the position of being manipulated by the student, and unintentionally, rewarding unwanted behaviors. As more appropriate behaviors are rewarded and generalized to other settings, natural reinforcers theoretically begin to sustain what was clinically taught.

Constructivist approaches require that positive relationships develop and that the teacher needs to be very intentional in this development in order for it to occur. First, the teacher must understand that this is a developmental process involving predictable stages of orientation, testing, and inclusion. Teachers must carefully study themselves by reflecting on their own appeal to the student—their nonverbal behaviors, their capacity to relate to the student's experiences and interests, their basic interpersonal skills of active listening, and demonstration of empathy and respect. Each teacher must learn to be an individual worthy of trust—someone who is consistently dependable, caring, supportive, honest, fair, and reasonable.

All of this is not alien to a systematic approach to challenging be-havior. It is more a matter of emphasis and priority. The behaviorist would focus on the power of the teacher to systematically shape ap-propriate behavior. The psychoeducator's focus, conversely, would be more on developing the trusting relationship. Regardless of the theo-retical perspective, teachers need to do both. Teacher preparation must strike a balance between contingency theory and relationship building so the teacher is prepared to operate in this middle ground.

Ways of Knowing

Behaviorists often contend that if something is not measurable, it lacks value. The systematic approach to education has focused closely on the importance and centrality of objective data collection as the basis for decision making. This is irrefutably rational and has been the basis for considerable progress in the education of individuals with disabilities (Kauffman, 1999). Planned interventions based on quantitative data, continuous assessment of task performance, and measurement of be-havior change has become a hallmark of good educational practice. Sole reliance on quantitative empiricism, however, neglects important issues that are revealed by employing other, more qualitative ap-proaches (Pugach, 2001). Preoccupation with quantitative data to the neglect of other forms of information may make a psychologist or an educator feel more like a scientist, but may result in a closing of the mind to other ways of knowing.

Including a constructivist influence in classroom pedagogy opens and encourages a more qualitative approach to understanding the context in which a child learns and expands the teacher's perspective on explanations for students' intentional behaviors. At this point the behavioral and psychoeducational perspectives begin to merge in the now-mandated process of "functional behavioral assessment." Later in this chapter we discuss functional behavioral assessment in much greater detail because this represents a particularly clear and useful outcome of melding perspectives in the enhancement of practice.

Control

Control is the essential nightmare for many new teachers, especially those serving students with emotional and behavior disorders. In *At the Schoolhouse Door* (Knitzer, Steinberg & Fleisch, 1990), a survey of the state of classroom instruction for students identified as "emotionally disturbed or behaviorally disordered" (ED/BD), the authors lamented that so many programs seemed to pivot around concern for maintaining control over students and never got any further; the classroom became dominated by a "curriculum of control." Students identified as ED/BD do, by definition, have problems controlling themselves. Therefore, the starting point for the typical special education intervention program is often to create an environment in which a student is maintained in a controlled state. The basic problem for such programs is to get beyond these external controls. Given that these students are sorely in need of self-control, how do you proceed once you have created a very controlling environment?

Through the use of coercion, threats, and sheer will, the teacher may try to control the student. And the teacher may succeed, but the student never develops self-control under these circumstances. Rather, the student may well come to resent the control, which generalizes to resentment toward the teacher, the school, and the whole educational enterprise, as well as other authority figures outside the school. This approach is chaotic because, so often, order in such programs deteriorates as resentment builds.

Most schools use behavioral principles to create environments that reward compliance. "Levels systems" and elaborate reinforcement schemes too often degenerate into sets of rules, and, as mentioned previously, the rules end up replacing the adult relationships the student so desperately needs. In both the chaotic and the behavioral environment, control is solidly external.

From a behavioral perspective, self-control must be taught. The basic paradigm for this teaching is a carefully managed environment, selectively responsive to the child's attempts at self-controlled behaviors. From a child-centered perspective, what is missing is a nurturing environment in which a child can feel secure, safe, and accepted, in which teachers and peers confirm feelings of belonging in human terms. Can educators teach self-control through any of the many self-control curricula now available (Campbell & Siperstein, 1994; Cartledge & Milburn, 1986; Goldstein, 1999; McGinnis & Goldstein, 2000; Walker, et. al., 1983)? Research equivocates (Gresham et al., 2001). Teachers sensitive to issues of child development enhance the possibility of developing student's self-control with curricula and pedagogy that focus on this as a skill. In a behavioral paradigm, self-control is something to be shaped. From a psychoeducational perspective, self-control is something to be nurtured. The approaches are not mutually exclusive, as external controls need be employed and enforced in certain situations.

By honoring the centrality of relationship building, respecting ways of knowing that go beyond simple measurement, and understanding the paradox of control, we can discern two principles. When operationalizing an intervention to a challenging behavior in a more blended environment, the teacher must align teacher strategies to student concerns, and induce more responsible action in the student by employing techniques that move away from "other-managed" behavior toward "self-managed" behavior.

FUNCTIONAL BEHAVIORAL ASSESSMENT AND POSITIVE BEHAVIOR SUPPORT PLANS

Reauthorization of the Individuals with Disabilities Education Act (IDEA; PL 101-476) in 1997 (PL 105-17) brought about new requirements for addressing the behavior problems of students with disabilities, including the implementation of functional behavioral assessment and the use of behavior intervention plans:

> If the local education agency (LEA) did not conduct a functional behavioral assessment and implement a behavioral plan for the child... the agency shall convene an IEP meeting to develop an assessment plan. (34 CFR 300. 520[b][1]['])
> [A]fter developing the plan described in paragraph (b)(1)(i) of this section, and completing assessments required by the plan, the LEA shall convene an IEP meeting to develop appropriate behavioral interventions to address that behavior and shall implement those interventions. (34 CFR 300.520[b][2])

A variety of perspectives exist for conceptualizing functional behavioral assessment. Iwata et al. (1990) described functional assessment in terms that stress reoccurrence and measurement. By contrast, Foster-Johnson and Dunlap (1993) took a more ecological view, stressing relationships between the person and the environment. To the extent that all behavior assessments and plans start with an identification of the student's concerns and resources, there is the potential to view the process as fundamentally constructivist. Before the process can be identified as truly constructivist, however, the construction of new behaviors must be considered as to their relevance for the culture, personality, and desires of the individual student, rather than their compliance with some expected norm for the school. The psychological construct, locus of control (Rotter, 1966), is useful in understanding how the student will perceive the process. A student who comes to this process with a more externalized locus of control will see this as one more thing being done to him. The degree to which the student is actively involved in the process, however, not only challenges the student's thinking but also builds more internal control systems.

Together, functional behavioral assessment and behavioral intervention planning constitute a problem-solving process. The techniques used to identify and solve the problem may be varied, reflecting the orientation of the person who facilitates the process. The process itself, however, remains constant. The steps are listed in Table 8.1, and discussed in the following pages. Several *assumptions* undergird this process regardless of the process facilitator's orientation:

- *Challenging behaviors serve a function for the student.* Whether this function is determined to be "reinforced behavior," "social communication," or an "expression of a need," all viewpoints recognize the behavior as purposeful.
- *Both behavioral and psychoeducational viewpoints identify context as an important variable.* In behaviorist terms; "setting events" or "antecedents" are sought out as clues. In a psychoeducator's frame, relationships play a vital role in the context.
- *Behavior patterns are thought to be observable or recognizable, though the patterns may not be evident to those performing or most closely affected by the behavior.*
- *The ultimate goal of functional behavioral assessment and behavior intervention planning is to preclude and/or replace challenging behaviors with more acceptable ones.*

As each step in this process is examined, it is evident that elements of several different approaches may be employed; however, the ultimate success will depend on thorough analysis of information, the identification of a valid hypothesis, and a good match between the strategies employed, the context of the problem, and concerns of the student.

STEP 1: GATHER INFORMATION

The first step in gathering information is to identify and define the problem behavior. For years, behaviorists have tried to teach educators to identify the behavior in objective, observable terms. The bulk of incident and discipline reports that cross the average principal's desk, however, are lacking in such objectivity and specificity. It is clear that educators have a ready-made data source in the form of these narratives. The fact that emotionally driven incident reports tell more

Table 8.1. Steps in functional behavioral assessment and behavior intervention planning

1. Gather information.
2. Develop a hypothesis statement.
3. Design a positive behavior support plan.
4. Evaluate effectiveness.
5. Modify the plan as needed.

about the writer's (i.e., the educator's) state of mind than the student's is often overlooked. To this end, it is important to acknowledge the synergy of the individuals in conflict. Qualitative researchers engaged in participant observation recognize that they must distinguish their own voices from those that they seek to observe and record. One way to do this is to create a subscript or commentary that is separate from the text.

In disaggregating a personal response from the observation, it is possible to more accurately represent the events surrounding the behavior. To deny the observer's emotional engagements in incidents of challenging behavior is to deny human nature. If educators learn to record both the observable, "objective" behaviors of students while identifying and recording their own thoughts and behaviors, this recording will provide a deeper and richer source of information, thereby empowering professionals to problem solve more fully. A truly complete understanding of a behavior event is unlikely to be accomplished until the educational climate acknowledges that teachers are integral parts of discipline scenarios rather than neutral figures.

Many teachers are ashamed of their "emotional" responses to students with challenging behaviors and view such responses as "unprofessional." Although the mental health community has long recognized the need for debriefing, educators seem to hold the view that they need to remain above emotional involvement. It is rare that teachers reflect on their own responses to students with challenging behavior in any fashion other than self-admonition or self-defense. If we, as adults, are unwilling or unequipped to engage in self-examination, how will our students learn to reflect on their own behavior for the purpose of making better choices? Consequently, within the documentation process, room exists both for the behaviorist's skill in observation and detail and the psychoeducator's desire to holistically examine the relationships involved in the event. Note this excerpt from an incident report of a teacher assistant on an end-of-the-year picnic with her elementary-level class, which included Matt, a boy with emotional and behavior problems:

On the Friday that we went to the lake, I was paired up with our most difficult 7-year-old student. The bus trip was fine, which made me relax a little bit. Once we arrived, things were okay at first. My student partner at one point became agitated at something and walked over to another little girl on the beach lying on her belly and proceeded to kick sand in her face. I yelled at him and told him that he needed to take a break from everything and sit for a few minutes. He bolted away from me and started to act uncontrollably. . . kicking more sand among other reckless acts. I was behind him and was going to follow him to try and restrain him when he suddenly stopped short and turned toward me. I then fell on top of him. He shouted out some nasty words and dug both hands in the sand and threw it in my face. At that point, the teacher of our classroom intervened. I took a walk to get cleaned up.

The teacher assistant acknowledged that, from the start, she was a little tense to be paired with this student. It would be helpful to know what other feelings she experienced prior to the incident, as the incident began to unfold, and afterward. To frame a hypothesis about what happened here and what sort of behavioral intervention plan is needed, it would be helpful to hear from Matt, his teacher, and others. In the meantime, if the teacher assistant would explore her emotions, she might uncover some clues about how to proceed and what to monitor in herself when dealing one-to-one with this boy in the future.

Resources, Interests, and Difficulties

A general examination of the resources, interests, and skill impairments of a student (and other relevant individuals) may provide clues to the occurrence of certain behaviors. Without knowledge of the social situation with family and peers, important information might be overlooked. For example, an 11-year-old girl was identified as being noncompliant because she refused to participate in physical education classes. The teacher later learned that the refusal had nothing to do with whether she liked or disliked sports or her teacher. Rather, the girl's refusal to participate stemmed from the fact that her slightly older sister excelled in sports and the student sought to avoid comparison. If the teacher had persisted in identifying this problem as simple noncompliance, and addressed it with unpleasant consequences, the teacher would have missed the opportunity to encourage the student by addressing the student's fears of inadequacy. Although symptoms of both issues are the same (refusal to participate), solutions based on relevant information are very different.

Forster-Johnson and Dunlap (1993) encouraged teachers to examine good behaviors as well as problem behaviors. In our special education tradition, we tend to focus on the impairments and problems, and then try to "fix" the negative. All who have worked in schools can recall students who seemed to be perfectly content in one environment or with one teacher but totally out of control in another situation. Matt, the boy who misbehaved during his class field trip, is considered to have emotional and behavior problems; therefore, it is not unusual for the teachers to find his behavior challenging. Still, his team would learn a great deal by examining what is present (or absent) in a successful situation that is not present when problems occur. If his behavior is more problematic during field trips than during activities at school, what is different about school? If some field trips have been more successful than others, what were the features of the successful trips? Does it make a difference if Matt is assigned to a partner or whom that partner is? How do the more successful partners interact with Matt? Analysis of these situations in which problems do not occur can elicit important insights and provide the keys to successful behavioral intervention.

General Health and Well-Being

Often, the first sign that a child is tired, hungry, or sick is deterioration in the child's behavior. When a child routinely misbehaves, it becomes easy to attribute it to the child's "personality." Medical conditions such as allergies, food intolerances, chronic infections, or dental problems can develop gradually, go undetected, and create a level of discomfort that increases the likelihood of conflict. Poor diet or insufficient sleep will likely increase irritability and/or activity levels. Some children live (and sleep) in settings that do not feel safe to them. If physical health and safety issues exist, they must be addressed before other types of interventions are likely to be successful.

Effects of Medication

As growing numbers of children take medication, educators must inform themselves about the medications their students take. For example, medication can be quite helpful for some children with attention-deficit/hyperactivity disorder (ADHD), but the wrong medication or the wrong dosage can wreak havoc. Furthermore, "hyperactivity" and "noncompliance" may be symptoms of other conditions (e.g., depression, obsessive-compulsive disorder) or side effects of other medications. In such situations, medications intended to manage ADHD are, at best, ineffective and, at worst, dangerous for the student. Therefore, it is important for teachers to learn what medications their students take, the intended effects, and the possible side effects. The most complete source of information on medications is the *Physicians' Desk Reference (2002)*, available in many public libraries.

The Student's Context

Imagine a doctor who based the diagnosis of your medical condition on the opinion of your parents and employer without meeting you or examining you. Such conduct might be considered malpractice. Yet, individuals and committees that write behavior intervention plans without ever observing the student, visiting his or her classroom and home, or interviewing the student directly are making the same mistake: prescribing treatment from second-hand information. If the functional behavioral assessment and behavior intervention plan are based on the perceptions of teachers and school personnel alone, the decisions are not well informed. Understanding the nature of the general context can lead to questions regarding the specifics of a setting, situation, or event.

Behaviorists use terms such as *setting events, antecedents,* and *consequences* to describe what happens before and after an incident, as viewed from an external perspective. These details are recorded using various charts and counting techniques. Unfortunately, these methods are often associated with highly regulated, self-contained special education classroom settings, in which the general context of the special class and the use of novel recording techniques may be variables that actually contribute to the problem behavior. Nonetheless, these data can provide useful information, especially when unobtrusive methods are used to gather information. A remarkably unobtrusive way to record such data in an inclusive classroom is to keep a video camera running throughout the school day. Staff and students quickly forget about the camera and, when incidents occur, the activities and interactions before, during, and after the event can be viewed and relevant data can be recorded.

In contrast, the psychoeducational perspective encourages more use of narratives and interviews to yield clues about the function of a behavior. The goal of this data collection is to view the incident from the perspective of the student. Why does the student behave in this manner? What does the individual's behavior communicate? What occurs as a result of the behavior? Natural, existing data sources include student journals and interviews, parent conversation and correspondence, and teacher narratives. Unfortunately, these data sources are not used consistently, and some professionals seem reluctant to value the viewpoints of these "nonprofessional" individuals.

Just as both quantitative and qualitative research has the potential to yield insight, so too can both forms of data collection inform functional behavioral assessment. A full examination of information from the psychoeducational and behavioral approaches permits us to view the situation from the inside and the outside. For this reason, the tools used to conduct a functional assessment may include the following:

- Team discussions (e.g., other teachers, an instructional support team, a pre-referral team)
- Interviews with the student, peers, staff, parent and other service providers (e.g., coaches, day care providers, mental health providers, court-appointed officers, doctors)
- Rating scales, ABC analyses, function tests, charting and scatterplots
- Skills assessment, academic tests, performance tests, student portfolios, and samples of student products
- Social skills inventories, videotapes, and direct observation
- A review of historical records, social records and other archived information
- Lesson plan records, attendance records, grade books

STEP 2: DEVELOP A HYPOTHESIS STATEMENT

The ultimate purpose of a functional behavioral assessment is to determine why an incident occurs. Every rationale, however, must be a hypothesis, because neither an observer nor an individual involved in an incident may know the definitive reason the event occurred. The behavioral approach tends to assess the problem from an external point of view, so it often focuses on changing the individual at the center of the event. From this perspective, it is important that the person-centered planning used for academic assessment should not become person-centered blaming when it comes to behavior assessment. The psychoeducational perspective examines the factors that influence

behavior as viewed from the individual's perspective, including an intense analysis of the role of the environment and others related to the
individual or event. This approach has been criticized as permitting or
excusing the individual from personal responsibility. Did Matt's behavior on the field trip cause the rest of the environment to respond
with a ripple effect? Or did the situation cause Matt to respond in a
predictable fashion? In reality, both orientations are necessary to acknowledge the dynamic nature of behavior, so both perspectives must
be considered when generating hypotheses about why challenging behavior occurs.

The choices of hypotheses and subsequent interventions often
have as much to do with the nature of the student as with the preferences and orientations of the educators. From a constructivist view, a
teacher most likely will not, and perhaps cannot, implement an approach or plan that is in stark contrast to his or her own viewpoint. If
the hypothesis focuses on the student as the source of the problem, it
is more likely to be acceptable to the teacher than the student. If the
hypothesis identifies the problem as stemming from classroom
arrangements or instructional practices, however, it is likely to be
more favorable to the student than the teacher. In order to develop a
hypothesis that is mutually acceptable, all interests need to be represented. This approach mediates both the behavioral (external) and the
psychoeducational (internal) orientations.

Determining why challenging behavior occurs has been an important issue for teachers, psychologists, and psychiatrists. Glasser
(1989) viewed student behavior as motivated by one or more of four
basic needs: belonging, freedom, power, and fun. Dreikurs (1968,
1972), extending Adlerian theory, also understood school behaviors to
be motivated by internal needs: attention, power, revenge, or helplessness. Durand and Crimmins (1992) developed and validated a scale
to determine the function of a behavior. Although the scale was developed to assess students with severe and/or multiple disabilities, it is
useful with other populations. With careful attention to students and
the circumstances surrounding their behavior, these motivational
schemes are all helpful in formulating hypotheses about the functions
of a behavior. Despite the range of functions to be considered, however,
some bias exists to label challenging behavior as "attention-seeking,"
even with contrary evidence. Although some students just want to be
the center of attention, more often challenging behavior is an attempt
to communicate a message (Donnellan, Mirenda, Mesaros, & Fassbender, 1984). Donnellan et al. (1984) identified 30 different messages
that a student may try to communicate through challenging behavior.
Evaluation of children and youth with emotional and behavioral prob-

lems revealed significant but previously unnoticed impairments in receptive and expressive language (Ruhl, Hughes, & Camarata, 1992; Warr-Lieper, Wright, & Mack, 1994). These findings suggest that students with challenging behavior may struggle with some communication, reifying the need for educators to carefully consider the full range of possible functions for challenging behavior.

Hypothesis generation is not limited to professionals. Anyone associated with the student, including parents, siblings, or playmates, may have insight into the possible cause of a problem. In any case, the ultimate purpose of this stage of the process should be to answer the question "Why is this happening?" with the intent of solving a problem rather than assigning blame.

STEP 3: DESIGN A POSITIVE BEHAVIOR SUPPORT PLAN

No one set of strategies or approaches best meets the concerns of all students with emotional or behavior difficulties. Each positive behavior support plan is unique to the student, the teacher, and the situation and based on the findings of the functional behavioral assessment. The positive behavior support plan model developed by Syracuse University's Child-Centered In-service Training and Technical Assistance Network (Janney, Black, & Ferlo, 1989) and refined by Janney and Snell (2000) provides a framework for generating possible solutions. In this model, all participants (including the student) work together to identify strategies to prevent behavior difficulties, teach alternative responses, and respond in crisis situations. What makes this model so appealing is that its proactive components seek to support and develop the student. Too often, behavior plans consist solely of consequences, rewards, or emergency intervention strategies (Amos, 2000). Although some reactive elements may be necessary for some students, they can only come into play after an event (i.e., after the damage is done to one's self, one's environment, or others). Prevention and teaching are proactive strategies that stem the escalation of situations and reduce the need for reactive measures. As illustrated in Figure 8.1, the bulk of the behavior plan should be prevention and teaching. A school wide discipline plan should provide elements that support both the prevention and crisis intervention elements of this plan while teaching the student, peers, and others to handle situations differently. Although the philosophical orientation of educators may vary from behaviorism to a psychoeducational approach, a plan that clearly identifies the intended outcome for the student must result. Also, strategies that are effective and culturally and personally respectful, and that provide a means for evaluating the effectiveness of implementation must be present. For these reasons, we refer to this type of behavior intervention plan as a positive behavior support plan. In the following pages, we discuss a wide variety of strategies that could comprise the plan.

Many "expert" plans fail because they are neither fully understood nor embraced by those expected to implement them. No single individual nor even any group of adults should be responsible for conducting the functional behavioral assessment or developing the positive behavior support plan. Group consensus is essential to ensure that strategies are amenable to all of the parties involved, including the student. Ultimately, a desired outcome is self-management, with the locus of control moving from the teachers and parents to the student. If a student can achieve self-management, the likelihood of increasing successful interactions across multiple settings is greatly enhanced. For this reason, student participation in the planning process is critical.

Positive behavior support plans may be developed for any environment or circumstance, including classrooms, the cafeteria, the school bus, or field trips. The selection of strategies is particular to the

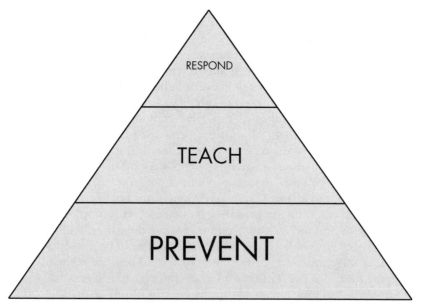

Figure 8.1. The model of a positive behavior support plan can be represented in triangular form.

Table 8.2.   Criteria for the selection of behavior support strategies and interventions

Ensures both physical and psychological safety

Maintains and enhances dignity

Builds on strengths

Is culturally responsive, age appropriate, and socially acceptable

Is minimally intrusive to the learning and social environment and is generalized

Is congruent to or a close of approximation of typical expectations

Builds capacity; increases opportunities for self-management

Enhances opportunities for positive interaction with others

Has consensus for support and sustainability

Uses realistic amounts of resources (e.g., time, personnel, materials)

Is supported by research

circumstances, concerns, and personalities of those involved, but should meet certain guidelines. Building on the work of Meyer and Evans (1989), Table 8.2 lists general criteria that should guide selection of components for the plan. Clearly, aversive procedures such as electric shock, restraint, and corporal punishment do not meet these criteria and are not endorsed. Likewise, it is important to note that if any party imposes the plan without stakeholders buying in, the plan is less likely to succeed. For this reason, educators are strongly encouraged to use outside consultants only as group facilitators. People who do not have a direct stake in the outcome of a plan and do not have first-hand knowledge of the individual and the circumstances can only guess at what best suits the situation. Table 8.3 shows a plan generated for Matt after the incident on his class picnic. Although Matt's behavior on the class picnic was serious, his positive behavior support plan responded to a persistent pattern of problem behavior under similar circumstances, not one isolated incident. Although additional information may be needed, this is the type of comprehensive plan that a group effort can produce.

STEPS 4 AND 5: EVALUATE EFFECTIVENESS AND MODIFY THE PLAN AS NEEDED

Everyone involved in developing the plan should be involved in evaluating and modifying it. The process of developing, evaluating, and modifying Matt's plan offers opportunities for peer involvement and

Table 8.3.   A positive behavior support plan for Matt

Problem statement: During field trips, Matt refuses to follow instructions from adults and is aggressive toward adults and other students.

Hypothesis: Matt doesn't like being paired with an adult. Matt doesn't know how to initiate social interactions in unstructured environments and activities

Prevent	Teach	Respond
Adequate adult supervision	Student participation in preparation	Discipline plan in case of misbehavior, including how to monitor students
Buddy system established	–Group lists possible activities during field trip	
Information given to students and adults prior to the field trip	–Group lists materials needed	Alternate transportation arrangements for emergencies
–Review seating arrangements on the bus with the class.	–Identify possible resources that will be needed (including personnel) and draw or locate a map.	Plan and assignments in place to search for missing children
–Review general rules for field trip (including safety, swimming, bathroom, and food rules) and bus ride, as dictated by school-wide policy and student discussions	–Packing	Training in restraint techniques that will not injure either party, including clear guidelines for use
	Rules and expectations for the field trip, defined by peer group (including Matt)	Parent and emergency personnel notification
–Review a map of the facility or grounds to locate Bathrooms Parking area Eating areas Active play zone Water play zone Shady areas Off-limit territory Adult resources (including first-aid) Places for rest, reflection, and quiet play	Problem solving strategy that considers specific ways to initiate conversation and play, to be used by peer group (including Matt)	
	Problem solving strategy that considers specific ways to respond to verbal abuse, teasing, and other provocations on the field trip, to be used by peer group (including Matt)	
Procedures for emergency responses to rain, injury, and so forth	–Ignore	
Proper supplies, including	–Select an alternative activity	
–Extra food and drink	–Swap partners	
Extra clothes, towel(s), blanket	–Identify safe solo or parallel play options	
–Sunscreen and insect repellent	–Choose strategies to select alternate play activities without alienating others	
–Quiet play alternatives (e.g., cards, dominoes)	–Self-induced time out	
–Sand toys	–Ask adult for help	

Table 8.3.   *(continued)*

Prevent	Teach	Respond
–Emergency telephone numbers, cellular, or mobile telephone	Discussion of resources available during the field trip.	
–Medical supplies (e.g., student medications such as allergy medication, Epi-Pens, insulin)	Role play before the field trip, including ways to generate conversation and play.	
–First aid supplies	Role play self-management scenarios.	
Environment in which group and personal play preferences are honored, mutual respect and responsibility is expected.	Staff discussion and role play	
Job sharing plan (e.g., carrying supplies, clean up, attendance)	–Strategies to cue appropriate behavior	
Backup adult personnel for emergencies or cancellations.	–Nonthreatening ways to interrupt behavior likely to become a problem	
Communication plan with chain of response and responsibility		
Discussion of authority adults do and do not have		

decision making, and can be a learning experience for the class. Parental and professional involvement should model cooperation and communication and facilitate the development of relationships with, and for, students. This is a recursive process, so the relationships and processes initially established to develop the plan lay important foundations for how the plan will later be evaluated and modified.

STRATEGIES TO PREVENT, TEACH, AND RESPOND TO CHALLENGING BEHAVIORS

As discussed previously, positive behavior support plans include three categories of interventions: prevent, teach, and respond. A strong investment in strategies to prevent and teach reduces the frequency when planned strategies to respond must be instituted. The following sections introduce a range of strategies commonly used in schools.

Strategies to Prevent Behavior Disruption

Designing and orchestrating an environment with high rates of student success and low rates of failure should be a goal of every teacher. It is also the key to realizing low rates of challenging behavior. So, in many ways, other chapters of this book may be thought of as a collection of "preventive strategies." Other chapters have discussed ideas about grouping, appropriate curriculum, and child-centered pedagogy in great detail, reflecting approaches that are both constructivist and systematic. Figure 8.2 presents a series of interventions, some described in greater detail in other chapters of this text.

Beginning at the base of the triangle, interventions are ordered from the more fundamental prerequisites for any sort of workable classroom to more student-centered opportunities to exercise and build interpersonal resources and skills. Thus, addressing basic physiological needs for bodily comfort, including accessible, satisfying environmental arrangements, is the essential foundation, without which other interventions will be less successful, if successful at all. Children need rest and food, adequate light, reasonably comfortable surroundings and so forth in order to learn. Next in the triangle are the considerations for predictable classroom routines, structures, and learning rituals that allow students to frame their days and to anticipate what will happen next. Thorough planning and preparation by the teacher is an essential ingredient in a classroom designed to minimize challenging

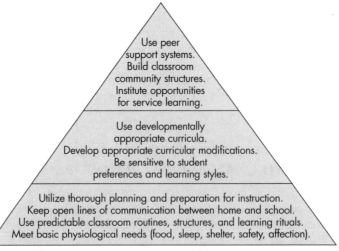

Figure 8.2. Practical strategies for preventing challenging behaviors follow the triangular model of a positive behavior support plan.

behavior. The absence of such preparation is a good predictor of a long and difficult day for everyone in the classroom. The positive behavior support plan developed after Matt's field trip illustrates several of these prevention strategies. Rounding out this group of preventive interventions are open lines of communication between the teacher and the student's home. When properly conceived as a framework for support for the student's academic welfare, these lines help to bind the student in an ecology of caring.

The next group of preventive interventions, a developmentally appropriate curriculum, sensitivity to student preferences and learning styles, and appropriate curricular modifications or adaptations for individual learners, are in no particular order, but collectively represent a second level of prophylaxis to challenging student behavior. These interventions are neither particularly behavioral nor especially psychoeducational; they simply represent the essence of good teaching. Students who can become appropriately engaged in a lesson have less reason or need to act out, even if their self-control is minimal. Simply offering students choices has proven to be an especially powerful strategy, greatly underutilized in classrooms governed by rules.

A third group of interventions can be characterized as more pedagogically imaginative and psychoeducationally healthy approaches to addressing the curriculum. A variety of small peer group designs have been successfully used to enhance student learning. Such peer support systems utilize mutual responsibility toward completion of a task. A classroom becomes transformed from a large group of individuals who must independently navigate learning challenges to several small groups who take responsibility for portions of an academic task or activity. A student with emotional or behavior problems may find this more supportive environment less threatening, or surrounded by peers unintentionally modeling appropriate interpersonal skills, such a student may learn these skills from the others.

Building a sense of community in the classroom is an intervention similar, in many ways, to peer support systems. In this case, a variety of activities such as regular classroom meetings or class-wide projects that build an identity of oneness and collective support by the whole group can foster an important, supportive environment for all students, particularly those who have not experienced this through a family or a sport team. (See Kreidler, 1991, 1997, for guidance in adopting strategies of this type.)

Service learning activities are a further extension of classroom practice in which feelings of responsibility are generated through peer support and classroom community. Ongoing activities such as tutoring younger students or growing vegetables for a community food pantry in the context of a science or social studies unit provide opportunities for all students to experience the virtue of being helpful to others. These experiences bind students in a compact of healthy feelings of community, enhance learning, and deter challenging behaviors that might have resulted from more competitive and less supportive environments.

Unfortunately, students with challenging behaviors are frequently excluded from these opportunities to work in groups because they lack the requisite social skills. Proponents of cooperative learning stress that the benefits of group work do not come automatically from just telling students to work together, even for students with "good" behavior (e.g., Johnson & Johnson, 1998; Slavin, 1995). First, learning activities must be structured to ensure interdependence, so each member of the group has clear roles and responsibilities essential to completing the group task. Then, students must be taught to work together, to use questioning and active listening effectively, to negotiate and problem solve, and to ensure that all contribute and no one dominates or withdraws. Therefore, the strategies to prevent challenging behaviors start to overlap with teaching.

Strategies to Intervene on Challenging Behaviors Through Teaching

A variety of comprehensive models (e.g., Mendler, 1992; Savage, 1999) provide guidance to teachers seeking help with managing challenging behaviors. These authors typically describe a context or set of ecological prerequisites in order for the model to be logically consistent. Such models then go on to present, in detail, a philosophical stance and how that can be actualized, often utilizing some combination or iteration of some of the interventions listed in Table 8.4. Such models rep-

Table 8.4. Strategies for intervention based on teaching

Positive reinforcement

Differential reinforcement

Self-awareness and self-control

Self-reinforcement

Contracting

Social skills training

Cognitive restructuring

Cooperative learning

resent systems of thinking about children or youth. Wolfgang (2001) classified many of these models as relationship/listening, confronting/ contracting, rules/consequences, or coercive/legalistic.

The purpose of this chapter is not to provide a comprehensive model for each of the proven interventions a teacher might use to meet challenging behavior. Instead, it is to suggest a representative range of interventions and discuss how they might be used in a constructivist classroom that can include students whose behavior is challenging. We suggest that a continuum exists among more behavioral and more psychoeducational interventions, between more systematic and more constructivist approaches. We assert that constructivist teaching and systematic behavior management can coexist, that explicit teaching of behavior for some students can be accommodated in an environment in which students actively construct learning. In Figure 8.2, we have identified only those interventions that are doable, that can be utilized with resources existing in the average classroom, that are not so complex as to be beyond the skills of the average teacher, and that, properly utilized, are culturally respectful of all students.

A staple intervention strategy is the use of specific procedures for teaching new social skills (e.g., Campbell & Siperstein, 1994). The model is well established, with a clear definition of the skill to be learned, followed by a small group discussion of the skill's potential utility in the students' worlds. Then the teacher or a respected peer of the students models the skill in a role-play format. Students then engage in their own role-play, practicing the new skill and critiquing each other. Finally, the teacher designs a program for generalization to real-life situations. Skill-building programs may address specific skills such as "accepting criticism" or "handling teasing," or more general skills like "self-control" might be taught as such a skill could be useful across a variety of environments and contexts. In a global sense, social skills instruction and the ability to get along with other people is analogous to phonics and reading. One must have the basic skills to enjoy and effectively participate in the social world just as phonics skills are necessary as a condition for literacy. Also, just as phonics skills can be taught in the context of a whole language process, basic social skills can be taught in the process of participating in the social world. Unfortunately, students with challenging behaviors may not have acquired some social skills, may act in ways that schools do not tolerate, and may get themselves into trouble as a result. When students do not know appropriate social skills, punishments will not correct the situation any more than punishment will teach a child to read. Very explicit instruction might be required. A classroom designed around constructivist principles must also provide direct instruction for accommodating the learning needs of students who are deficient in social skills and who have not learned new skills through implicit modeling.

Social skills instruction may be thought of as teaching the individual how to behave in certain problematic situations in ways that are in his or her best interest. Each skill involves remembering several common sense steps, or learning points, to guide thinking and verbal behavior. Sometimes, students' challenging behaviors represent not so much a situational skill deficiency as they do an inadequate approach to thinking through a social problem. It is less a question of how to behave, but rather an absence of cognitive organization about how to think about the social situation. Various programs and curricula have been developed under the general category of cognitive restructuring (e.g., Eggert, 1994; ICPS, 1992; Kaplan, 2000; Nichols, 1996, 1997). Through a variety of materials for self-analysis, impulse control, and simplified problem-solving procedures, a student learns a process, a general cognitive strategy, for problem solving. The student might be taught to be alert to certain situations that are especially problematic for him or her, such as interactions that put him or her in danger of becoming an object of teasing. The student then initiates a strategy employing physiological relaxation followed by a set of questions to him- or herself. What do I want to happen? What do I have to do if this is to happen? What are the short- and long-term costs/benefits of such a plan, and what is the likelihood that the plan will unfold as I want it to? If that is not a good plan, what else can I do? The presumption is that a student, once taught these cognitive structures, will be better able to handle the challenges of a typical classroom and school.

From an educational perspective, children with emotional and behavior problems (as well as children from other cultures) have learned sets of interaction patterns that differ from what is expected in U.S. schools. Although many children will learn preferred social and problem-solving skills incidentally, some children will need them taught directly. Healthy classroom environments support and encourage such behavior, but many students who present challenging behaviors need more explicit feedback about whether their behaviors meets class and school norms, with a more intense and intentional approach to reinforcement. Rewards may take many forms, from food to privileges to tokens, and be offered on various schedules. Still, the fundamental principle is that the reward must be something the student values enough to continue performing the behavior that preceded the reward. Systematic functional behavioral assessment, as discussed previously, might identify reinforcers for specific behaviors within a variety of environments from very structured to more open settings.

Similarly, differential reinforcement designs may be utilized to reduce problem behaviors by reinforcing more desirable alternatives. Such structured interventions have been employed successfully in a variety of real classroom environments, not just the clinical environments in which they were originally developed and refined. During functional behavioral assessment, for example, a team may hypothesize that a student would be more capable of learning social studies if she were present for the discussion than if he or she were wandering about the room. In addition to strategies to prevent the problem behavior (e.g., more hands-on learning), the team may agree on a differential reinforcement procedure to help teach desired behavior during class discussions. During group discussions of recently completed reading in social studies, the student may receive differential reinforcement for "in-seat behavior," which simultaneously reduces "out-of-seat behavior," for example. Particular behaviors lend themselves to specific structured reinforcement interventions in a wide variety of contexts including those using constructivist pedagogy.

Constructivist principles promote maximal opportunity for individuals to make decisions about their learning. This value is supported by the behaviorist paradigm in which the teacher incrementally shifts some data collection and reinforcement responsibilities from the adult to the student. Although individuals vary in their ability and readiness to engage in self-measurement and reinforcement, these self-monitoring behaviors are the essential overt structures requisite for self-control and eventual self-reflection. Selectively adopting these types of "behavioral tools" enables educational environments, including those grounded on constructivist principles, to accommodate the concerns of students with more challenging behaviors.

Contracting for behavior change has become a popular form of intervention among teachers dealing with challenging behaviors. Because this intervention, in principle, requires the active participation of the student, it represents something of a cusp between more teacher-devised and controlled approaches and more student-involved approaches. One can imagine a continuum with, on one end, the teacher taking near sole responsibility for identifying and defining the target behavior, a scheme for monitoring, and the terms for reinforcement, with the student participation limited to little more than signing the document. At the other end is full collaboration between student and teacher regarding all aspects of the process. Initially, some students may need the teacher to play a large role in the process until they become more comfortable with what is expected of them as collaborators. As a teaching strategy, however, the teacher would never impose a contract on a student; instead, the teacher engages the student in a reflective process, consistent with functional behavioral assessment. The behavior contract may be seen as a vehicle through which the student and the teacher develop a relationship. The document and the terms of reinforcement become less important as motivation to behave differently becomes more internalized through the process of negotiation and sharing between teacher and student. This is analogous to scaffolding arrangements that could be employed between a teacher and a student when any new content is learned.

Strategies for Responding to Challenging Behaviors

We have discussed a number of ways in which challenging behaviors might be prevented in a classroom through ecological, curricular, and pedagogical interventions. We have also presented a number of interventions that fall under the category of "teachable skills" to address specific problems that might be identified through functional behavioral assessment. Several of these were used in the functional behavioral assessment illustration developed for the field trip incident. In order to avoid future problems, a teacher must be capable of preventing as much challenging behaviors as possible and teaching new skills to students that are likely to engage in such behavior. In some instances, however, that will not be enough. Teachers must also be prepared to respond to unacceptable behavior when it does occur. A responsive and healthy environment and a capacity to teach new skills that students need to function in that environment does not mean that some students will not make bad choices, misinterpret actions of others, or act badly on the basis of habit or desperation. Table 8.5 presents a representative sample of ways in which the teacher and the school may respond to challenging behaviors. Some of the interventions are more behavioral; some are more aligned with a psychoeducational paradigm. All conform to the requirements of being doable by a classroom teacher in the context of a typical school, although some may require additional time or space that would be possible only with assistance through special education support or other community agencies.

Since Redl and Wineman (1952) first described "techniques for the manipulation of surface behavior," verbal and nonverbal interventions have been revisited and reworked several times (Charles, 2001; Fagen & Hill, 1977; Savage, 1999). The core ideas have held up well for 50 years. Many effective teachers intuitively use the strategies of "planned ignoring," "proximity and touch control" (unobtrusively moving closer to a student), and "tension decontamination through humor" (joking to lighten the mood). The notion of identifying specific verbal and nonverbal behaviors in one's repertoire, and consciously

Table 8.5. Strategies for responding to challenging behavior

Nonverbal and verbal interventions
Logical consequences/response cost and time out
Life space intervention
Back-up systems

arranging them from those that are mild to those rather intrusive has been a helpful way of conceptualizing how teachers have coped with classroom behavior without losing the academic momentum and damaging a fragile ego or a teacher–student relationship. This extends and expands on the work of Kounin (1977) and others who sought to understand how it is that some teachers possess skills that enable them to influence groups better than others, and how, to some degree, such skills can be taught to new teachers. From a psychoeducational perspective, Redl and his successors remind us how important it is to catch misbehavior early and match it with a specific intervention that provides the offender with a graceful opportunity to stop.

Some of these verbal and nonverbal interventions also fit nicely into the behavioral paradigm. A nonverbal intervention such as planned ignoring, for instance, may be interpreted in terms of simple reinforcement theory. During functional behavioral assessment, a team hypothesized that the function of a student "calling out" in class was to get attention, and the teacher's unwitting responses maintained the behavior. If the hypothesis was correct, denying the reinforcement of the attention would result in the eventual discontinuation of the behavior. When this occurs, of course, a more acceptable alternative (preferably one that fulfills the same function) needs to be taught and reinforced. A verbal intervention such as the use of humor to relieve class tension around an incident may be viewed as a stimulus/response that cues laughter and reinforces smiling and laughing behaviors in the group. The point is that many of these interventions may be understood as either psychoeducational or behavioral. They are all part of orchestrating a class through an educational activity and coping with unwanted behavior when it occurs in a manner that encourages self-control or is at least not psychologically destructive.

Teachers enter into tricky territory when employing consequences to reduce the likelihood of future unwanted behavior. Ideally, the world operates in such a way that negative consequences are naturally occurring responses to bad choices—a headache following an evening of too much drinking, for instance, or a fall following skiing too fast. Nature, however, usually does not provide such sorts of consequential events following challenging behaviors in classrooms, so teachers and administrators attempt to create them by contriving punishments. But the prohibitive problems with using punishments are amply documented in nearly every text on behavior management. (e.g., Hoover & Kindsvatter, 1997; Martin & Pear, 1999; Martin, Sugarman, & McNamara 2000; Wolfgang, 2001). Punishment characteristically loses its deterrent properties while increasing resentment. The resultant resentment from frequent applications of punishment eventually generalizes to the whole educational enterprise. That is, the punished child begins to hate school and, over time, learns how to be punishing and cruel. But what is a teacher to do if punishment is so strongly contraindicated, assuming there is ongoing attention to the prevention and teaching interventions, and unacceptable behavior still occurs? An intriguing constructivist alternative to punishment is logical consequences. As described by Levin and Shanken-Kaye, "a logical consequence is a consequence that, although requiring the intervention of the teacher or another person, has some logical connection to the behavior that precedes it, and so it is not viewed as arbitrary or capricious" (1996, p. 122). A student must make up work missed when he or she is late to class, for instance, or a child is told that he or she must work individually because he or she has been uncooperative within the group. The teacher announces the consequence matter of factly, without rancor. The logical connection between the challenging behavior and the consequence is sufficiently obvious that students are able to understand clearly how they got themselves into the unwanted predicament.

Behaviorists, working within the rules of reinforcement, have at their hands a very similar intervention. In the response-cost strategy, specific amounts of a reinforcer are withdrawn from the student (in the form of some quantifiable unit like chips or time) contingent on an inappropriate behavior. By the use of prescribed rules for presentation or withdrawal of quantities of the reinforcer, contingent on student behavior, students can clearly make the connection between their behavior and their circumstance. So, response cost and logical consequences operate in much the same manner. After experiencing interventions such as logical consequences or response cost, students learn to anticipate the future and, presumably, make adjustments in their behavior. Whether learned in the natural and everyday sequence of classroom events, or in a more systematic and planned fashion through logical consequences and response cost, anticipation of costs and consequences is a necessary prerequisite to self-control.

Time out bears discussion here as it is so frequently used as an after-the-fact intervention, but also routinely misused. Procedurally, time-out is fairly simple: A student is removed from a group or activity for a certain amount of time after an unacceptable behavior. As a behavioral strategy, however, it is important to recognize that time out is the abbreviation of time out from positive reinforcement. For time out to be effective, then, the student must perceive the group or activity from which he or she is being removed as reinforcing. If nothing in the learning situation is reinforcing, however, the student may not mind leaving. If the learning situation is downright unpleasant, or if the function of the student's behavior is to assert some power or have some fun at the teacher's expense, the student may actually experience removal as rewarding. If the student is giving his or her best effort but continues to disappoint the teacher, removal is not time out from positive reinforcement, but just another corrosive and punishing experience. As with other interventions, time out is best used when functional behavioral assessment indicates that it will be an effective component of a positive behavior support plan.

Life space crisis intervention (LSCI) is a counseling approach specifically developed for use by teachers and staff in schools or other environments in which children and youth experience crises and their behavior unravels (Long, Wood, & Fecser, 2001). Conducting an LSCI requires specific training. The adult employs basic counseling skills such as active listening and empathic responding while drawing out the perceptions and feelings of the student regarding the immediate incident in which he or she was involved. A mental time line is constructed, and the central issue is clarified through carefully listening to the student. Often, the central issue is very different from what initially seems apparent to both the student and the adult. Children and youth crises tend to fall into one of several generally predictable patterns of self-defeating behavior. The insight the student gleans from understanding how his or her behavior is connected to his or her feelings and perceptions and the environmental responses provide the opportunity for the student to learn new skills or consider different ways of viewing his or her world.

This is clearly an intervention within the realm of a constructivist philosophy. It is respectful of alternative interpretations of events, although generally more structured and goal-directed than most counseling approaches. The child's perceptions and feelings are clearly central to the intervention process. Interestingly, there is still great latitude for other systematic interventions within the LSCI approach. In the process of an interview, it may become apparent that the crisis in which the child was involved was a situation in which the child acted badly because he or she lacked more appropriate social skills, for instance. At this point, the adult and the child arrive at a teachable moment. They both realize, or the adult realizes and helps the child to understand, that things could be better in the future if the child could learn some appropriate new skills. Enter systematic social skill instruction. Such a chain of events is the apotheosis of addressing challenging behavior in the "middle ground" among psychoeducational and behavioral models.

No teacher can be expected to manage all forms of challenging behavior. Schools need to formalize a system of back-up support for assisting a teacher who is coping with resistant challenging behavior in his or her classroom. Levin and Shanken-Kaye (1996) described agreements among teachers in which one teacher agrees to accept a disruptive student from another class on a short-term basis until the student makes a written commitment to return and use more acceptable behavior. Such arrangements are preferable to the more widely used in-school suspension model that is often characterized by an atmosphere of punishment and provokes counter-aggressive tendencies in the student. The teacher buys for the student and him- or herself a little time and space, whereas the onus of responsibility for returning to the classroom rests with the student. Details for such arrangements are idiosyncratic to the individuals involved, the school climate, and the resources available. Making such arrangements calls for the same precautions as for time out: the teacher must ensure that his or her classroom is somewhere this student wants to be, through ongoing attention to prevention and teaching strategies, and functional behavioral assessment.

Using a different sort of back-up system, the teacher with the difficult student arranges to meet with other teachers of that student and other school staff such as the school psychologist, counselor, and administrator. Many schools have formalized this arrangement in the form of teacher assistance teams. The process of functional behavioral assessment is initiated just as discussed earlier in this chapter. Outcomes from such an assessment might involve any sort of feasible response to the function of the challenging behavior—rearranging antecedent or consequent events, adjusting pedagogical practices, better planning, and so forth. Colleagues, as a part of their duties as teachers, can be of real assistance to each other in responding to challenging behaviors. Teachers must never feel that they need to deal with their students solely by themselves. Expansions of this concept are full-service schools (Dryfoos, 1998), in which health, mental health, child protective services, and other social services are provided within schools; in which children and families in need can gain access to them easily; and in which wraparound services (Eber, Nelson, & Miles, 1997) are available that work together to devise a coordinated, interagency plan of care to address the complex, interrelated concerns affecting the family system (including the child's education). The essential feature of all of these back-up support systems is that they offer assistance to teachers and schools committed to including students with challenging behaviors.

CONCLUSION

We believe that with functional behavioral assessment and an open-minded, eclectic approach to the choice of interventions comprising a positive behavior support plan, it is possible to successfully meet the needs of students with very challenging behaviors in inclusive elementary schools. Preventing, teaching, and responding constitute a framework entirely consistent with both constructivist pedagogy and systematic instruction. Selecting interventions that acknowledge multiple perspectives to understanding the circumstances of a behavior, that match and extend a student's capacities for self-control, and that seek to deepen the human relationship between student and teacher should not be held captive to whether that intervention fits a particular behavioral or psychoeducational perspective. The assessment, planning, and intervention processes offered here are recursive, so student (and staff) responses to each intervention inform future assessment and planning. Although the initial investment may seem demanding, the payoff is the creation of learning environments that satisfy both teachers and students.

REFERENCES

Alberto, P.A., & Troutman. A.C. (2002). *Applied behavior analysis for teachers* (6th ed.). Upper Saddle River, NJ: Prentice Hall.

Amos, P. (1999). What restraints teach. *TASH Newsletter, 25*(11), 28–29.

Bandura, A., & Walters, R.H. (1963). *Social learning and personality development.* New York: Holt, Rinehart & Winston.

Brendtro, L.K., & Ness, A.E. (Eds.). (1983). *Re-educating troubled youth: Environments for teaching and treatments.* New York: Aldine.

Brendtro, L.K., Ness, A.E., & Milburn, J.F. (1983). Psychoeducational management: Individualizing treatment. In L.K. Brendtro & A.E. Ness (Eds.), *Re-educating troubled youth: Environments for teaching and treatments* (pp. 127–177). New York: Aldine.

Campbell, P., & Siperstein, G.N. (1994). *Improving social competence: A resource for elementary schoolteachers.* Needham Heights, MA: Allyn & Bacon.

Cartledge, G., & Milburn, J.F. (Eds.). (1986). *Teaching social skills to children: Innovative approaches* (2nd ed.). New York: Pergamon.

Charles, C.M. (2001). *Building classroom discipline* (7th ed.). White Plains, NY: Longman.

Donnellan, A.M., Mirenda, P., Mesaros, R.A., & Fassbender, L. (1984). A strategy for analyzing the communicative functions of behavior. *Journal of The Association for Persons with Severe Handicaps, 9*(3), 201–212.

Dreikurs, R. (1968). *Psychology in the classroom: A manual for teachers* (2nd ed.). New York: Harper & Row.

Dreikurs, R. (1972). *Discipline without tears: What to do with children who misbehave.* New York: Hawthorn.

Dryfoos, J. (1998). *Full-service schools: A revolution in health and social services for children, youth, and families.* San Francisco: Jossey-Bass.

Durand, V.M., & Crimmins, D.B. (1992). *The motivation assessment scale administration guide.* Topeka, KS: Monaco & Associates.

Eber, L., Nelson, C.M., & Miles, P. (1997). School-based wraparound for students with emotional and behavioral challenges. *Exceptional Children, 63*(4), 539–555.

Eggert, L.L. (1994). *Anger management for youth: Stemming aggression and violence.* Bloomington, IN: National Education Service.

Erickson, E. (1968). *Identity, youth and crisis.* New York: Norton.

Fagen, S.A., & Hill, J.M. (1977). *Behavior management: A competency-based manual for in-service training.* Washington, D.C.: Psychoeducational Resources.

Foster-Johnson, L., & Dunlap, G. (1993). Using functional assessment to develop effective, individualized interventions for challenging behaviors. *Teaching Exceptional Children, 25*(3), 44–50.

Glasser, W. (1989). *Reality therapy: A new approach to psychiatry.* New York: Harper & Row.

Goldstein, A. (1999). *The prepare curriculum: Teaching prosocial competencies.* Champaign, IL: Research Press.

Gresham, F.M., Sugai, G., & Horner, R.H. (2001). Outcomes of social skills training for students with high-incidence disabilities. *Exceptional Children, 67*(3), 331–344.

Homme, L.H. (1969). *How to use contingency contracting in the classroom.* Champaign, IL: Research Press.

Hoover, R., & Kindsvatter, R. (1997). *Democratic discipline: Foundation and practice.* Upper Saddle River, NJ: Prentice-Hall.

Individuals with Disabilities Education Act (IDEA) of 1990, PL 101-476, 20 U.S.C. §§ 1400 *et seq.*

Individuals with Disabilities Education Act Amendments of 1997, PL 105-17, 20 U.S.C. 1400 *et seq.*

Iwata, B., Pace, G.M., Kalsher, M.J., Cowery, G.E., & Cataldo, M.F. (1990). Experimental analysis and extinction of self-injurious escape behavior. *Journal of Applied Behavior Analysis, 23*(1), 11–27.

Janney, R., Black, J., & Ferlo, M. (1989). *A problem solving approach to challenging behaviors: Strategies for parents and educators of people with disabilities and challenging behaviors.* Syracuse, NY: Syracuse University and Syracuse City School District.

Janney, R., & Snell, M.E. (2000). *Teachers' guides to inclusive practices: Behavioral support.* Baltimore: Paul H. Brookes Publishing Co.

Johnson, D.W., & Johnson, R.T. (1998). *Learning together and alone: Cooperative, competitive, and individualistic learning* (5th ed.). Needham Heights, MA: Allyn & Bacon.

Kaplan, J.S. (2000). *Beyond functional assessment: A social-cognitive approach to the evaluation of behavior problems in children and youth.* Austin, TX: PRO-ED.

Kauffman, J.M. (1999). The role of science in behavioral disorders. *Behavioral Disorders, 24*(4), 265–272.

Kauffman, J.M. (2001). *Characteristics of emotional and behavioral disorders of children and youth.* (7th ed.). Upper Saddle River, NJ: Prentice Hall.

Knitzer, J., Steinberg, Z., & Fleisch, F. (1990). *At the schoolhouse door: An examination of the programs and policies for children with behavioral and emotional problems.* New York: Bank Street College of Education.

Kounin, J.S. (1977). *Discipline and group management in classrooms.* New York: Kriegar.

Kreidler, W.J. (1991). *Elementary perspectives 1: Teaching concepts of peace and conflict.* Cambridge, MA: Educators for Social Responsibility.

Kreidler, W.J. (1997). *Conflict resolution in the middle school.* Cambridge, MA: Educators for Social Responsibility.

Kunc, N. (2000). Rediscovering the right to belong. In R.A. Villa & J.S. Thousand (Eds.), *Restructuring for caring and effective education: Piecing the puzzle together* (2nd ed.). Baltimore: Paul H. Brookes Publishing Co.

Levin, J., & Shanken-Kaye, J.M. (1996). *The self-control classroom.* Dubuque, IA: Kendall-Hunt.

Long, N.J., & Morse, W.C. (1996). *Conflict in the classroom: The education of at-risk and troubled students* (5th ed.). Hawthorne, NY: Aldine.

Long, N.J., Wood, M.M., & Fecser, F.A. (2001). *Life space crisis intervention: Talking with students in conflict* (2nd ed.). Austin, TX: PRO-ED.

MacCraken, M. (1977). *Lovey: A very special child.* New York: Signet.

Marek, E. (1988). *The children at Santa Clara.* New York: Penguin.

Martin, G., & Pear, J. (1999). *Behavior modification: What it is and how to do it* (6th ed.). Upper Saddle River, NJ: Simon & Schuster.

Martin, J., Sugarman, J. & McNamara, J. (2000). *Models of classroom management: Principles, applications and critical perspectives* (3rd ed.). Bellingham, WA: Temeron.

McGinnis, E., & Goldstein, A.P. (2000). *Skillstreaming the elementary school child: New strategies and perspectives for teaching prosocial skills.* Champaign, IL: Research Press.

Meichenbaum, D. (1977). *Cognitive-behavior modification: An integrative approach.* New York: Plenum.

Mendler, A.N. (1992). *What do I do when...? How to achieve discipline with dignity in the classroom.* Bloomington, IN: National Education Service.

Meyer, L.H., & Evans, I.M. (1989). *Nonaversive intervention for behavior problems: A manual for home and community.* Baltimore: Paul H. Brookes Publishing Co.

Miltenberger, R.G. (2001). *Behavior modification: Principles and procedures* (2nd ed.). Belmont, CA: Wadsworth.

Morse, W. (1996). Crisis intervention in schools. In N.J. Long & W.C. Morse (Eds.), *Conflict in the classroom: The education of at-risk and troubled students* (5th ed., pp. 418–428). Austin, TX: PRO-ED.

Nichols, P. (1996). *Clear thinking: Clearing dark thought with new words and images.* Iowa City, IA: River Lights Publishing.

Nichols, P. (1997). Problem-solving for personal power. *Reclaiming Children and Youth, 6*(2), 75–81.

Paley, V.G. (1989). *White teacher.* Cambridge, MA: Harvard University Press.

Pelzer, D. (1995). *A child called "it."* Deerfield Beach, FL: Health Communications.

Physicians' Desk Reference. (2002). Montvale, NJ: Thomson Medical Economics Company.

Pugach, M.C. (2001). The stories we choose to tell: Fulfilling the promise of qualitative research for special education. *Exceptional Children, 67*(4), 439–454.

Redl, F. (1966). *When we deal with children.* New York: Free Press.

Redl, F., & Wineman, D. (1952). *Controls from within: Techniques for the treatment of the aggressive child.* New York: Free Press.

Rogers, C. (1969). *Freedom to learn.* Columbus, OH: Merrill.

Rotter, J. (1966). Generalized expectancies for internal versus external control of reinforcement. *Psychological Monographs, 80,* 1–28.

Ruhl, K.L., Hughes, C.A., & Camarata, S.M. (1992). Analysis of expressive and receptive language characteristics of emotionally handicapped students served in public school settings. *Journal of Childhood Communication Disorders, 14*(2), 165–176.

Savage, T.V. (1999). *Teaching self-control through management and discipline* (2nd ed.). Needham Heights, MA: Allyn & Bacon.

Skinner, B.F. (1953). *Science and human behavior.* New York: Macmillan.

Slavin, R.E. (1995). *Cooperative learning: Theory, research and practice* (2nd ed.). Needham Heights, MA: Allyn & Bacon.

Walker, H., McConnell, S., Holmes, D., Todis, B., Walker, J., & Golden, N. (1983). *The Walker social skills curriculum: The ACCEPTS program.* Austin, TX: PRO-ED.

Warr-Lieper, G., Wright, N.A., & Mack, A. (1994). Language disbilities of ant-social boys in residential treatment. *Behavior Disorders, 19*(3), 159–169.

Wolfgang, C.H. (2001). *Solving discipline and classroom management problems* (5th ed.). New York: John Wiley & Sons.

CHAPTER NINE

Using Activity Routines to Design Inclusive Education for Students with Severe Disabilities

BEVERLY RAINFORTH

Tara sits in an adapted wheelchair at her desk in the back of her fourth-grade classroom, with an aide by her side. Tara's electronic communication device sits on a counter nearby. The teacher distributes construction paper, cut in half, and envelopes containing 30 beans to all the students. She gives Tara full sheets of construction paper and a bag of 30 one-inch cubes. The teacher instructs the class to count their beans by making 3 piles of 10 each. Tara's aide does not realize that these instructions apply to Tara too, so she talks quietly to Tara about the colors of their wooden cubes. The teacher introduces a lesson on division by asking how the children might divide pies among themselves. Most of the children seem interested in the idea of sharing a pie, and volunteer ideas about how it would be done. Now the teacher asks Tara if she likes pie, trying to draw her into the lesson. Tara smiles and says, "Ehh," approximating "Yes."

Next comes a series of word problems such as, "If you want to divide 21 pieces of pie among 3 friends, how many pieces would each friend get?" The students count out 21 beans and distribute them on 3 pieces of paper to make 3 groups of equal size. With some direction from the teacher, the aide understands that Tara is also expected to count and distribute her blocks on the large sheets of paper, so she physically assists Tara to point to the blocks and encourages Tara to count with her. Unfortunately, there is no real system to the counting and no grouping of blocks, and Tara seems to resist participation. The teacher

241

*focuses her instruction on the class as a whole and helps students who do not
have an aide. As the class moves on to written problems, the aide gets Tara
ready to go to music class.*

This scene from an elementary school in a small city shows both
the efforts that can go into including children with severe disabilities
in general education classes and the ways in which some of those efforts fall short. Whenever the needs of students with severe disabilities
are not well met, or even detract from the teacher's ability to meet the
needs of the rest of the class, the rationale for inclusion will be ques-
tioned. When the needs of all students are not being met, however, it
is inappropriate to refer to the arrangement as inclusion. Despite many
positive efforts by the teacher and aide, the reality is that Tara is not
included; she is excluded from both the classroom community and the
active learning opportunities the class offers.

This chapter presents strategies for planning and implementing
the inclusion of students with severe disabilities in elementary education classrooms, taking into consideration the concerns of educational
team members, including parents. Active, learner-centered classrooms, such as those described throughout this book, provide count-
less opportunities for students with severe disabilities to participate in
rich communities of learning. Too often, however, the potential of
these learning communities is not realized for these students. Too
often, a student with severe disabilities is welcomed into a classroom
community, but the intentionally designed instruction he or she needs
is not provided. Then, if the student does not progress, the educational
team concludes that he or she needs a different environment in order
to receive appropriate instruction. As illustrated throughout this book,
it is not necessary to choose between the systematic methods that
some students need and constructivist approaches. This chapter focuses on the systematic strategies that can be provided for students
with severe disabilities in the context of classrooms in which children
engage in interactive learning activities, such as those presented in this
book. Particular attention is given to development of a curriculum that
is meaningful for each student, the social context of learning, and the
need for highly intentional instruction.

CHARACTERISTICS OF
STUDENTS WITH SEVERE DISABILITIES

Students with severe disabilities are a small but very diverse group,
made up of individuals who have significant needs related to develop-

ment of cognition, communication, social interactions, and sensori-motor abilities. Often they have two or more disabilities, such as moderate, severe, or profound mental retardation; cerebral palsy; autism; developmental disability; or deaf-blindness. Having these labels does not necessarily mean that a child has severe disabilities; this is reserved for 1% of the population with the greatest functional limitations (Brown et al., 1983). Early research on teaching children and adults with severe disabilities showed that, in general, they tend to learn slowly, have difficulty transferring learning to new situations, and forget skills that are not practiced frequently (Brown, Nietupski, & Hamre-Nietupski, 1976). This information has tremendous implications for effective instruction of students with severe disabilities in today's inclusive elementary schools.

First, instruction must focus on those skills that students really need to learn. The educational team for a student with severe disabilities must have a clear vision for the student's future and agree on the learning priorities that lead to those outcomes. Second, educators must use instructional methods that elicit the highest possible rate of skill acquisition, as determined through frequent assessment of the student's performance on his or her learning priorities. Third, instruction must be provided in the contexts in which students are most likely to use the skills they will learn. If a team wants a child to learn to communicate with others, for example, the team should teach communication skills in situations in which others can and will communicate with the child. This is less likely in a special education classroom, in which all the students have difficulty communicating, and more likely in general education settings, in which staff and many young allies will naturally model and elicit communication and assist with transfer to new activities and settings. Teaching these skills within school routines, rather than in isolated drill and practice sessions, also promotes acquisition, maintenance, and generalization (e.g., Brown, Holvoet, Guess, & Mulligan, 1980; McGee, Morrier, & Daly, 1999).

Finally, teachers and related services providers (e.g., occupational therapists, physical therapists, speech-language pathologists) with expertise in educating students with severe disabilities must be part of the general education team. Although general education classes are rich with learning opportunities for students with severe disabilities, taking full advantage of those opportunities requires that expertise be brought to general education environments. Specialists should work directly with students, guide other adults and children who support the students, and participate in planning lessons and specialized instructional strategies, when needed (Rainforth & York-Barr, 1997).

For many years, professionals assumed that students needing such specialized instruction and high levels of support were served best in separate classes or schools. A decade of research shows that, contrary to this belief, students with severe disabilities benefit tremendously from inclusive education when appropriate supports are directed toward learning priorities (McGregor & Vogelsberg, 1998). Furthermore, research shows the reciprocal relationships among teacher perspectives, student placement, program quality, and student outcomes. For example, the best predictor of where a student will be educated is not the type or severity of the student's disability, but teacher advocacy for a particular placement (Hunt et al., 1993). When the programs of matched pairs of students with severe disabilities were compared, the students in inclusive classroom had higher quality individualized education programs, were engaged in instruction a greater portion of their day, and had more and higher quality interactions with peers without disabilities than the students in special classes (Hunt, Farron-Davis, Beckstead, Curtis, & Goetz, 1994). In turn, the use of ecological curriculum and assessment models, such as those found in these high-quality inclusive classrooms, lead to higher teacher expectations than developmental models, which tend to create misconception that students with severe disabilities are "developmentally young" and less capable than students without disabilities (Bates, Morrow, Pancsofar, & Sedlak, 1984; Linehan, Brady, & Hwang, 1991). Furthermore, adults with severe disabilities are more likely to live and work in the community (versus segregated facilities) when they are educated in their home community and prepared to live and work there (Brown et al., 1987). Therefore, the choices teachers make about where and how students with severe disabilities will be educated have self-fulfilling and far-reaching implications for these students' lives. In comparison with segregated special education placements for students with severe disabilities, inclusion is associated with higher program quality, greater student achievement, and greater likelihood of community membership as an adult.

CHARACTERISTICS OF INCLUSIVE EDUCATION FOR STUDENTS WITH SEVERE DISABILITIES

Inclusion means far more than just placing a student in a general education class and is not just another name for mainstreaming. Inclusion has been described as an attitude or philosophy, but it also has several practical components, as discussed in Chapter 1. Four specific features of inclusive education are listed here:

1. All students attend the same schools and receive instruction in the same classes that they would attend if they did not have disabilities or disadvantages.
2. Remedial, special education, and related services are provided within general education, so specialists work closely with classroom teachers as they support students needing their services.
3. All students are provided adaptations, specialized interventions, and personnel support as needed to participate and learn in the general education environment and curriculum. Accommodations are made to the general education curriculum when needed, so all students can learn skills appropriate to their chronological age and developmental needs.
4. The curriculum is conceived to include academic, social-emotional, and other learning required for children to become contributing members of society. Educators hold high expectations for all students while recognizing needs for individualization rather than blind uniformity.
5. Classrooms are learning communities in which all students are valued members who support one another.

The chapter opening vignette of Tara illustrates some, but not all, of these features. For example, Tara does not attend her neighborhood school because it is not accessible to students in wheelchairs. She does attend the closest accessible neighborhood school and the same class she would if she did not have a disability. She has an aide for support, and the teacher has modified the curriculum to meet Tara's needs. Unfortunately, the special education and related service providers spend little if any time planning with the classroom teacher or working with Tara and her aide in the classroom. As a result, Tara is not able to work on the motor, communication, and cognitive skills she might have during lessons such as the one described in the vignette. Whenever she is unable to reach her communication device or sit with the rest of the class, she has no way to be part of the learning community.

School Routines as Curriculum

When teams commit to designing programs that are truly inclusive for students with severe disabilities, an effective starting point is a review of the daily routine for the class. Routines provide important organizing frameworks for classrooms and schools and, as such, can shape a curriculum rooted in the school or classroom ecology. During the first months of kindergarten, a great deal of time is devoted to teaching a variety of routines. When attention is turned to academic content, routines support that focus. Students' abilities to perform the peripheral tasks, such as moving into work groups and getting materials together, have a great influence on how well a class "works." Therefore, routines are as important to the curriculum as the academic content but, as the latter takes on greater importance, routines may be taken for granted. Then, if the academic content seems "beyond" a student, it may be assumed that the student cannot benefit from being educated in general education classes. Examining school routines offers another perspective. Systematic observations of children and adults have revealed that activity routines have a consistent set of components that, when analyzed, point out both the performance demands and the learning opportunities inherent in those routines (Brown, Evans, Weed, & Owen, 1987). The components are described next.

- Initiation: In schools, routines are often initiated by a teacher announcing it is time to start the next lesson, students noticing the time on the clock, or a bell. A student may also initiate a routine by, for example, asking permission to go to the bathroom. In general, students are expected to respond to instructions given to the entire class, or subtle cues (e.g., teacher's position in the room). Some students with severe disabilities will miss the teacher's cues, but will notice that other students are getting ready, and will follow their lead. Others will need a teacher or aide to give individual instruction and/or assistance to initiate the activity.
- Preparation: Students prepare for lessons or activities by going to the proper location, getting the materials they need, and arranging themselves and their materials. Teachers may assist with preparation by giving instructions or distributing materials. During this part of routines, it is particularly obvious when students (not just those with severe disabilities) have problems organizing themselves and their materials; some students need cue cards, direct instruction, and support from helpful peers to master this part of the routine. In school routines, initiation and preparation are often intertwined.
- Core: The scheduled lesson or activity is the core of the routine for students without disabilities. For students with severe disabilities, academic tasks may need to be adapted, and their learning objectives may differ from the rest of the class. For example, Tara's

teacher provided 1-inch cubes because Tara could not grasp the beans the other students used. While the other students were working on concepts related to division, Tara could do the same work, but with different objectives. In this case, Tara had the objectives of picking up cubes and placing them on a designated paper (motor), developing one-to-one correspondence and rote counting (cognitive), and answering questions with her communication device (communication).

- Termination: As with initiation, termination typically occurs when a bell rings, the teacher announces the end of a lesson, or students recognize the time. Reaching the end of a task or chapter in a reading book may also serve as termination. Some students, especially those with a disability such as autism, may need a signal that an activity will end in 5 minutes, 2 minutes, 1 minute, and so forth, so they can prepare themselves. Students may then collect their materials, put materials away, and/or line up at the door or move to another area of the room. Some students with severe disabilities, especially motor disabilities, will need additional time for transitions, so the team needs to determine if it is better for the student to end the first activity early or start the next activity late.

These four components of routines occur in a sequence (similar to a task analysis). The remaining seven components reflect abilities that are interwoven throughout activities, and full participation in routines demands use of these abilities and provides many opportunities to learn them. Often, teachers and therapists assume that general education offers few, if any, opportunities to teach abilities such as movement and communication, so students who need this type of instruction must be removed. When educational team members start noticing the rich teaching and learning opportunities that are interwoven throughout daily routines, they become empowered to address needs of students with severe disabilities within class routines.

- Movement: Movement is part of most school activities. Transitions require some form of mobility; sitting requires postural control, and participation usually requires movement of the hands (to manipulate materials), head and eyes (to look), and mouth (to speak). For most students, such abilities are taken for granted, but for students with severe disabilities, these may represent learning priorities. When students receive occupational or physical therapy services, their therapists need to be involved in planning to maximize learning opportunities in general education routines. Special educators and therapists have demonstrated that systematic instruction (described later in this chapter) is a highly effective approach to teaching motor skills to students with even the most severe disabilities, and that occupational and physical therapy services can be more effective in everyday routines than in a therapy room (Bidabe, 1990; Karnish, Bruder, & Rainforth, 1995).

- Preferences: Offering students opportunities to express preferences promotes self-determination and, in turn, reduces challenging behavior (Brown, Gothelf, Guess, & Lehr, 1998). In the course of daily routines, student choices can be as simple as where to sit, what color of folder to take, or which writing implement to use. Other choices may include whether to work with an aide or peer or whether to answer with one's voice or a communication device. It is important to emphasize that "choosing" between a teacher's demand and an unpleasant consequence is not what is meant here. When a student is faced with tasks that he or she finds unpleasant, however, allowing the student to decide the order or manner in which they will be done can reduce the struggle (Moes, 1998). For students with severe disabilities, choices may be offered by presenting two objects, two or more pictures or pictograms, or asking direct or indirect questions, depending on each student's abilities and needs.

- Communication: The only prerequisites for communication are something to communicate about, someone to communicate with, and a way to communicate. General education classrooms fulfill the first two criteria, with teachers and students talking about the curriculum and numerous other topics. Children practice all aspects of language development as they negotiate both conversational rules (e.g., how to extend conversation) and classroom rules (e.g., how much talking, how loud). Students with severe disabilities may communicate verbally, with sign language, with communication books or boards, or with electronic devices. Providing classmates with information about students with severe disabilities and instruction on ways to communicate with them has resulted in communication exchanges much like those among typical children (Hunt, Farron-Davis, Wrenn, Hirose-Hatae, & Goetz, 1997). Involving speech-language and/or augmentative and alternative communication specialists in planning is essential.

- Social interactions: Communication and social interactions are closely related, as children both expand their communication skills through their interactions and learn that certain types of communication can either extend or terminate those interactions. Social interactions often occur within routines through sharing, taking turns, offering and receiving help, and working toward shared goals. The opportunity to be involved in social interactions and to develop social competence has been identified as one of the greatest advantages of inclusive education for students with severe disabilities, but realizing these opportunities requires goal-directed instruction (e.g., Meyer et al., 1998).

- Problem solving: Problem solving is central to learning most subjects. Opportunities to solve problems also arise spontaneously throughout school routines. All children need to learn to address problems such as not having a pencil, losing one's place during a lesson, having too few chairs for all participants, and disagreeing with students. Although these may be treated as disruptions, they can also be reframed as incidental learning opportunities when problem solving is recognized as a legitimate, even essential, part of the curriculum. For many students with severe disabilities, instruction in problem solving will focus on recognizing when they need help and communicating distress in socially acceptable ways.

- Monitoring quality of performance: Students monitor quality when the teacher directs them to check their work, and through spontaneous self-correction throughout the school day. Monitoring quality also refers to social areas, such as being careful not to step on others when standing in line, or recognizing when to whisper and when to talk out loud. For some students with severe disabilities, monitoring quality may involve movement, such as pushing a microswitch hard enough to play the pre-recorded message at the proper moment.

- Monitoring tempo of performance: Most students routinely monitor their speed of walking, talking, eating, and working. Many students with severe disabilities seem to become aware of monitoring tempo when they start making transitions with classmates. Typically, students without disabilities are conscious of how much time is allowed to get to music class, for example, and convey their own sense of urgency to their classmate. When students need longer than the time usually allowed to complete work or make transitions, it is important to evaluate the relative priorities throughout the day and make thoughtful decisions about what can and cannot be missed.

Every class, whether dull and dry or rich and exciting, is organized into routines with the components that have just been described. When teaching teams design constructivist classrooms, analysis of routines is likely to reveal vast opportunities for students with severe disabilities to participate and learn.

USING ACTIVITY ROUTINES TO
PLAN INCLUSIVE EDUCATION FOR
STUDENTS WITH SEVERE DISABILITIES

Activity routines reveal a great deal about the culture of a classroom. Some aspects of the culture can be surmised from observation, but other aspects are understood most easily if the classroom teacher describes the routine, clarifying the underlying philosophies and goals. Although the content of instruction certainly changes during the year, classroom teachers have individual preferences about formats for instruction (i.e., the routines) and can usually describe the types of routines used in their classroom (e.g., introduce concept to whole class, then work in cooperative groups). This information is the starting point for planning how to include a student with severe disabilities in an elementary education classroom.

Consider Tara, for example, who has severe and multiple disabilities, including cerebral palsy and visual impairments, which have limited her development in all areas. Tara attended an inclusive preschool program, but when she entered the public schools, school personnel recommended placement in a special school. With strong parent advocacy, Tara has remained in general education classes since kindergarten, but her educational teams have had neither a vision for her inclusion nor an effective planning strategy. As a result, the professionals have felt pulled between allowing Tara to be present for and participate in general education activities, and providing Tara with an education that is individualized, intentional, and intensive. During the spring, when Tara was in third grade, her education team held a meeting to start planning her participation in fourth grade. Tara's third-grade teacher, fourth-grade teacher, speech-language therapist, occupational therapist, vision specialist, aide, and mother attended the meeting. Tara's mother gave a brief description of her hopes and dreams for Tara's life, to help create a vision for her inclusion. Although parent participation in this type of planning is always appropriate, Tara's mother left at this point. She understood that a byproduct of her strong advocacy for Tara was that staff were afraid of making a mistake or not appearing competent in front of her, and this early stage of learning would be enhanced if the staff felt free to ask questions and express concerns. In turn, the staff committed to keep Tara's mother informed and seek her input as they worked through the new planning process.

During this first planning meeting, a clear vision evolved of how staff could provide individualized, intentional, and intensive instruction in the context of the general class activities and routines. For the first time, the individuals attending the planning meeting took on the persona of a real team who would all contribute to Tara's participation and achievement in fourth grade. During their planning, the team considered the fourth-grade morning activities, identifying the classroom teacher's expectations for fourth graders, team expectations for what Tara could do fairly easily, and team expectations for what Tara could do with instruction or adaptations. Their analysis of the early morning routine is presented in Table 9.1. This general analysis helped set expectations for Tara's participation and gave the team a starting point when school began in the fall.

When Tara entered fourth grade, the team needed to plan each part of the daily routine more thoroughly to ensure her active participation and learning throughout the school day. The vignette at the start of the chapter is an example of one routine that her team had not yet addressed. Table 9.2 presents an analysis of the routine in Tara's

Table 9.1.   Analysis of general education routines for Tara: Morning activities

What fourth graders are expected to do	What Tara does now or easily could do	What Tara could do with instruction or adaptations
7:30–7:40: Arrival: Arrive and wait outside or go to cafeteria for breakfast	Arrives and is taken to classroom; if she says she is hungry, she has breakfast in classroom (due to commotion in cafeteria)	Create personal schedule for daily activities (identify named activity from choice of two printed on index cards)
Attendance and lunch count: Find clothespin with name and put on folder for lunch choice	Indicates lunch choice by yes or no response to questions, adult records choice	State lunch choice on Dynavox; find name from choice of two clothespins; reach, grasp, place clothespin on lunch choice
Opening: Take turns leading Pledge of Allegiance, review schedule for day (any special activities), put homework on desk	Leaves group for special education services	Press switch on Dynamite to lead Pledge, point to named activities on personal schedule, take homework from bag
8:30–10:00: Language Arts: Listen to new story read aloud, listen to same story on tape in small groups, independent reading; study spelling words from reading; complete worksheets, write in journals, do homework	Leaves group or room for special education, speech-language therapy, occupational therapy, and physical therapy services; drives wheelchair to bathroom at 9:15	Change position (preferably in stander), answer predetermined questions on Communicator, activate switch to play book on tape, use spelling words for sight vocabulary, use word prediction program to write on computer; do homework; check timer to see how much longer to work, cross activities off on schedule

Table 9.2.   Analysis of general education routines for Tara: Fourth-grade math

What fourth graders are expected to do	What Tara does now	What Tara could do with instruction, adaptations, or higher expectations
Initiation and Preparation		
When directed by teacher, clear desk except for pencil When teacher distributes other materials, put on desk	Passive participant: chair is pushed up to desk, materials are placed on desk, materials are arranged on desk	Drive chair to desk Hold hands to take materials from teacher Choose whether she or aide will arrange materials on desk
Core		
Count beans Put beans in groups of equal size Solve division problems, answer questions presented to class, write answers to written problems Work independently	Point to blocks with assistance Count blocks with verbal model	Point to blocks in order when arranged in rows of five Pick up blocks with assistance, release onto designated plate (vs. paper) Put one block on each plate (1:1 correspondence) Count three objects without verbal model Answer questions using Dynavox
Termination		
Finish when teacher announces time Put beans in envelope Put envelope in bin Put math paper in teacher's math folder Line up at door when called	Passive participant: materials are put in envelope, chair is pushed into hallway	Drop blocks in bag (aide holds open) Ask for assistance cleaning up (with Dynavox) Drive power wheelchair from desk to door
Movement		
Use pincer grasp to group beans Point at beans to count Print numbers in designated spaces	Point with full physical assistance	Point at, grasp, and release objects with prompt at wrist Press keys on Dynavox Drive power wheelchair in classroom

Table 9.2. *(continued)*

What fourth graders are expected to do	What Tara does now	What Tara could do with instruction, adaptations, or higher expectations
Preferences		
How to arrange materials on desk	None	Whether to speak or use Dynavox
Whether to volunteer answers		Whether to do tasks or ask for help
Whether to solve problems using beans or on paper		Who will help (peer or aide)
		Where helper will sit (right or left side)
Communication		
Listen to directions	Listen to discussion	Use Dynavox to answer questions (social, content), request help, comment, ask questions
Answer questions	Answer yes/no questions orally	
Talk quietly to neighbors		
Social Interactions		
Help pick up materials dropped on floor	Seating prevents interactions	With change in seating, share materials
Share materials		Fool around with friends
Offer to help peer if finished paper		Choose peer to accompany in hallway
Offer to distribute or collect materials		
Fool around without annoying teacher		
Problem Solving		
Regrouping for division	Refuses to participate if task too hard or not interesting	Dynavox out of reach
Not enough beans		Cannot see examples or hear explanation
Break pencil		Ask for help rather than refuse to do task
Cannot solve written problem		
Monitor Quality and Tempo		
Finish paper in allocated time	Monitored by adults	Complete work in allocated time
Check work for accuracy		Self-correct counting errors
Follow teacher directives fast enough to avoid discipline		Drive wheelchair to next class

math class, outlining the classroom teacher's expectations for fourth-graders, team expectations for what Tara currently does or easily could do, and team expectations for what Tara could do with instruction, adaptations, or higher expectations. Although the vignette focused on the core of the routine, the analysis looks at all the components of routines, in order to expand possibilities for Tara to participate and for her team to address her individualized education plan objectives. Notice how many opportunities are available in the course of this one routine—far more than time allows for instruction. As her team looks at each routine, they need to balance priorities so that all of Tara's needs get sufficient attention in the course of her school day.

At another school that uses this planning strategy, classroom teachers complete the first two columns in the chart seen in Figure 9.1, much as Tara's team did. In the first column, the classroom teacher outlines the routines of the day, listing how "typical" students are expected to participate. The second column lists how the student with severe disabilities currently does or easily could participate. The chart is then distributed to all other members of the student's team, including the child's family, so each person can list his or her ideas about how the student might 1) participate more fully and 2) work on priority skills within the routine. Ideas about instructional strategies, adaptations, and accommodations may also be recorded. When team members return their completed charts, the last columns from all of the charts are copied and everyone receives an expanded chart with ideas from all the team members as seen in Figure 9.1. The team then meets to decide on instructional priorities. In some instances, the team reconsiders the priorities listed on the individualized education plan; in other cases, the classroom teacher reconsiders some aspect of the class routine.

In the course of these discussions, team members teach one another about instructional strategies required to meet a student's unique needs. For example, the physical therapist might teach everyone how to position a student with physical disabilities, the speech-language therapist might demonstrate use of a student's picture communication system, the special education teacher might model the prompting sequence that has proven effective for the particular student, and the classroom teacher might explain how he or she uses cooperative learning groups. Although the process is time consuming, the teams have found that it saves them a great deal of time as the school year progresses. Not only do team members have a better understanding and agreement about how to meet the needs of an individual with severe disabilities in general education but also they found that the process provided them with a better perspective on the needs of and planning for all of their students.

Step 1: The classroom teacher completes the first and second columns.

What teacher plans for all students to do	What student with severe disabilities does now

Step 2: Each team member records his or her ideas in the third column. Ideas from all team members are pasted together into one large chart, which is distributed to all team members.

What teacher plans for all students to do	What student with severe disabilities does now	Ideas for participation and learning for student with severe disabilities (with instruction, adaptions, or higher expectations)			
		Parent	Special Education Teacher	Aide	Related Services	Related Services

Step 3: The team meets and decides which ideas to implement during this routine. Other ideas may be priorities during other routines in the day.

What teacher plans for all students to do	What student with severe disabilities does now

Step 4: Team members share information and skills needed to implement their plan.

Figure 9.1.   Teachers who use planning a strategy similar to Tara's would fill out a chart such as this.

ADAPTING CURRICULA FOR
STUDENTS WITH SEVERE DISABILITIES

When students are unable to complete academic tasks independently, one strategy is to provide more assistance by, for example, giving more verbal cues, modeling appropriate responses, or giving physical assistance. Although these strategies are appropriate sometimes, they can also push a student through a task without much opportunity for real learning. An alternative is to adapt the curriculum. One approach to curriculum adaptation is to consider, systematically, the theme of the lessons in a unit, the tasks in a lesson, the objectives of the tasks, and the materials (Salisbury, Mangino, Petrigala, Rainforth, & Syryca, 1994). The team examines the options and determines the least change needed to meet the student's needs. First, the team asks whether the student with severe disabilities should participate in the lesson as planned for the rest of the class. Although this may seem unlikely, some students with severe disabilities do rise to the occasion and learn the same material in the same way. When the team decides adaptation is necessary for a student, they ask next if the student's needs would be met by changing the materials. Enlarging the type, reducing the number of items on a page, color coding, or using a keyboard and word prediction program rather than writing may meet the student's needs.

If changing materials is not sufficient, would the student's needs be met by considering different objectives for the same tasks? In the fourth-grade math lesson, Tara's objectives could have been to grasp and release small objects and develop one-to-one correspondence. In a second-grade class, the spelling lesson became a reading lesson for Kyle, a boy with severe cognitive disabilities. While others wrote sentences using spelling words and worked with flash cards, Kyle was helped to dictate sentences using each word, reread his sentences and find his words, and read the words on flash cards. During the Friday spelling quiz, Kyle listened to the teacher say each word and use it in a sentence, then circled the correct word from a choice of two on his spelling paper. These adaptations allowed Kyle to learn alongside his classmates.

For most activity-based lessons, teams can identify alternate objectives that allow students with severe disabilities to participate and learn priority skills during the activity. Occasionally, a lesson that is important for the rest of the class does not lend itself to this type of adaptation, or the student with severe disabilities may have other important needs at that time. In the curriculum-adaptation model developed by Salisbury and colleagues (1994), the next question is whether the student could participate in another activity related to the same theme. Every effort is made to plan alternate activities that would allow the student to be viewed in valued roles, making contributions to the class. For example, Isaiah, a third-grade student with autism, was able to work quietly in close proximity to peers for a certain duration, but then needed changes in the type and pace of his activity if his success was to continue. During a unit on the local community, which integrated social studies, science, and math, Isaiah's team devised a related series of hands-on activities that he could work on in a quiet corner of the classroom while the rest of the class was involved in large group work. Isaiah could listen to the discussion while he was, for example, making a map of the community (with assistance from his aide or the occupational therapist) and learning key concepts; later in the unit, the class would refer to Isaiah's map. This level of adaptation kept Isaiah connected with his class even though he was not involved in the same activity.

Finally, a team may plan a separate activity for a student, but only after determining that different materials, objectives, and activities with the same theme are not appropriate for the student. For example, when Isaiah had not slept well the night before, his team knew he might have difficulty even with the alternate activities they had planned. On those occasions, he was offered the choice of working on the planned activity, taking trash to the school recycling center (which involved a long walk), or looking at books (which allowed him to sit in a beanbag chair and, sometimes, take a nap). To ensure that school was a successful experience for both Isaiah and his class, the teacher and aide made every effort to anticipate Isaiah's needs and offer choices before he became upset. (See Chapter 8 for more information on positive behavior supports.)

Students with severe disabilities may have other concerns that cannot be met in the context of the general education program. For example, Isaiah needed to see the school nurse for medication each afternoon. His teacher tried to plan the day's activities so the trip to the nurse would occur during something that was less important or interesting for him. Rather than just dispensing the medication, the school nurse might use this as a teaching opportunity, asking Isaiah to state his name and how he gets his medicine (Nurse: "Do you take your medication by yourself?" Isaiah: "I don't take any medicine unless an adult gives it to me."). Tara also has some concerns that take her away from her class, particularly for toileting, which requires her to use an accessible bathroom with assistance from two adults. In scheduling trips to the bathroom, Tara's team considered when she usually needed to go, when two adults were available, and when she would not miss priority activities with her class.

By using this step-wise approach to curriculum adaptation, teams ensure that student needs for both participation and learning are met, promoting true inclusion. When considering adaptations, however, teachers often express concerns about whether other students will think differing expectations are "fair." Research in inclusive elementary schools has demonstrated that children understand and respect individualized expectations (Evans, Goldberg-Arnold, & Dickson, 1998; Evans, Salisbury, Palombaro, & Goldberg, 1994). This is particularly true when adults model appreciation of differences, when classroom communities are firmly founded on values of cooperation and belonging (rather than competition and rejection), and when children have opportunities to understand the differing abilities and needs of their classmates. These conditions are supported when teams use curriculum adaptations judiciously, ensuring that every student experiences challenges as well as successes.

PROVIDING SYSTEMATIC INSTRUCTION IN INCLUSIVE EDUCATION

Many teachers have welcoming classrooms and accept students with a great range of abilities and needs. Although this is an important beginning, it is not sufficient to constitute a high-quality program of inclusive education for students with severe disabilities. The teacher and the entire education team must have clear expectations and provide instruction that is both intentional and intensive to ensure that students progress toward achieving learning priorities. Previous sections of this chapter focused on the context and content of instruction, with systematic strategies to identify learning opportunities in inclusive classrooms and to adapt the general education curriculum for students with severe disabilities. This section focuses on systematic strategies that can be used to teach priority skills.

Identifying Appropriate Prompts or Cues

Instruction for students without disabilities is usually provided through a combination of oral and written cues, supported by materials that may elicit use of other "intelligences" (Armstrong, 1994). Many students with severe disabilities have significant language disabilities and/or become over-reliant on verbal directions. Therefore, it is important to consider the cues, or prompts, that will be effective for each individual, given his or her abilities and disabilities. Generally, prompts may be categorized as verbal, visual, or physical, with many variations of each. For example, verbal prompts range from direct instructions (e.g., "Get your library book.") to indirect cues (e.g., "What do you need to take with you to the library?"). Visual prompts include sign language, pictures (e.g., book, student in library), models of correct performance, or pointing at actual objects or locations related to a task. Physical prompts include partial physical assistance (e.g., gently tapping the student's elbow to reach for book when offered) or full physical assistance (e.g., opening spastic hands and helping to grasp book). Some special educators have adopted one set of prompts for all students, but students vary too much for this to be effective. It is most appropriate for a student's team to select two or three prompts to use in sequence, based on that student's abilities and needs. The first prompt gives the student the least assistance that may elicit the correct response, with the expectation that the student is learning to respond to this prompt consistently. The last prompt is one the student responds to consistently, so it ensures the correct response without being overly intrusive.

For Tara, a prompt sequence would reflect that her performance is limited by her coordination and often by her motivation. Therefore, an important first prompt might be a "challenge" (e.g., "I don't know if there is enough pie to share it with you. Let's see."). The next prompt might be a direct instruction about how to do the task (e.g., "Put a block on each piece of paper."). Finally, physical assistance would be appropriate to help her pick up the blocks. Isaiah would have a very different set of prompts, reflecting that he responds inconsistently to verbal directions, responds very well to picture cues and choices, can be distracted easily, and does not tolerate having his hands touched (so physical prompts are to be avoided).

Pausing briefly between prompts will increase the effectiveness of a prompt sequence (Carter & Grunsell, 2001; Westling & Fox, 2000). The duration of this "time delay" or "wait time" is also individualized, taking into consideration how long it takes the student to process cues and initiate a response without getting distracted. Tara might need 10 seconds or longer to initiate movement, whereas Isaiah would need only approximately 3 seconds. Although some students may need different kinds of prompt sequences for different kinds of tasks, it is often possible to establish a generic prompt sequence for a student that could be used to teach almost any task. For Isaiah, the following generic prompt sequence is effective:

1. Verbal direction (e.g., "Isaiah, it's time to go to the library. Get your book.")
    Wait 3 seconds for response.

2. Picture cue (e.g., show pictures of library and book)
   Wait 3 seconds for response.
3. Material cue (e.g., hand book to him and point toward the door)

If Isaiah started to respond incorrectly, the instructor would move immediately to the next prompt. At first, Isaiah responded most consistently to the material cues but, over time, the quick and consistent succession of prompts is teaching him to respond more consistently to the picture cues and then verbal directions.

Collecting Data on Student Performance

Another important aspect of systematic instruction is data collection to provide the team with information about student abilities and needs as well as feedback about effectiveness of instructional strategies. Some teams rely heavily on annual assessments using formal instruments, anecdotal records, and subjective impressions of student performance. None of these provide enough accurate information. A study of staff who insisted their impressions were accurate, for example, showed that they usually reported student progress, even when students were making no progress or even regressing (Holvoet, O'Neil, Chazdon, Carr, & Warner, 1983). Unfortunately, many practices used in special education have not been validated (Rigby & Schwellnus, 1999) and, even when a practice has been validated, that does not guarantee its effectiveness with every member of this very diverse population. Just as teachers are highly accountable for the achievement of their other students, teams must become more accountable for achievement of students with severe disabilities. Most states have adopted alternatives to mandated testing for students with severe disabilities, usually in the form of a student portfolio (Kleinert, Haig, Kearns, & Kennedy, 2000). Portfolios may include work samples, audio- or videotapes that capture qualitative aspects of student performance (e.g., reduction in Isaiah's "agitation" during noisy activities, increased intelligibility of Tara's speech), and graphs that demonstrate measured changes in student performance.

When appropriate, the kinds of data kept for the rest of the class should also be kept for students with severe disabilities (e.g., number or percent correct on Kyle's spelling quiz, list of words learned). Other types of data include frequency (e.g., number of times Isaiah initiates interactions with other children), duration (e.g., how long it takes Tara to drive her wheelchair to the cafeteria in her wheelchair), and latency (e.g., how long a pause before Tara requests the material she wants). Another type of data collection is to record which prompt a student responds to in a prompting sequence. As noted previously, Isaiah responded to object cues most consistently at first but, over time, data showed that he responded more consistently to picture cues and, eventually, to verbal directions. If the data did not show progress, however, his team would need to reconsider the types of prompts they had chosen, the length of the time delay, and other features of instruction. Regular graphing of all objective data provides a visual display that is quite powerful in conveying student performance trends.

Just as these data provide essential feedback to school personnel, data provide important indicators of performance for family members and students. Research indicates that feedback on goal attainment can be far more helpful and motivating than rewards such as praise, stickers, or privileges (Larin, 2000). Not all students with severe disabilities will understand goal attainment, but some will. Tara's aide might tell her, for example, "You got to the cafeteria in 3 minutes and 45 seconds last week. Do you think you can break your record today?" On arrival at the cafeteria, the aide could report the time as well as information about how many stops Tara made and how straight she drove her wheelchair. Some students with severe disabilities also benefit from daily review of behavior charts or periodic review of graphs.

As important as data collection is, it is also time consuming. Collecting too much data can become onerous, interfering with instruction, reducing the accuracy of the data, and reducing the likelihood that anyone will actually use it to make decisions. A good guideline is to record data once a week on acquisition of skills reflected in IEP objectives, but daily on challenging behaviors that are of concern. This guideline is consistent with grading practices and discipline procedures for students without disabilities.

Numerous variations on the prompting and data collection strategies are introduced here, and the literature on systematic instruction in special education is extensive. Readers are directed to Snell and Brown (2000) for more guidance on using systematic instruction to teach motor, communication, social, and academic skills to students with severe disabilities.

THE NEED FOR A TEAM APPROACH TO PROVIDE INCLUSIVE EDUCATION FOR STUDENTS WITH SEVERE DISABILITIES

Planning and providing the kind of instruction described in this chapter requires collaboration among classroom teachers, special educators, related service providers, and the parents of students with severe disabilities (Jackson, Ryndak, & Billingsley, 2000; Rainforth & York-Barr, 1997). Unfortunately, many professionals who are expected to form these educational teams have been taught to work alone, so planning, teaching, and solving problems together may be a new and challenging venture. In addition to "willingness" to work with others, effective teaming requires time to plan and teach together, as well as "models" of coplanning, coteaching, and problem solving that support teamwork. Without these, teams never get past "quick fixes" for their students, and will likely face interpersonal problems due to poor communication and coordination, disagreements about goals, and inadequate support to implement plans, all of which detract further from meeting student needs (Snell & Janney, 2000).

Fortunately, research has validated several practices that support and enhance teaming. For example, Giangreco (1994) taught teams to use a consensus-building process. When he evaluated the effects, he found that nearly half the team decisions were different from decisions that each person had made alone, with team members reporting high levels of confidence in their new decisions and better understanding of the roles each person on the team would play. This chapter recommends a model for team members to plan curriculum and instruction together. Part of this model is for team members to engage in "role release," that is, to teach one another the skills necessary to implement the comprehensive plan they have devised. Although there has been resistance to role release in the past (Rainforth, 1997), Utley and Rapport (2000) found that special education teachers and therapists do support teaching others many areas of knowledge and skill traditionally associated with their professional disciplines.

Just as it is challenging for professionals to team with one another, both professionals and parents have expressed a similar frustration with parent–professional collaboration. Some of this difficulty may arise from parents having varied visions of what is appropriate for their child. Some parents of children with severe disabilities are strong advocates for inclusive education whereas others fear that the general education system cannot or will not meet their child's needs (Palmer, Fuller, Arora, & Nelson, 2001). The lives of some parents have been filled with struggles—both to sustain their child's life and to obtain appropriate services—which may spill over into relationships with other professionals. Families whose culture and social class differ from that of white, middle-class educators may have different visions of what constitutes a "normal life" for their child with a disability and, therefore, may have different expectations for how school should contribute to realizing that vision (Harry, 1998).

Despite great variations among parents, steps can be taken to strengthen partnerships among parents and professionals. One group

of parents of children with severe disabilities made the following recommendations (Pollock & Stewart, 1998, pp. 64–65):

1. Change the environment, not the child. Focus on adapting the
    environment and the activity so the child can be more success-
    ful, not more "normal." Don't invest your energies in trying to
    "fix" the child.
2. Incorporate your ideas and suggestions into your daily routines
    and activities. Make them practical and easy to accomplish.
3. Individualize your programs. Recognize our individuality and
    offer flexible programs that allow us to select options or make
    choices.
4. Prepare us. Help us plan ahead, to think of issues that we might
    be facing in the future but are unaware of at present.
5. Support us in our decisions, our actions, and our ideas. Tell us
    when we are doing a good job or have a good idea.
6. Share your ideas and your knowledge with us. You bring a
    wealth of experience to each of our individual situations. Share
    that wealth.
7. Educate us about child development, about disabilities, and
    about systems. We need adequate and appropriate information
    in order to make good decisions.
8. Communicate with us. Keep us informed about what you are
    doing and help us be part of the team. You can facilitate com-
    munication between home and school.
9. Network with us, and promote opportunities for us to network
    with each other.
10. Advocate on our behalf. Work with us to advocate for more/bet-
    ter services, for improved access to services, for flexibility in the
    services offered, and help us cut through the red tape.

Planning and implementing inclusive education is more effective
when parents are central members of their child's educational team.
Although these recommendations do not all apply to what goes on at
school, honoring parents' priorities increases the likelihood that they
will support the educational program. Furthermore, although some of
these recommendations are unique to parents, many also support
partnerships among professionals.

CONCLUSION

This chapter has presented strategies to educate students with severe
disabilities in inclusive elementary schools. A rich elementary educa-

tion curriculum offers an excellent context for addressing the individ-ualized education plan objectives of students with severe disabilities while offering opportunities for these students to participate in every-day routines and activities. To ensure student learning, however, each student's team must identify systematic instruction strategies that con-sider the ways the individual student learns best. Meeting the range of needs presented by a student with severe disabilities requires collabo-ration among the student's classroom teacher, special education teacher, related service providers, and parents. With this collaboration, students, as well as their teams, benefit.

Before closing, imagine Tara involved in the same lesson that started the chapter. This time, however, her education team had en-gaged in planning that incorporated the strategies outlined throughout the chapter. During this planning they identified learning priorities and taught one another the relevant methods associated with their particular expertise. They considered Tara an important member of the fourth-grade learning community, and conveyed this to all of her classmates.

Tara sits in an adapted wheelchair at a cluster of four desks in her fourth-grade classroom. Tara's group is the one closest to the door, with a wide aisle to the computers so Tara will have easy access in her wheelchair. The aide has checked to make sure Tara is positioned well in her chair, and that Tara's Talker (elec-tronic communication device) is positioned where she can reach it. The aide con-tinues to notice if Tara needs her assistance, but encourages other children to hang out with Tara and provide the kinds of support that children typically offer each other.

Angela, a girl who often fills idle moments by drawing on her desk and her fingernails, sits next to Tara. A student from each group gets a bin of sup-plies, with paper plates and plastic bags containing 30 objects. Angela holds up a bag of macaroni and a bag of 30 one-inch cubes, and asks Tara which she would like to use. Tara indicates her choice by focusing on the cubes. Although the cubes are easier for her to grasp than the smaller objects, and might have just been given to Tara, offering her the choice respected her need to express preferences. The teacher instructs the class to count their objects by making 3 piles of 10 each. Angela asks Tara if she needs help pouring out her cubes. Tara scowls (which Angela understands as "No"), reaches for her bag, and gradu-ally gets the bag far enough off of the desk so the cubes fall out. Angela puts her macaroni in 3 piles of 10 each, picks up some cubes that have fallen off Tara's desk, and asks Tara if she may count her cubes, to which Tara agrees.

The teacher introduces a lesson on division by asking how the children might divide cookies among themselves. One solution involves counting the num-ber of kids in the group. The teacher asks different groups, "How many piles of cookies would you have to make for your group?" Then, moving from the concept of division to counting, asks, "Tara, how many kids are in your group?" Tara's aide bends down near her and helps her to point to each child as she whispers the numbers in her ear, "One, two, three, four. Find it on your Talker." Tara presses the button, and answers, "Four." The teacher reiterates, "Yes, so your group would make four piles of cookies." As the class moves on to distributing "cookies" onto paper plates for different numbers of friends, Tara's aide instructs her to put all the "blueberry cookies" on one plate and all the "red cherry cookies" on another plate. Angela alternates between doing her own work and encouraging Tara to keep separating her cubes by color. The two responsibilities keep Angela occupied and, neither intimidated nor indulgent, she is proving to be an excellent buddy for Tara. The teacher continues leading the class and starts circulating to help individual students, as does Tara's aide. When the teacher reaches Tara's table, she arranges the "cherry cookies" in a horizontal line, guides Tara's hand to point to each, and counts them with Tara. She asks who the "cherry cookies" are for and, although she reminds Tara to answer with her Talker, she clearly understands Tara when she replies, "Me."

As the class moves on to written problems, the aide asks Tara to start cleaning up by putting her cubes back in the plastic bag and all her materials in the bin. She asks Tara if she wants to drive her own chair to music, or have the aide push her. Again, Tara answers clearly, "Me." The aide asks Tara who she wants to go with and, using her Talker, she selects Dante. Dante declines today, and Tara chooses Nydia, who beams. The aide moves Tara's wheelchair into the doorway and the teacher has the class line up, with Nydia by Tara's side. The aide turns on the power for Tara's wheelchair, and follows at a distance as the class goes to music.

REFERENCES

Armstrong, T. (1994). *Multiple intelligences in the classroom.* Alexandria, VA: Association for Supervision and Curriculum Development.

Bates, P., Morrow, S.A., Pancsofar, E., & Sedlak, R. (1984). The effect of functional vs. non-functional activities on attitudes and expectations of non-handicapped college students: What they see is what we get. *Journal of The Association for Persons with Severe Handicaps, 9*(2), 73–78.

Bidabe, L. (1990). *MOVE: Mobility options via education.* Bakersfield, CA: Kern County Superintendent of Schools.

Brown, F., Evans, I.M., Weed, K., & Owen, V. (1987). Delineating functional competencies: A component model. *Journal of The Association for Persons with Severe Handicaps, 12*(2), 117–124.

Brown, F., Gothelf, C.R., Guess, D., & Lehr, D. (1998). Self-determination for individuals with the most severe disabilities: Moving beyond chimera. *Journal of The Association for Persons with Severe Handicaps, 23*(1), 17–26.

Brown, F., Holvoet, J., Guess, D., & Mulligan, M. (1980). The individualized curriculum sequencing model (III): Small group instruction. *Journal of The Association for the Severely Handicapped, 5*(4), 352–367.

Brown, L., Nietupski, J., & Hamre-Nietupski, S. (1976). Criterion of ultimate functioning. In M.A. Thomas (Ed.), *Hey, don't forget about me! Education's investment in the severely, profoundly, and multiply handicapped* (pp. 2–15). Reston, VA: Council for Exceptional Children.

Brown, L., Nisbet, J., Ford, A., Sweet, M., Shiraga, B., York, J., & Loomis, R. (1983). The critical need for non-school instruction in educational programs for severely handicapped students. *Journal of The Association for the Severely Handicapped, 8*(3), 71–77.

Brown, L., Rogan, P., Shiraga, B., Zanella Albright, K., Kessler, K., Bryson, F., Van Deventer, P., & Loomis, R. (1987). *A vocational follow-up evaluation of the 1984 to 1986 Madison Metropolitan School District graduates with severe intellectual disabilities.* Seattle, WA: The Association for Persons with Severe Handicaps.

Carter, M., & Grunsell, J. (2001). The behavior chain interruption strategy: A review of research and discussion of future directions. *Journal of The Association for Persons with Severe Handicaps, 26*(l), 37–49.

Evans, I.M., Goldberg-Arnold, J.S., & Dickson, J.K. (1998). Children's perceptions of equity in peer interactions. In L.H. Meyer, H.S. Park, M. Grenot-Scheyer, I.S. Schwartz, & B. Harry (Eds.), *Making friends: The influences of culture and development* (pp. 133–147). Baltimore: Paul H. Brookes Publishing Co.

Evans, I.M., Salisbury, C., Palombaro, M., & Goldberg, J.S. (1994). Children's perceptions of fairness in classroom and interpersonal situations involving peers with severe disabilities. *Journal of The Association for Persons with Severe Handicaps, 19*(4), 326–332.

Giangreco, M.F. (1994). Effects of consensus-building process on team decision-making: Preliminary data. *Physical Disabilities: Education and Related Services, 13*(1), 41–55.

Harry, B. (1998). Parental visions of "una vida normal/a normal life": Cultural variations on a theme. In L.H. Meyer, H.S. Park, M. Grenot-Scheyer, I.S. Schwartz, & B. Harry (Eds.), *Making friends: The influences of culture and development* (pp. 47–62). Baltimore: Paul H. Brookes Publishing Co.

Holvoet, J., O'Neil, C., Chazdon, L., Carr, D., & Warner, J. (1983). Hey, do we really have to take data? *Journal of The Association for Persons with Severe Handicaps, 8*(3), 56–70.

Hunt, P., Farron-Davis, F., Beckstead, S., Curtis, D., & Goetz, L. (1994). Evaluating the effects of placement of students with severe disabilities in general education versus special classes. *Journal of The Association for Persons with Severe Handicaps, 19*(3), 200–214.

Hunt, P., Farron-Davis, F., Wrenn, M., Hirose-Hatae, A., & Goetz, L. (1997). Promoting interactive partnerships in inclusive education settings. *Journal of The Association for Persons with Severe Handicaps, 22*(3), 127–137.

Hunt, P., Haring, K., Farron-Davis, F., Staub, D., Rogers, J., Beckstead, S.P., Karasoff, P., Goetz, L., & Sailor, W. (1993). Factors associated with the integrated placement of students with severe disabilities. *Journal of The Association for Persons with Severe Handicaps, 18*(1), 6–15.

Jackson, I., Ryndak, D.L., & Billingsley, F. (2000). Useful practices in inclusive education: A preliminary view of what experts in moderate to severe disabilities are saying. *Journal of The Association for Persons with Severe Handicaps, 25*(3), 129–141.

Karnish, K., Bruder, M.B., & Rainforth, B. (1995). A comparison of physical therapy in two school-based treatment contexts. *Physical and Occupational Therapy in Pediatrics, 15*(4), 1–25.

Kleinert, H.L., Haig, J., Kearns, J.F., & Kennedy, S. (2000). Alternate assessments: Lessons learned and roads to be taken. *Exceptional Children, 67*(l), 51–66.

Larin, H.M. (2000). Motor learning: Theories and strategies for the practitioner. In S.K. Campbell, D.W. Vander Linden, & R.J. Palisano (Eds.), *Physical therapy for children* (2nd ed.) (pp. 170–197). Philadelphia: W.B. Saunders.

Linehan, S.A., Brady, M.P., & Hwang, C. (1991). Ecological versus developmental assessment: Influences on instructional expectations. *Journal of The Association for Persons with Severe Handicaps, 16*(3), 146–153.

McGee, G.G., Morrier, M.J., & Daly, T. (1999). An incidental teaching approach to early intervention for toddlers with autism. *Journal of The Association for Persons with Severe Handicaps, 24*(3), 133–146.

McGregor, G., & Vogelsberg, R.T. (1998). *Inclusive schooling practices: Pedagogical and research foundations.* Baltimore: Paul H. Brookes Publishing Co.

Meyer, L.H., Park, H.S., Grenot-Scheyer, M., Schwartz, I.S., & Harry, B. (1998). *Making friends: The influences of culture and development.* Baltimore: Paul H. Brookes Publishing Co.

Moes, D.R. (1998). Integrating choice-making opportunities within teacher-assigned academic tasks to facilitate the performance of children with autism. *Journal of The Association for Persons with Severe Handicaps, 23*(4), 319–328.

Palmer, D.S., Fuller, K., Arora, T., & Nelson, M. (2001). Taking sides: Parents' views on inclusion for their children with severe disabilities. *Exceptional Children, 67*(4), 467–484.

Pollock, N., & Stewart, D. (1998). Occupational performance needs of school-aged children with physical disabilities in the community. *Physical and Occupational Therapy in Pediatrics, 18*(1), 55–68.

Rainforth, B. (1997). An analysis of physical therapy practice acts: Implications for role release in educational settings. *Pediatric Physical Therapy, 9*(2), 54–61.

Rainforth, B., & York-Barr, J. (1997). *Collaborative teams for students with severe disabilities: Integrating therapy and educational services.* Baltimore: Paul H. Brookes Publishing Co.

Rigby, P., & Schwellnus, H. (1999). Occupational therapy decision making guidelines for problems in written productivity. *Physical and Occupational Therapy in Pediatrics, 19*(l), 5–27.

Salisbury, C., Mangino, M., Petrigala, M., Rainforth, B., & Syryca, S. (1994). Promoting the instructional inclusion of young children with disabilities in the primary grades. *Journal of Early Intervention, 18*(3), 311–322.

Snell, M.E., & Brown, F. (2000). *Instruction of students with severe disabilities* (5th ed.). Columbus, OH: Charles E. Merrill.

Snell, M.E., & Janney, R.E. (2000). Teachers' problem-solving about children with moderate and severe disabilities in elementary classrooms. *Exceptional Children, 66*(4), 472–490.

Utley, B.L., & Rapport, M.J.K. (2000). Exploring role release in the multidisciplinary team. *Physical Disabilities: Education and Related Services, 18*(2), 89–118.

Westling, D.L., & Fox, L. (2000). *Teaching students with severe disabilities* (2nd ed.). Columbus, OH: Charles E. Merrill.

CHAPTER TEN

Creating and Sustaining Inclusive Classroom Communities

BEVERLY RAINFORTH & JUDY W. KUGELMASS

Each chapter in this book presents images of inclusive classroom communities and describes strategies for educating all children in those communities. In Chapter 1, we define *inclusion* as an approach that addresses the needs of *all* children within a school, not just students with disabilities. In this broadened definition of inclusion, we identify several ways of organizing services, approaching instruction, and honoring diversity in order to meet the needs of all children within the general education classroom and curriculum. Because the ultimate purpose of inclusion is to promote human rights and social justice through education, we also discuss what we call a pedagogy of success—curricula, instructional materials, and methods that are thoughtfully planned and implemented to meet the needs of individual students as well as support their classroom and school communities.

Unfortunately, the history of education has been replete with competition between approaches that have been considered incompatible. In Chapter 1, we identify and discuss features of two such approaches: constructivism and systematic instruction. We believe that a pedagogy of success requires shifting from either/or thinking to reflective understanding; from automatically rejecting or accepting either approach to adopting a thoughtful blend of constructivism and systematic instruction. This book demonstrates how children with a wide range of abilities, interests, and needs can be educated in constructivist classrooms in which instruction is intentionally designed and implemented. Within these classrooms, some instruction is direct and systematic, as appropriate to the individual child and the work at hand. Some children require more support and guidance, others need to learn to work more cooperatively, and still others need to learn to manage themselves and their work more independently. Because the adults in these classrooms recognize the varied abilities, interests, and needs of their students, they recognize that one size can never fit all; they must tailor their approach to education from the threads that suit their unique group of learners. To fully recognize how principles of inclusion, constructivism, and systematic instruction can be incorporated into a pedagogy of success, it is useful to consider highlights from each chapter and make connections among the chapters. After presenting this synthesis, guidance is offered on initiating and sustaining the practices described throughout this book.

ADVANCING ISSUES OF CULTURAL AND LINGUISTIC DIVERSITY IN THE EARLY CHILDHOOD CLASSROOM

In Chapter 2, Monica Miller Marsh discusses how developmentally appropriate practice (DAP), an early childhood model grounded in constructivism, has inadvertently limited opportunities for children from nondominant cultures to succeed in U.S. schools. Miller Marsh introduces "social constructionism," Vygotsky's (1978) theory that learning does not occur within children, but through interaction with others for co-construction of knowledge. The teacher featured in this chapter, Ms. Gonzales, models systematic instruction, constructivism, and social constructionism as she guides the learning of 26 children with diverse ethnicities, languages, social classes, and learning abilities. She recognizes that such a diverse group of children may not enter her first-grade class knowing the behavioral norms of schools, so she teaches those norms intentionally. In small-group and partner work, she carefully selects which children will work together, designs learning activities that require student interaction, and gives explicit guidance and feedback about how to work together well. Ms. Gonzales also uses modeling, direct instruction, literature, and a variety of projects to explore and validate languages other than English, nondominant cultures, nontraditional gender roles, and other aspects of diversity.

Within this rich cultural backdrop, Ms. Gonzales offers a challenging academic curriculum with many ways for children to learn and demonstrate understanding of important content. She has high expectations for all of her students and motivates them to do their best. This integration of sociocultural and academic objectives was seen when she challenged Grace, whose first language is Spanish, and Dionne, who has learning difficulties, to write the numbers 1 to 20 on the blackboard together and name them in order. She recognizes that some children will learn some content more slowly or may not learn everything that others do. With extensive use of small-group and partner work, Ms. Gonzales creates ongoing opportunities for co-construction of knowledge, yet she monitors for accuracy and makes corrections when needed. When children become frustrated, as Charlie and Dionne did during center work, she notices and adjusts her teaching, giving more time, more encouragement, more help, or more direct instruction. Through this blend of constructivist and systematic approaches, Ms. Gonzales offers an effective education for a large and diverse class of first-graders.

PROJECT-BASED INSTRUCTION

In Chapter 3, Judy W. Kugelmass introduces an approach to teaching that is generally associated with constructivism. Project-based instruction (PBI) is built on the constructivist concept that learning is a social experience. The examples provided from two classrooms demonstrate how children solve intellectual and social problems through interaction with one another and their physical environments. In these classrooms, learning is linked to real-life experiences that have meaning and purpose. They also illustrate the wide range of possibilities and contexts in which PBI can be applied. In one situation, a schoolwide kindergarten project on birds is planned as a year-long event by an instructional team that includes classroom teachers, special education consultants, and related services staff. In the other situation, a project emerges spontaneously in a fourth-grade class, inspired by student interest and concern about homeless children. In both cases, every child is included in a meaningful way that both supports the completion of the project and meets his or her individual needs.

These examples (and the projects Lamash and Regenspan describe in Chapters 6 and 7) differ from projects that develop solely out of student interest. For the projects described in this book, teachers intentionally design the classroom investigations with their students to address specific learning objectives. Instruction is based in the activities that take place within the context of these classroom projects. For example, language arts, social studies, and mathematics objectives are integrated into the bird project. The fourth-grade project on homelessness integrates language arts requirements with student and teacher interest in social action. Objectives for each project came from mandated curricula, state or school district learning standards, and/or individualized learning objectives such as those found in students' individualized education programs (IEPs). Teachers facilitate activities that help develop knowledge, skills, and/or dispositions, while simultaneously reinforcing and applying children's existing cognitive, linguistic, and social skills. PBI deepens and expands on what children already know, motivates their desire to learn more, and provides opportunities for all children to participate successfully in a shared learning experience.

FINDING THE MIDDLE GROUND
IN LITERACY INSTRUCTION

In Chapter 4, Karen Bromley borrows the term *thoughtful eclecticism* (Duffy & Hoffman, 1999) to describe literacy instruction that incorporates both systematic (teacher-directed) and constructivist (teacher-guided) approaches. Snapshots of kindergarten, first-grade, and fourth-grade classes, and interviews with their respective teachers, illustrate this school's commitment to "balanced literacy instruction," which is explicit, systematic, mindful, and contextualized (Cambourne, 1999). In each of these classrooms, teachers teach reading and writing processes and skills explicitly, by, for example, showing one-to-one correspondence between speech and print while reading a "big book" in kindergarten, strengthening decoding and spelling in first grade by making new words from the letters in a target word, and exploring with prefixes, suffixes, roots, and whole words in fourth grade. These teachers are also systematic in that they assess their students' literacy skills formally, interpret results carefully, and develop written plans for lessons and activities to address student concerns. They carefully select literature, for example, according to the reading ability of each student, and have clear goals when they use reading groups—sometimes grouping students with similar abilities, sometimes mixing abilities. The teachers are mindful of students' metacognitive processes, particularly as children learn to make sense of print and, when print does not make sense, to draw on a variety of "word-solving" strategies.

These strategies and examples may seem more aligned with what we have termed *systematic instruction*, yet there is a strong emphasis on children co-constructing knowledge through group work, building on their knowledge and interests to strengthen comprehension, and using personal experience to inspire writing. The next element of balanced literacy instruction is that it is contextualized. Thus, Miss Davis guides her kindergarten students to use literacy in their imaginary play, engaging them to read menus, newspapers, and recipes, take orders, and use the cash register in their restaurant. In her fourth-grade classroom, Miss Murray teaches literacy as an integral part of the study of science and social studies.

Like the other schools described in this book, the student population in this school has great racial, ethnic, linguistic, and socioeconomic diversity. Literature becomes an important means to validate this diversity, although the teachers recognize that the students' diversity is reflected in development of their reading and writing abilities. These students require an array of support services and, in this inclusive school, ESL teachers, literacy specialists, special education teachers, and speech-language therapists work within general education classrooms. Although many refer to this as a "push-in" model (specialists push themselves in rather than pull students out), such vernacular suggests that specialists are unwelcome intruders. Instead, Bromley refers to this approach as "pull-in," suggesting that classroom teachers value these resources and actively seek their participation.

BEYOND CONSTRUCTIVISM AND BACK TO BASICS: A CULTURAL HISTORICAL ALTERNATIVE TO THE TEACHING OF THE BASE TEN POSITIONAL SYSTEM

In Chapter 5, Jean Schmittau examines mathematics instruction in American public schools from the perspective of cognitive learning theories and identifies significant weaknesses in our current approaches. Applying a cultural-historical model, she explains why neither algorithmic drill, which characterizes the "back-to-basics" movement, nor constructivist approaches, featuring use of manipulatives such as base ten blocks, is adequate to develop the concepts underlying the base ten positional system. Both approaches have inadvertently led children to construct misconceptions that interfere with learning more advanced mathematical concepts.

Schmittau explains why understanding of bases and positional systems is absolutely central to the understanding of addition, subtraction, multiplication, and division of whole numbers. She then offers an alternative model that has been researched for more than 40 years and used with thousands of students with wide ranges of abilities in other countries. Examples from an American classroom, in which the cultural-historical approach has been applied, illustrate the importance of providing an intentionally designed curriculum consisting of a carefully sequenced collection of problems. Although this chapter is distinct in many ways from other chapters in this book, it shares the perspective that students will become actively engaged in deep learning when they are challenged to solve real problems. The curriculum requires skill on the part of the teacher in tailoring the inquiry method to the needs of all students. Not only are there observable and measurable objectives, but children also learn to evaluate their individual and collective growth toward meeting these objectives. This approach transcends both the basic skills and constructivist orientations while addressing the features advocated by both, thereby eliminating the foundation for the basic skills versus constructivism debate.

SOCIAL HISTORY, TECHNOLOGY, AND THE BUILDING OF INCLUSIVE CLASSROOM COMMUNITIES

Throughout Chapter 6, Laura Lamash demonstrates what others are saying in this book: No one theory, method, instructional approach, or curriculum can guarantee the success of every student in an inclusive classroom. As she shows how digital technology can sustain a thriving community of heterogeneous learners, she also alerts us to its limitations and dangers. She reminds us to view technology as an instructional tool that, like all tools, reflects the context in which it is used. Technology can help create a community of learners who construct knowledge through interactions and dialogue with others, and it can support the diverse learning styles, interests, and needs of children in an inclusive classroom. If these are a teacher's goals, however, the teacher must intentionally create this context.

Lamash illustrates how digital technology was integrated into a yearlong project to help develop this kind of classroom. The project, Time Travel, is another example of PBI that supports the integration of academic content with the development of children's creative, interpersonal, and intrapersonal skills. Lamash also introduces social history as an approach to social studies instruction that uses primary sources and personal narratives to tell the stories of ordinary people; social movements; and cultural, social, and political institutions. Through documentation and critique of historical phenomena, students focus their historical investigations on the lives of everyday people and, ultimately, link history with current conditions and their own lives. As their culminating event for Time Travel, Lamash's fourth-grade students examined the impact of the Industrial Revolution on the lives of working class children and adults. They also established connections between the Industrial Revolution and the Digital Revolution, further relating social history to themselves and their community. The chapter demonstrates how integrating social history and technology can support the social, emotional, conceptual, and skill development of students with diverse abilities and needs in the context of a general education classroom.

INCLUSIVE EDUCATION THROUGH THE ARTS IN A COLLABORATIVE, COMMUNITY-RESPONSIVE ELEMENTARY TEAM: A DAY IN THE LIFE

In Chapter 7, Barbara Regenspan illustrates that children and adults have lives and relationships outside of school that are multifaceted, often complicated, and do not stop at the school door. Variables include race, language, country of origin, religion, family structure, and family income. Rather than deny these influences, the teachers in this chapter find ways for lives outside of school to contribute to a pulsating classroom community. The children's experiences and relationships outside of school also become important sources for rich and challenging curricula. Like many other teachers featured in this book, the teachers in these multiage classrooms use PBI, this time with the arts as a central medium in their curricula.

Regenspan notes that instruction in these classrooms alternates between development of basic skills through "practice for" and practical applications through "the real thing." Sufficient attention is given to both aspects of learning so that students remain engaged with real-life challenges as they acquire the fundamental academic knowledge and skills required to respond to those challenges. Woven throughout these experiences is the development of interpersonal skills for clarifying expectations with teachers and negotiating with classmates. Although teachers plan activities with specific objectives for development of subject-matter knowledge and skills, as well as individualized objectives from IEPs, curriculum also spirals from a variety of planned and unplanned events. Regenspan and Lamash both acknowledge the challenge of managing such complexity, but show how this spontaneity generates student ownership for and engagement in the curriculum.

MEETING THE NEEDS OF STUDENTS
WITH CHALLENGING BEHAVIORS

In Chapter 8, Robert Carpenter and Melissa Price address the population of students who are most often removed from general education
classrooms: children with challenging behaviors. This is unfortunate
because these children have a great deal to gain from being in the kinds
of classrooms described in this book. Children with challenging behaviors may need specialized interventions, but they also need many opportunities to observe and interact with children who can model appropriate social and problem-solving skills, opportunities that are
inherently lacking in classes that serve only children with challenging
behaviors. In other respects, children with challenging behaviors have
the same range of learning abilities, interests, and needs as other children, and the kinds of constructivist classrooms described in this book
offer far-richer learning environments than most special classes.

Carpenter and Price review several systematic behavioral intervention strategies that come from the field of applied behavior analysis. They emphasize, however, that these are not "quick fixes." Clearly
defining standards for behavior and systematically giving or taking
away rewards may be necessary for some students, but these structures are only as effective as the relationships that adults develop with
these children. Furthermore, the best intervention is prevention
through designing curriculum and instruction (including social skills
instruction) that are appropriate for each student, constructing behavior as positive, and offering graceful ways for children to stop misbe-
having. Miller Marsh demonstrates these points in Chapter 2, in the
way Ms. Gonzales approaches classroom management as well as Ivan's
and John's misbehavior when they toss game pieces around the room.
Regenspan also illustrates these principles, particularly in explaining
Mrs. D.'s interactions with Larry. As most readers can imagine, the
paint spill incident in Chapter 7 might have been constructed as more
evidence of Larry being endless trouble. Instead, Mrs. D. takes responsibility for the accident, and makes Larry a star of sorts, with many
adults rallying to help clean up Larry and his classroom.

Carpenter and Price discuss two other important strategies:
1) functional behavioral assessment (FBA), leading to creation of a
positive behavior support plan, and 2) life space crisis intervention
(LSCI). Both FBA and LSCI are systematic approaches. Both also recognize that "challenging behavior" and its causes are the constructions
of several people, including the student. Fully understanding and respectfully considering the child's perspective are essential to resolving

the issue. As Schmittau's chapter illustrates, misconceptions are also "constructions." LSCI is one strategy that guides students to see their own misconceptions as they justify their behavior, whereas FBA can help adults see the misconceptions they hold about preventing and responding to challenging behavior.

USING ACTIVITY ROUTINES TO DESIGN INCLUSIVE EDUCATION FOR STUDENTS WITH SEVERE DISABILITIES

In Chapter 9, Beverly Rainforth addresses students with severe disabilities who are rarely considered for inclusion in general education classes. Their exclusion is not because they disrupt classes or cannot be educated there satisfactorily, but because teachers have so little personal or professional experience with the population that they may assume that true inclusion is not reasonable. Rainforth details how students with severe disabilities can receive a purposeful and meaningful education in the context of constructivist classrooms such as those described throughout this book. Like Kugelmass, Rainforth illustrates how individualized objectives can be addressed and direct, systematic instruction provided within classroom activities and routines designed for children without disabilities. For students with severe disabilities, responsibility for this process does not fall on individual classroom teachers. Just as Kugelmass, Bromley, and others have noted, planning and implementing inclusive education for students with disabilities rests with a team, which includes the classroom teacher, special education teacher, and related services professionals (e.g., speech-language pathologist, occupational therapist, physical therapist).

Cuban noted that public schools must ensure benefits both to individuals and to society as a whole (Willis, 2002). For individual benefits, every student needs a challenging curriculum, requiring many levels and many ways to participate. Societal benefits accrue when every student learns the importance of contributing to their community and experiences the joys of making contributions. Although children with severe disabilities often have specific learning needs that differ from other children in general education classes, they also need many of the same opportunities for learning as other children, such as a rich and engaging environment that encourages communication, negotiation, and social interactions with other children and adults. Furthermore, decisions about where children with severe disabilities are educated have profound implications for where they will live and work as adults and, ultimately, the extent to which they will contribute to society.

It is not, however, only students with severe disabilities who need these opportunities. As discussed in Chapter 1, inclusive schools are not created just to serve students with disabilities. Inclusive schools are designed to meet the unique abilities and needs of *all* children in the increasingly diverse communities found in the United States. Adopting a thoughtful blend of systematic instruction and constructivist approaches enables public schools to ensure benefits both to individual students and to society as a whole.

INITIATING CHANGE TO CREATE INCLUSIVE ELEMENTARY SCHOOLS

Although the examples presented in each chapter and the research cited throughout the book support the effectiveness of these kinds of classrooms, we recognize that some teachers may be reluctant to initiate practices that do not already exist in their own schools. This reluctance may be further reinforced by school policies that focus on meeting uniform sets of standards and monitoring student achievement through high-stakes testing. In these contexts, educational reform is not directed toward instructional innovation, but at accountability. In some places, this has led to scheduling instructional time for test preparation and/or requiring teachers to "teach to the test." In these schools, developing children's capacity for critical thinking, creativity, and social skills is relegated to the back burner.

Teachers working in these kinds of school environments are understandably wary of innovations that do not directly teach what will be tested. If they are working in classrooms with diverse populations of students, they are faced with an additional contradictory demand: to meet external standards and/or the individual needs of the child. This false dichotomy has once again created a pedagogical dilemma that teachers must resolve. Some teachers have tried to address these conflicting demands by moving away from heterogeneous groups engaged in cooperative and collaborative learning to homogenous grouping of students. Others are increasing the use of special classes and/or pull-out services for remedial or special education. These teachers have not been provided with alternative instructional strategies such as those presented in this book. The instructional approaches described and illustrated throughout this book demonstrate that it is possible to teach academic skills and address established standards while providing experiences that enhance children's overall development by blending systematic instruction with constructivist practices.

Teachers who want to use these approaches in their own classrooms will, however, still need to consider where, when, and how to begin. Although the approaches described here are best accomplished when implemented by an instructional team, individual teachers have initiated these approaches successfully in their own classrooms. An individual teacher can also share the ideas presented in this book with her or his colleagues, a curriculum coordinator, and/or the building principal. Many routes to change are possible, from innovation by individual teachers to site-based decision-making, to administrative mandate. Whatever the route, change still occurs one person at a time, and is a highly personal experience. Research on school change shows that each individual goes through predictable "stages of concern" and "levels of use": from learning about an innovation to managing the tasks involved in the innovation to striving to improve benefits of the innovation for students (Hall & Hord, 2001). Bringing new instructional practices into a school also represents significant change, and it is important to understand that "change is a process, not an event" (Hall & Hord, 2001, p. 4). Fully adopting a new curriculum or institutionalizing a broader reform such as inclusive education typically takes 3–5 years.

Although change takes place with individual teachers, adopting and sustaining a reform involves learning and integrating knowledge from many different people (O'Neil, 1995). Studies of change also show that targets of change, such as a curriculum, are influenced by many other elements in a school, so changing multiple elements may be more successful than an isolated change (Spillane, Halverson, & Diamond, 2001). Therefore, simultaneously committing to inclusive education, adopting a new teaming model, and exploring new approaches to curriculum and instruction can have a more positive effect than any one innovation in isolation.

The school principal is often cited as the key person in creating and sustaining inclusive schools (e.g., Brown & Moffett, 1999; Lipsky & Gartner, 1997; Udvari-Solner & Keyes, 2000). Unfortunately, a narrow focus on principals can create the impression that leadership resides only with administrators. Hall and Hord (2001) noted that the principal, as positional leader of the school, is the primary person to sanction a change as important, to keep priorities clear, and to provide ongoing support by allocating resources and addressing bureaucratic issues. Yet everyone involved in a reform has responsibilities in adopting and sustaining change. Teachers, whether or not they are formally designated as "change facilitators," help support reform by modeling new strategies, coaching and encouraging other teachers, and sharing information with audiences outside the school (e.g., school board, PTA, professional conferences). Although some teachers may lead by formally sharing methods and materials in a curriculum workshop or demonstration lesson, others may share strategies over lunch in the teacher's room, or present their process when they put student work in a hallway display case. Teachers are also the primary source of information about whether a reform is working, and often know what adjustments would make the reform more effective in their school. Even while some teachers may avoid leadership roles, they still influence the change process as followers (Spillane et al., 2001).

SUSTAINING INNOVATIONS IN CHANGING TIMES

A great deal has been written about how to change schools but relatively little has been written about sustaining change, as though once adopted, innovations would sustain themselves. This assumption ignores the constant shifts that have occurred in public education reform in the United States during the 20th century. As described in the first chapter of this book, these shifts have been characterized by the ascendancy of conflicting innovations that focus on either academic achievement or the development of the "whole" child. The pendulum has shifted from right to left, from skills to affect, from uniform standards to individual interest. These ideological movements have not allowed for the emergence of approaches that balance the needs of individual children with assuring the development of basic skills. Therefore, we must expect that sustaining a balanced approach will be as difficult as sustaining other innovations.

Staying true to the basic principles of an innovation while adjusting to ever-changing circumstances is no small feat. The political climate is not the only factor that affects the ability to maintain practices long enough to refine and improve their implementation. A teacher who once labored long hours preparing lessons such as those presented in this book may be unable to keep such a pace after becoming a parent or encountering health problems. A school that had celebrated diversity may discover growing intolerance as economic downturn creates an exodus of middle-class families, with deepening poverty and despair among the families who remain. State-mandated testing programs may convince teachers they must abandon effective teaching strategies and just drill for the tests, even though they know their students retain little of what they were taught. Even when teachers do sustain innovations, failure to adapt to changing times can threaten the fidelity of teachers' work. Teachers and schools must find ways to adapt to changing personal circumstances and to the changing social, economic, and political realities impacting their school community.

Recent literature identifies several influences on a school's ability to sustain change, including 1) shared vision and beliefs, 2) the school culture, 3) program coherence, 4) teachers as learners, 5) collegial relations, 6) mentoring, 7) shared leadership, 8) integration of the broader policy context, and 9) adaptability. Each of these influences is discussed in the following sections.

Shared Vision and Beliefs

The starting point for school change is to have a vision for the school. Absence of such a vision will create confusion. Sustainable reforms grow from understanding of and support for that vision by the entire school community, including school board members, administrators, families, teachers, and other school staff. For innovations such as a new curriculum, Hall and Hord recommended "innovation configuration maps" (2001, p. 41) to clearly articulate what the innovation is and what it is not. This approach has appeal for broader reforms such as inclusive education, because there are so many misconceptions about what really constitutes "inclusion."

Although the vision is essential, it is neither complete nor powerful until those involved in the reform also articulate their core values, or "covenant of beliefs" (Glickman, 2002, p. 42). Because this "covenant" is developed and affirmed by the school community, it is an important guide for decision making, especially when practices are challenged. Kugelmass (2000, 2001) described an elementary school, Betsy Miller, which was able to sustain reforms despite several changes, including the departure and subsequent death of the principal who had led the school through its transformation. After the teachers clarified their core commitments to collaboration and inclusion, they determined that they could adjust some of their practices without violating their core values. The experience of another elementary school, Charles Washington, illustrates what can happen when these commitments are compromised. Charles Washington had also committed to including all children, even those with the most severe disabilities and challenging behaviors. Like Betsy Miller, it went through several difficult transitions, during which its vision of inclusion was challenged. Rather than studying their earlier vision and beliefs and questioning whether their practices really supported the vision and beliefs, the staff at Charles Washington began espousing what they called "responsible inclusion," in which high rates of exclusion were accepted without question.

School Culture

Over a period of years, the teachers at Betsy Miller (Kugelmass 2000, 2001) embedded their values into every part of their school and developed practices that supported those values, which were tangibly illustrated in posters and projects displayed in the school, schoolwide activities and celebrations, and the literature describing the school. When faced with challenges, the school's culture was strong and able to sustain the reforms the teachers had invested so much to establish. Hargreaves and Fink (2000) described another school, Lord Byron High School, which demonstrated remarkable innovations for its first 7 years of operation. Other schools in the district resisted adopting the structures that had distinguished Lord Byron and, eventually, several factors led this school to revert to very traditional practices. When some of Lord Byron's best teachers took leadership positions in other schools, however, they brought their vision, values, and supporting practices with them, making a great impact on the school district by "reculturing the system" (Hargreaves & Fink, 2000, p. 33).

Program Coherence

The central commitment in school reform must be to deepen student learning, and not just results on mandated tests (Fullan, 2002; Hall & Hord, 2001; Hargreaves & Fink, 2000). Thus, the vision for the school, its covenant of beliefs, and educational practices must support one another around this commitment. As illustrated throughout this book, schools committed to inclusive education define student learning in terms of traditional academic outcomes, but do not stop there. Inclusive schools are also concerned with every child's physical and emotional health, aesthetic development, and the social and communication abilities that support the culture of classroom and school as communities. This broad view of the curriculum promotes the societal benefits that are the responsibility of public schools (Willis, 2002). "Overload and fragmentation are natural tendencies of complex systems" (Fullan, 2002, p. 19), so school communities must check their vision, beliefs, and practices regularly for consistency. Some of Lord

Byron's (Hargreaves & Fink, 2000) and Charles Washington's failures to sustain reforms grew out of overload and fragmentation related to changes in the student population and staff turnover. Some schools add layer on layer of innovation, without examining how the latest addition complements or competes with the existing culture. Even when all practices are complementary, a school will collapse under the weight of numerous separate initiatives unless teachers take care to fully understand, integrate, and adopt these promising practices.

Teachers as Learners

Reform is more likely to be sustained when teachers take an active part in learning about the specific practices they adopt, study the efficacy in their school and classrooms, and adjust the practices based on their findings. Conferences, workshops, and visits to other schools can be important strategies for introducing an innovation. The most useful learning about a new practice occurs at the school and in the classrooms in which the practice will be adopted, however, because the unique circumstances of the school shape how the practice will become most effective (Fullan, 2002). Any forum that encourages teachers to exchange ideas helps break down the "egg carton" structure of schools, which isolates teachers from one another and limits their growth (Spillane et al., 2001). Study groups, in which teachers read books or articles together and have weekly professional discussions about the specific educational focus of their reading, bring staff development into the local context and raise teachers' interest in learning (Lambert, 2002; Routman, 2002). Another powerful approach to staff development is a "critical friends group" that meets monthly to examine student performance and the related teacher practices and to explore alternatives (Bambino, 2002; Easton, 2002).

As teachers deepen their interest in evaluating their current efforts and learning about new approaches, action research is an effective tool to study and refine practice (Calhoun, 2002; Glickman, 2002). In action research, teachers read research on teaching (not just how-to descriptions) and conduct small studies in their own classrooms. Although teachers may learn a great deal from action research conducted individually, the power of the study groups and critical friends groups described above is tapped when action research is a collaborative endeavor, especially when studying a school wide effort such as inclusive education. Calhoun (2002) and Routman (2002) both warned that teachers often are reluctant to admit they struggle with some practices or to share student performance data that may reflect poorly on their best efforts as teachers, and may avoid such discussions for months or even years. When teachers cross this hurdle, however, they become a community of learners who can affect deep and lasting change.

Collegial Relations

Gossen and Anderson (1995) described three types of schools: traditional, congenial, and collegial. Traditional schools are hierarchical organizations in which the expectation is that principals will lead and teachers will follow; in classrooms, teachers will lead and children will follow. Although some teachers (and students) accept this hierarchy, conflict is evident and practice stagnates. Congenial schools are characterized by a social atmosphere, with friendly conversations, snacks in the teacher's room, and recognition of birthdays and other personal events. Considerable conflict may lurk under the surface, however, because there is no forum or culture to wrestle with difficult issues, and there is fear that discussing issues openly will damage relationships. In collegial schools, teachers are respectful of one another as they focus on their primary purpose: teaching well. Teachers have personal relationships, but these do not interfere with tackling the issues that face their school. Rather than weakening relationships, a culture of problem solving extends to resolving conflicts with teachers, administrators, students, and students' families. As discussed throughout this section, thoughtful processes of school reform strengthen collegial relationships and school–community relationships. The depth of these relationships helps sustain schools as they address challenges to their reforms (Fullan, 2002; Kugelmass, 2001).

Mentoring

Johnson and Kardos (2002) identified three types of professional cultures: veteran oriented, novice oriented, and integrated. Veteran-oriented professional cultures are dominated by experienced teachers who have tremendous knowledge and skills, but there is no mechanism for experienced teachers to share their expertise with new teachers. Schools of this type are at high risk for schisms to develop between veteran and novice teachers, and for practices that were well-established to be lost. When a school such as Lord Byron (Hargreaves & Fink 2000) suddenly finds itself in this situation, it may be too late to regain the culture that made it exemplary. Newly established schools or disorganized schools with high turnover tend to have novice-oriented professional cultures, in which many inexperienced (and often uncertified) teachers may have great enthusiasm but lack professional grounding. In these schools, no culture exists to transmit to new teachers.

Schools with integrated professional cultures use veteran teachers as mentors to help orient new teachers to the culture of the school and to guide their professional development. Even in schools without formal mentoring programs, experienced teachers can offer tremendous support to new teachers by talking about the vision and values of the school, describing practices that support its culture, sharing materials, and inviting new teachers to observe their teaching. Without formal mentoring programs, novice teachers may not welcome observation by and feedback from their senior colleagues, but invitations to team teach can create opportunities to plan together, to evaluate the success of co-taught lessons, to strategize about more effective methods, and to create the kind of trusting relationships that characterize effective mentoring. In these ways, new teachers can learn the vision, core values, and practices that support reforms such as inclusive education.

Shared Leadership

Fullan noted that "charismatic leaders are actually a liability for sustained improvement" and "a school leader's effectiveness in creating a culture of sustained change will be determined by the leaders he or she leaves behind" (2002, p. 20). Sharing leadership increases teachers' ownership for reforms, and thereby makes them more sustainable as administrators and policies change. When principals share leadership, however, teachers need a clear understanding of the district and building governance structure, that is, which roles and responsibilities are being shared and which are not (Glickman, 2002). Teachers in one school may be *asked to make decisions* about adapting curriculum and grading for students with disabilities, *asked to make recommendations* about student groupings and use of school space (but the final decision rests with the principal), and *advised* that district or state policy determines certain decisions about class size and staffing. When teachers understand the arenas in which leadership is shared, they can have a great and lasting influence on how their school works.

As noted previously, everyone involved in a reform needs to take responsibility for adopting and sustaining the reform. For some teachers, this will mean focusing on their own students and practice while others will look at broader school interests. Teacher-leaders, who are interested in deep learning and sharing their learning with others, will emerge from the kinds of work groups described here. Teacher-leaders also may be formally appointed as mentors or curriculum specialists or may assist with implementation or evaluation of mandated programs (Feiler, Heritage, & Gallimore, 2000; Lambert, 2002). Teacher-leaders are most effective when the strengths of individual teachers are matched with the identified needs of the school, when their roles and responsibilities are defined clearly, and when their focus is not distracted by unrelated (even if important) issues (Feiler, Heritage, & Gallimore, 2000).

Integration of the Broader Policy Context

Every school is subject to national, state, and local policies and regulations. Hargreaves and Fink (2000) offered examples of schools that were given special support or waivers as they adopted innovations. Although dispensations can be crucial during a start-up period, relying on them long-term will undermine reform because new administrations, tight budgets, and other political realities eventually will prevail. Rather than basing innovations on exceptional circumstances, Hargreaves and Fink advised that "educators will do better to capture the public imagination on which governments depend by making their practice and improvement efforts highly visible and by helping create a broad social movement for large-scale, deep, and sustainable transformations in public education that will benefit all students" (2000, p. 33). When teachers seek information about regulations, written policies, and other political realities affecting their school, they can help create structures that will support and sustain their reforms.

Adaptability

Kugelmass (2001) described a school that was able to sustain reforms despite several changes, including the departure and subsequent death of the principal who had led the school through its transformation. The teachers in this school clarified their core commitments, which were to collaboration and inclusion, and agreed that they could adapt certain practices to comply with bureaucratic demands without violating their core values. An important part of their experience was that the teachers at Betsy Miller Elementary School wrestled with the changing environment. By understanding the need for compromise and arriving at consensus about how to alter some features of their practice without violating their core beliefs, they were able to sustain the reforms they had initiated. In this case, adaptability related to the broader policy context. In other situations, adaptability might apply to collegial relations, shared leadership, or any of the other factors discussed here.

Teachers may resist adaptation either because change is difficult or because they see the adaptation as synonymous with "selling out" to bureaucratic expediencies or political whims. Some situations may require compromise, that is, giving up something to gain or keep something (Wilmot & Hocker, 2001). The teachers at Betsy Miller recognized that, if they refused to make any adjustment, they might lose even more of what they had worked to create, so compromise was necessary. In other situations, however, the need to adapt can lead to truly collaborative, or "win-win" solutions. For example, federal monitoring of implementation of the Individuals with Disabilities Education Act of 1990 (PL 101-476) has revealed high rates of segregated services for African American and Latino students with learning and behavior difficulties (Office of Special Education Programs, 2001). A school district cited for this issue would need to develop a corrective action plan with tight timelines. Change under such circumstances would be very stressful and, initially, might seem like a losing proposition for students and teachers. If the school district chose to examine their practices carefully and consider a range of alternatives, however, the need to adapt might lead them to explore the kinds of curriculum and instructional practices described throughout this book, adopt a strong model for teamwork, and create truly inclusive schools. The outcomes would not be a compromise, but winning solutions for students and teachers.

CONCLUSON

Creating schools that are truly inclusive is not a matter of putting all students in general education classrooms. It is a matter of thoughtfully creating the conditions under which all children, and all adults, can thrive. This book shares numerous illustrations of the results of that process and offers guidelines for creating and sustaining such schools. Each individual teacher has tremendous power to either influence change or maintain the status quo. We hope that readers of this book will take up the challenge to change their own practice, create a single classroom that responds to diverse student abilities and needs, provide systematic instruction in the context of constructivist practices, document the results with numerical data and exciting student work, and share their experiences with others. One teacher at a time, one team at a time, one school at a time, we believe we can create public educational systems that ensure benefits both to individual students and to society as a whole (Willis, 2002).

REFERENCES

Bambino, D. (2002). Critical friends. *Educational Leadership, 59*(6), 25–27.

Brown, J.L., & Moffett, C.A. (1999). *The hero's journey: How educators can transform schools and improve learning.* Alexandria, VA: Association for Supervision and Curriculum Development.

Calhoun, E.F. (2002). Action research for school improvement. *Educational Leadership, 59*(6), 18–23.

Cambourne, B. (1999). Conditions for literacy learning. *The Reading Teacher,* 53, 126–127.

Duffy, G.G., & Hoffman, J.V. (1999). In pursuit of an illusion: The flawed search for a perfect method. *The Reading Teacher, 53,* 10–16.

Easton, L.B. (2002). How the tuning protocol works. *Educational Leadership, 59*(6), 28–30.

Feiler, R., Heritage, M., & Gallimore, R. (2000). Teachers leading teachers. *Educational Leadership, 57*(7), 66–69.

Fullan, M. (2002). The change leader. *Educational Leadership, 59*(8), 16–20.

Glickman, C. (2002). The courage to lead. *Educational Leadership, 59*(8), 41–44.

Gossen, D., & Anderson, J. (1995). *Creating the conditions: Leadership for quality schools.* Chapel Hill, NC: New View.

Hall, E.G., & Hord, S.M. (2001). *Implementing change: Patterns, principles, and potholes.* Needham Heights, MA: Allyn & Bacon.

Hargreaves, A., & Fink, D. (2000). The three dimensions of reform. *Educational Leadership, 57*(7), 30–33.

Johnson, S.M., & Kardos, S.M. (2002). Keeping new teachers in mind. *Educational Leadership, 59*(6), 12–16.

Kugelmass, J.W. (2000). Not made for defeat. *Educational Leadership, 57*(7), 25–28.

Kugelmass, J.W. (2001). Collaboration and compromise in creating and sustaining an inclusive school. *International Journal of Inclusive Education, 5*(1), 47–65.

Lambert, S. (2002). A framework for shared leadership. *Educational Leadership, 59*(8), 37–40.

Lipsky, D.K., & Gartner, A. (1997). *Inclusion and school reform: Transforming America's classrooms.* Baltimore: Paul H. Brookes Publishing Co.

Office of Special Education Programs. (2001). *Twenty-third annual report to congress on implementation of the Individuals with Disabilities Education Act.* Washington, DC: Author.

O'Neil, J. (1995). On schools as learning organizations: A conversation with Peter Senge. *Educational Leadership, 52*(7), 20–23.

Routman, R. (2002). Teacher talk. *Educational Leadership, 59*(6), 32–35.

Spillane, J.P., Halverson, R., & Diamond, J.B. (2001). Investigating school leadership practice: A distributed perspective. *Educational Researcher, 30*(4), 23–28.

Udvari-Solner, A., & Keyes, M.W. (2000). Chronicles of administrative leadership toward inclusive reform: "We're on the train and we've left the station, but we haven't gotten to the next stop. In R.A. Villa & J.S. Thousand (Eds.), *Restructuring for caring and effective education: Piecing the puzzle together* (2nd ed., pp. 428–452). Baltimore: Paul H. Brookes Publishing Co.

Vygotsky, L.S. (1978). *Mind in society: The development of higher psychological processes.* Cambridge, MA: Harvard University Press.

Willis, S. (2002). Customization and the common good: A conversation with Larry Cuban. *Educational Leadership, 59*(7), 6–11.

Wilmot, W.W., & Hocker, J.L. (2001). *Interpersonal conflict* (6th ed.). Columbus, OH: McGraw-Hill.

INDEX

Page numbers followed by *f* and *t* indicate figures and tables, respectively.